The Democracy Reader

To Bert Luwyn
with best wishes,
Sondra Myers

The Democracy Reader

Sondra Myers, *EDITOR*

International Debate Education Association
New York • Amsterdam • Brussels

The Democracy Reader

Published in 2002 by
The International Debate Education Association
400 West 59th Street
New York, NY 10019

ISBN 0-9702130-3-4

Library of Congress Cataloging-in-Publication Data

The democracy reader / Sondra Myers, editor.
        p. cm.
Includes bibliographical references.
ISBN 0-9702130-3-4
1. Democracy. I. Myers, Sondra.
JC423 .D4344 2002
321.8--dc21
        2002017288

Printed in the United States of America.

Acknowledgements

My thanks go to the many friends and colleagues, from Newark to Mongolia, who led me to stories of civic transformation. My aim in *The Democracy Reader* was to demonstrate through stories the variety, vitality, determination, and ingenuity that have animated the democratic movement at this moment in history. My gratitude, too, to my associates at the Democracy Collaborative at the University of Maryland, who have been most encouraging and supportive of my work on the book.

Connecticut College was the publisher of the *Democracy is a Discussion* handbooks, which are included in *The Democracy Reader*. I owe special thanks to the College and its immediate past president, Claire Gaudiani, for their support of my work in conceiving and editing the handbooks.

The advisory committees for both handbooks included some of the most distinguished scholars and practitioners in the field. Their willingness to work with me on the project and the quality of their advice were crucial to the high marks the books have received. I am deeply appreciative of the time and consideration they gave so generously to the project.

The United States Information Agency (now the International Information Program at the Department of State) translated and printed the handbooks for distribution abroad, making them available in U.S. embassies worldwide, increasing exponentially the scale of the Democracy is a Discussion project and the scope of its influence. My thanks go to George Clack and Chandley McDonald in the Publications office; to Pen Agnew, who served as civic education coordinator for USIA; and to its former director, Joseph Duffey, who gave high priority to civic education in the agency.

Thanks go, too, to Sandra Chalk, whose advice on editorial and logistical matters has been invaluable; and to Katie Roman for her research assistance. My deepest appreciation goes to Jane Rostov, my executive assistant, who knows more about publishing and "getting things right" than anyone I know. She has been a true partner in this endeavor.

Finally, I thank my husband, Morey Myers, for his encouragement and advice on this project as well as past ones—and future ones, too!

Table of Contents

An Album of Civic Stories

Democracy on the Ground

The Long Road

Bold Moves

The Handbook

Basic Elements of Democracy

Challenges

Promise

Documents

Foreword

In the new climate of civil uncertainty in which the reality of terror can overwhelm the aspirations to democracy, it is bracing to recall that democracy's sturdiness comes not just from written constitutions or the leadership of politicians but from the vigorous on-the-ground engagement of citizens. Just as democracy is born in struggle from below rather than handed down from generous elites making a gift from above, so too its durability depends on bottom-up activity by ordinary citizens.

Thus it was that when Alexis de Tocqueville toured America in the rousing days of Andrew Jackson's presidency in the early 1830s, he observed again and again that the responsibility for America's vaunted new liberties depended not on the federal government but on the vitality of America's burgeoning towns and municipalities. "Liberty is local!" he proclaimed, offering what has been a simple rule for democracy ever since.

In this compendium volume on democracy, bringing together a new album of civic stories with a revised and updated version of the *Democracy is a Discussion* handbooks, readers will discover democracy's roots in the ordinary. Although we regard democracy as an extraordinary system of government—in Churchill's ironic description, "the worst form of government in the world except for all the other forms"—it is in fact a system that depends on the actions of ordinary women and men. It is quite the opposite of a system rooted in heroism. Heroic leaders may be required in an oligarchy or an aristocracy where the quality of leadership will determine political destiny. But democracy means quite literally government without heroes, and its stability and its freedoms depend on the quality not of its leaders but of its citizens.

In his play *Galileo*, Bertolt Brecht has one frightened soldier say to another: "Pity the country that has no heroes." No, replies his wise comrade, "pity the country that *needs* heroes." Dictatorship and monarchies may need heroic tyrants and courageous kings; democracies need only engaged citizens and competent voters. Government without heroes means, however, a truly active and engaged citizenry who as ordinary individuals can together achieve extraordinary things. This album compiles examples from throughout the world. A city too near New York finds its own voice in Clement Price's story of Newark. An individual launches a global NGO to combat corruption at Transparency International. A village finds a path to democracy inside theocratic Iran. Sicilians rebel against the long corrupt tyranny of the criminals over their island. A nation nearly destroyed by apartheid finds a way to forgive, bottom up.

The Album includes stories from around the world, and from deep within America. They reflect the variety of the global governance tapestry, but share a single theme: the necessity for democracy to begin with individual citizens and their mobilized communities. Liberty is never the gift of tyrants but always the fruit of civic and political struggle. It is about citizens no less than about constitutions, which is why at the time of the American founding both Thomas Jefferson of Virginia and John Adams of Massachusetts—who were for the most part political foes—could both agree that no democracy in the new land of America could flourish unless schools and universities made the education of citizens their first priority. It is why today efforts like those of George Soros' Open Society Institute to create a robust civil society in lands emerging from communism or from poverty are far more likely to create a foundation for democracy than the mere opening of privatized economic markets or the import of a constitution.

Indeed, what these stories also show, as they are illuminated by the wonderful collections from the two democracy handbooks, is that there is no one way to democracy, no single model—whether American or French or British—that must be followed. The roads to democracy are many, but they all begin with indigenous cultural and civic activities by ordinary women and men seeking to gain control over their destinies.

BENJAMIN R. BARBER
New York City
October 22, 2001

Introduction

After the publication of *Democracy is a Discussion: Civic Engagement in Old and New Democra*cies 1996 and *Democracy is a Discussion II: The Challenges and Promise of a New Democratic Era* in 1998, I intended to step away from the extraordinary events of the late twentieth century—events of what seemed to be "millennial" significance—to return to other projects. However, the energies unleashed by these events—the collapse of communism and totalitarian regimes throughout the world and the dynamic "What next?" atmosphere that resulted—called for a hiatus in business as usual. The end of the Cold War, combined with the revolution in telecommunications technologies, offered a unique opportunity to join others in helping to build the foundation for a new world order. Would the twenty-first century be a new democratic era? Could democracy take hold in nations where people had been deprived for decades—if not for generations—of their rights as citizens? That seemed to be, for the first time in the world's history, a distinct if elusive possibility.

That open question, a decade after the Velvet Revolution, continues to call out to me for contemplation and discussion. Hence, in the spring of 2001 I began working on *The Democracy Reader*, a book that would feature "An Album of Civic Stories" from around the world—and include "The Handbook," a consolidated and updated version of the widely used *Democracy is a Discussion* handbooks. Insofar as "completion" is possible when following the progress of democracy, *The Democracy Reader* completes the project begun in 1996. But the daily changes in the geopolitical landscape, and in particular the changes resulting from the September 11th terrorist attack on the U.S., present new challenges to democracy—and call for new solutions and, inevitably, new projects.

With the attacks on the World Trade Center towers and the Pentagon, the question "What next?" took on new meaning. "Next" for the U.S. government was developing a national strategy that included strengthening our international alliances, devising and implementing a plan of retaliation, offering support for families of victims, and rebuilding the destroyed areas.

"Next" for proponents of democracy and civil society must be a powerful civic response. Although a call for strengthening the democratic fabric of the world seems pale in the face of the innocence-shattering debacle of September 11th, I believe that such a life- and reason-affirming response has its own logical and moral authority. The psychological and ethical vacuum created by the terror is as palpable and haunting as the emptiness we "see" where the twin towers stood. People are yearning for reinforcement of their connectedness to the world and its people. Globalizing democracy and civil society is more important than ever before.

One can argue about democracy's inherent weaknesses—its perpetual lack of resolution, its messiness, its reliance on ordinary people for decisions of extraordinary importance. But by the end of a century in which we saw not only the unspeakable brutalities of Hitler's Holocaust and Stalin's reign of terror, but alarming new examples of mass murder and genocide, I knew I wanted to be an active member of the opposition to all forms of political, religious, and economic tyranny.

I have come to believe that democracy must be our generation's legacy to the future. Our children and grandchildren, indeed, all people on this planet, deserve no less than their right as human beings to control their own destinies, and to work toward "liberty and justice for all."[1] Abraham Lincoln saw democracy as our last and best hope; Benjamin Barber claims it as our first and only hope. I agree with both of them—and add only that, with all its faults and in its many forms, democracy offers the best protection we have against "ethnic cleansing" and genocide, racial and religious discrimination, terrorism, and the ever-present hegemonic impulse of the powerful to dominate the weak. At the personal level, it affords us the opportunity to use our considerable skills to make the world a better place.

We must bring into the fold of the open society a much wider swath of the world's population. The particular tyrannies of the present and future have already reared their heads, inevitably and forcibly insinuating themselves into our lives. Terrorism, we are warned, may be the twenty-first century's answer to the art and science of warfare. But even wars have rules—and terrorism has only carefully orchestrated "random" violence—

---

[1]The United States Declaration of Independence

mostly against innocents; and death to losers and winners alike. We, the "second front in the war on terrorism,"[2] must understand its origins and the reasons for its rise as a resistance to modernity. The choice of the World Trade Center towers as the target for the 9/11 terror is not accidental. It warrants our reflection. The secularism and materialism that the towers represented to the terrorists cannot be ignored. It must be addressed by creative scholars and community practitioners committed to routing out the causes of terror along with its manifestations, and to sowing the seeds of social justice.

We are facing an economic tyranny that has the potential to be no less destructive than the political tyrannies of the twentieth century. Commerce that is not contained in a democratic context—both nationally and internationally— is accountable to no moral principle but the ethic of the bottom line. In that universe the greatest good, the standard by which actions are judged, is profitability.

The globalization of democracy and civic engagement must be accelerated if it is to keep apace with the globalization of markets and, regrettably, of crime, corruption, and terrorism. Hence, strengthening democracy where it exists and fostering its development in nations newly released from oppressive governments is the work we must do. The task is monumental; the stakes, after 9/11, much higher than we imagined. There is nothing more important to our future than working toward a global democratic community.

With that goal in mind, *The Democracy Reader* looks at democracy from three perspectives, inviting readers to examine through separate lenses what democracy is, what it can be, and how essential citizens are to its success. It is meant to be a kind of primer that brings democracy to life by exploring its values, its challenges, and its many faces.

Part One, "An Album of Civic Stories," brings a collection of snapshots to the reader's attention—portraits of people and places, institutions and ideas, lit from within by the glow of civic inspiration. Part Two, "The Handbook," is a series of texts by distinguished authors and discussion questions on the basic elements of democracy, focusing on the role that citizens play in making democracy work, the challenges faced in the process of democratization, and the dimensions and dynamic of globalization. Part Three contains historical documents relevant to the ongoing struggle for democracy, e.g. the Universal

---

[2]Benjamin R. Barber, "The Second Front in the War on Terrorism: Democratizing Globalism." Inaugural 2001 Civil Society Lecture, University of Maryland, College Park, September 24, 2001.

Declaration of Human Rights, the preamble to the U.S. Constitution, and the 1996 Founding Provisions of the Constitution of the Republic of South Africa.

I applaud Tomas Masaryk's wisdom in declaring that "democracy is a discussion"[3]—a discussion that leads to compromise and consensus; and Christopher Lasch's observation in *Changing Places* that "Self-governing communities, not individuals, are the basic units of democratic society." What both authors imply is that democracy is neither an abstract ideal nor an individualistic value. It is, rather, a collective commitment to the common good, translated into a collective set of actions. And it is always a work in progress—a collaborative work of people in their communities who understand that the rights they enjoy are possible only if they assume responsibility for protecting the rights of all members of the society.

Americans have always struggled as a people to balance the individualism that accounts for much of our can-do ingenuity with a commitment to the common good, which is what we owe to all members of a society that offers us unprecedented freedoms. Alexis de Tocqueville, that canny observer of democracy in America, recognized only forty years after the birth of the United States, the traits that define it as a democratic society even today. He understood the virtues of democracy as well as its shortcomings and perils. He worried about American individualism, which he described as a "deficiency of mind and a perversity of heart." How would he judge us today? And how would Benjamin Franklin, that most prophetic of our founding fathers, judge our retreat from civic responsibility? It was Franklin who cautioned his colleagues even as he asked for their unanimous support of the U.S. Constitution in 1787, that a constitutional government "can only end in despotism, as other forms have done before it, when the people shall have become so corrupted as to need despotic government, being incapable of any other." Communities, large and small, are the places where those defining struggles occur—every day.

Grateful that our "old" democracy, with all its failings, endures as a work in progress at the start of the twenty-first century, and energized by the unprecedented number of nations attempting to make the difficult transition to democracy after years of domination by totalitarian or authoritarian regimes, I am pleased to introduce *The Democracy Reader*. It is my hope that it will be used as a tool for educating and inspiring men, women, boys, and girls in every part of the world to join the struggle to make democracy work. It can serve as a gateway

---

[3]Tomas Masaryk, founder and first president of Czechoslovakia, serving from 1920–1935.

to democracy's ideas and ideals, the difficulties it is likely to encounter as it progresses, and to the stories of people's creative and determined efforts to make democracy work in every part of the world—every day.

While people in emerging democracies work hard to shed the culture of bondage and acquire the habits of heart and mind that citizenship requires, those in old *and* new democracies must use their civic power to combat globalization's tyrannies and build on its enormous potential. We are not, after all, so different from one another. And the fact that we are interconnected has, in the information age, taken on literal as well as figurative meaning. We are engaged in a lifetime endeavor to translate an idealistic vision into pragmatic actions and policies that respect, protect and serve all members of society. In a globalized, interconnected and interdependent world, our endeavors are linked and our concept of community enlarged. We must be prepared to act according to the new realities of our interdependence.

The moment calls upon us, citizens of all nations, to work together to build a more just and peaceful world, where human dignity and mutual respect prevail over fundamentalist intolerance and economic inequities; where human beings are free to fulfill their potential as individuals and citizens, and as members of a global civic community. We cannot assign these tasks to someone else. They are ours to do.

SONDRA MYERS
Editor

An Album of Civic Stories

Introduction

These stories reflect the civic essence of the thinking and/or actions of people in all parts of the world who have made the decision to join the struggle for human rights and social justice. The stories are mostly modern, but their geographic and cultural range is vast. The common thread among them is their "civicness," articulated in as many ways as there are places and people.

Democracies are very different one from the other, which speaks to their freedom to be themselves—indeed, the necessity to be themselves. It speaks, too, to the infinite capacities of the human imagination and will. Those who worry about the United States or other powerful nations foisting their particular brand of democracy on others have the wrong concern. I don't worry about other societies becoming too American, but rather about their not becoming democratic enough. Robust and sustainable democracies are not given to people by great powers. They are created by people with the skills and the will to assume responsibility for their own destinies. The Album of Civic Stories is a small fragment of the rich and variegated "landscape" that is democracy.

FROM
"Thinking and Living"
BY THOMAS MANN

Lying before me on a piece of velvet is a memento from my travels, a small ornamental object I was awarded as an honor. It is a little gold key with rings attached to it, engraved on one side with three stars forming a triangle, a pointing hand, and between them the Greek letters ΦΒΚ. The other side bears the name of the owner, the date 1941, and also the year when the society of American scholars that uses this key as its emblem was founded: It has been in existence for 165 years, and last March I was admitted to the chapter in Berkeley [California, USA].

It was a kind gesture for which I am most appreciative—how could I not be? A capacity for appreciating life and all that life brings with it is the chief and most fundamental capacity of a writer; for being a writer does not involve inventing things, it involves taking things that occur and making something out of them. And that, in turn, involves thinking about what they mean. But "think" and "thank" are related words; thinking has a great deal to do with thanking. We show thankfulness for life by writing about it thoughtfully....

To my sense of gratitude it appears as if many thoughts could be attached to the small gold emblem on my desk. Phi Beta Kappa stands for "Philosophia biou kubernetes," "Philosophy, the guide of life." A fine, meaningful maxim, it seems to me, and one enormously relevant today, even though it is the legacy of a bygone century....I would call it a democratic maxim, for the high form of pragmatism that makes philosophical reflection—*thinking*—responsible for human life, and for the consequences in life and reality, is something fundamentally democratic. The most profound cause for the weakness of democracy in Germany and for the country's present catastrophic state lies not in the political sphere, but rather in the psychological and intellectual sphere. It lies in the lack, perhaps on the most basic and essential level, of a kind of pragmatism that boils down to respect for real life, a sense of intellectual responsibility for life and for the effects that ideas have on reality, on the social and political lives of real people....

Philosophy shares the fate of democracy. It is forced to be militant from the simple motive of self-preservation. In the world that Hitler's victory would bring about, in a Gestapo world of universal enslavement, there would be no philosophy at all any more, just as there would be no democracy. There would also be no religion and no morality....

Does this mean that philosophy must subordinate itself to politics and itself become political? That is not what I am saying. What I mean to say is that the problem of humanity forms a unity whose various spheres and forms of expression cannot be separated from one another. The fatal error of the educated German upper class was to draw a sharp dividing line between the intellect and life, between philosophy and political reality....

Philosophy as the guiding force of life means something else as well: It means that philosophy must take life as its point of orientation and pole star. The glorification of "life" at the expense of intellect, so fashionable only a short while ago, was folly, and it is no less a folly for the intellect to indulge itself in sterile, uncaring games at the expense of life....

From an article of the same title, Summer 1941, reprinted in We Write for Our Own Time: Selected Essays from 75 Years of the *Virginia Quarterly Review, edited by Alexander Burnham (University Press of Virginia, 2000), pages 59-62. Reprinted with permission of the University Press of Virginia.*

THOMAS MANN *(1875-1955) was a German novelist and critic. He received the Nobel Prize in literature in 1929, principally for his novel* Buddenbrooks *(1901). He is the author of numerous books, including* Reflections of a Nonpolitical Man *(1918) and* The Magic Mountain *(1924).*

"Where, After All, Do Universal Human Rights Begin?"
BY ELEANOR ROOSEVELT

Where, after all, do universal human rights begin? In small places, close to home—so close and so small that they cannot be seen on any map of the world. Yet they *are* the world of the individual person: the neighborhood he lives in; the school or college he attends; the factory, farm or office where he works. Such are the places where every man, woman, and child seeks equal justice, equal opportunity, equal dignity without discrimination. Unless these rights have meaning there, they have little meaning anywhere. Without concerted citizen action to uphold them close to home, we shall look in vain for progress in the larger world.

Eleanor Roosevelt was a member of the U.S. delegation to the United Nations and chair of the Commission on Human Rights. She was First Lady of the United States from 1933 to 1945 and wrote numerous books, including On My Own *and* This Is My Story.

Democracy on the Ground

The Long Road

The Democratic Legacy of Genghis Khan
BY PAULA L.W. SABLOFF

Democracy is not just about democratic constitutions and processes, it's about people who believe in and practice democratic values. When democratic values are aligned with democratic practices, democracy can be achieved and sustained. Democracy is about citizens who have the capacity and the will to enjoy the rights to freedom and equal justice and, in return, assume the responsibilities for the welfare of the community. Sometimes it takes years to connect democratic principles with democratic government; sometimes it takes centuries. Mongolia is an example of the latter.

Although Mongolia was the first Soviet satellite with a communist government and socialist economy,[1] it was among the first to make the transition to democracy. In December 1989, a month after the Berlin Wall was torn down, Mongolians began demonstrating for open government and multi-party elections. By June 1990, Mongolia held its first free, multi-party elections, and in 1992, the Mongolian people ratified a democratic, parliamentary constitution. In the 1990s, former Secretaries of State James Baker and Madeleine Albright along with former First Lady Hillary Rodham Clinton were impressed with the level of democracy they observed in Mongolia; and a 1999 Freedom House survey categorized it as a democratic nation based on its record of political rights and civil liberties. Furthermore, when Mongolia's former Communist Party regained power in July 2000, its leaders sought legitimacy by pledging their commitment to democracy, the 1992 Constitution, and civil society.

---

[1]Mongolia became the second communist nation, when, in turning to the Bolsheviks to help free Mongolia from the Chinese, Mongolian leaders accepted Soviet support and influence (1921). In 1924, Mongolia rewrote its constitution to match Russia's communist form.

Clearly Mongolia is actively building the institutions necessary for maintaining a liberal democracy, the kind of democracy recognizable to the West. In addition, recent anthropological research[2] suggests that Mongolians believe in democratic values similar to those of Americans. Mongolians want personal freedom (of religion, speech, etc.), multi-party elections, rule of law, a free-market economy, human rights, freedom of the media, transparency in government (no secrets, no corruption), and equality under the law.

Where did these liberal democratic values come from? Were they imported from the West? Certainly they were reinforced by Western contact, but Mongolians' democratic values have a long history. They derive partly from their nomadic heritage, but I would argue that the main reason Mongolians adopted democracy so rapidly and successfully at the end of the 20th century is that they pulled from an 800-year-old tradition of democratic values. These values were encoded in their culture by their great leader, Genghis Khan (1162-1227), who introduced them into the Mongolian consciousness, although he did not erect a democratic society.[3]

How did Genghis Khan predispose Mongolians to democracy? First, he instituted two necessary preconditions for government "by the people." By making the Mongol tribes a unified and independent nation, he gave his people the right to make their own laws. And by adapting the writing of the preceding Uigher tribe to the Mongolian language, his sons and officials were no longer dependent on foreign scribes. Instead, they could write down the laws for all to follow and could assume control over the writing of their own history.

Having established the preconditions for democracy, Genghis Khan instituted some of the values and practices of liberal democracy into his government. Some, indeed, were already traditional parts of Mongolian culture. Among them were:

---

[2]We interviewed 867 people in the two urban centers and surrounding countryside, using quota sampling. We worked to get voting-age citizens who would be representative of the following demographic categories: age, gender, occupation, education, religious and ethnic identity, and political affiliation. Our sample closely matched the national demographic profile of Mongolia according to the National Statistics Office.

[3]Please note that I am NOT saying Genghis Khan ran a democratic society. No one credits King John with establishing a democracy when he signed the Magna Carta, yet we trace the beginning of Western democracy to this event. Genghis Khan preceded the Magna Carta by nine years, and he instituted democratic principles willingly rather than under duress as King John did. But Genghis Khan did not institute a democratic government as we would recognize one today.

Participatory government He established the Great Assembly, the Ih Hural, which met regularly, helping him to make decisions of war and peace. He also created a Council of Wise Men who advised him regularly.

The rule of law Once Genghis Khan had consolidated the Mongolian federation of tribes (1206), he established rule by law and a judicial system, which eventually operated throughout his kingdom.

Equality Genghis Khan initiated forms of political and economic equality, although he never fully institutionalized them. He did, however, create a meritocracy for his army and Council, whereby men he believed to have merit, regardless of their birth or rank, could be invited to join his Council of Wise Men. He also respected women, which was highly unusual at that time in any part of Eurasia. *The Secret History of the Mongols,* the epic story that includes the rise of the Mongol people and a biography of Genghis Khan, gives several examples of women making key decisions, telling Genghis Khan how to live and what political actions to take.

Human rights and personal freedoms While Genghis Khan did not grant his people the basic human rights and freedoms that today's Mongolians prize so highly, he did allow *some* freedom of speech. In addition, enacting the shamanic concept of freedom of religion, he extended a welcome to all known religions in his city of Harhorin.

Through 600 years of conquests, oppression, and hardship, Mongolians never forgot the story of Genghis Khan or the democratic values that were his true legacy to his people. From the fall of the Great Mongolian Empire in 1368 to the 20th century, Mongolians constantly sought independence. All through the 20th century, they tried to combine their struggle for freedom with the building of democratic government. This goal was finally achieved in 1990, when Mongolian government and democratic values became aligned. It is that alignment that makes many scholars and Mongolians believe that Mongolia will remain a democratic nation.

PAULA L.W. SABLOFF *is senior research scientist at the University of Pennsylvania Museum of Archaeology and Anthropology, where she curated the 2001 exhibition "Modern Mongolia: Reclaiming Genghis Khan."*

"The Project of Democracy"

BY ALEXANDER KEYSSAR

This notion of democracy as a project, as well as the contested history of democracy, ought to inform American—and other—efforts to promote democratic regimes in nations with different political traditions and troubled recent pasts. The business of exporting democracy has been booming since the end of the cold war, and American experts and consultants have been dispatched throughout the globe to offer advice regarding the erection of new political institutions. Thus far, the track record of such efforts has been mixed: blueprints drawn up in Washington do not necessarily fit foreign landscapes, and the creation of formally democratic electoral procedures does not guarantee a redistribution of power and influence. Military leaders, party bosses, and business moguls have been endlessly inventive in devising methods of circumventing or overriding procedural democracy. Our own history suggests that this ought not be a surprise. Growing a democracy takes time, and it is often easier to pay lip service to popular government than to live with its decisions. This is not to say that the United States ought to be tolerant of abuses or cast a blind eye to oligarchies masquerading in constitutional garb. But if Americans are to be involved at all in such international efforts, and if our goal truly is to promote democracy—and not simply capitalism—we must recognize the real scope of the endeavor and be prepared to provide long-term support to those individuals and forces who will be struggling for popular government for some time to come.[1]

At home too, there is, and always will be, much to be done. The ideal of democracy—that all individuals are not only born equal but remain equally worthy—surely is an admirable one. The principle that no person's interests and needs are more important than those of anyone else—and thus that all individuals should have an equal chance of influencing government policy—seems well worth fighting for.[2] The project of democracy has never been unanimously embraced in the United States, but it has animated and shaped a great deal of our history. For more than two centuries, men and women who were committed to that project have pressed it forward, despite ceaseless and sometimes forceful opposition. The history of the right to vote is a record of the slow

---

[1]Regarding our efforts overseas see the *New York Times*, 25 October 1999.

[2]Sidney Verba, Kay L. Schlozman, and Henry E. Brady, *Voice and Equality: Civic Voluntarism in American Politics* (Cambridge, MA, 1995), 10.

and fitful progress of the project, progress that was hard won and often subject to reverses. The gains so far achieved need to be protected, while the vision of a more democratic society can continue to inspire our hopes and our actions.

From "Conclusion: The Project of Democracy," The Right to Vote: The Contested History of Democracy in the United States *(New York, Basic Books, 2000), pages 322-324.*

ALEXANDER KEYSSAR *is the Matthew W. Stirling Jr. Professor of History and Social Policy at Harvard University. His current research interests include election reform, the history of democracies, and the history of poverty.*

෯

FROM
"A Blood American"
BY ROGER WILKINS

I often tell my students that the opportunity to engage in active citizenship is the greatest gift of their country. I tell my black students that they are far more than the sum of their pain and their grievances, my white students that they are more than the sum of their privileges and their resentments. And finally, I tell them all that it is a lie that "there's nothing certain but death and taxes." Nothing is certain but death, taxes, and *change.* We can either effect the change that is sure to come or stand immobile and be swept away by the change that others have shaped. Consequently, I try to pound into my students' minds the idea that democracy is precious and fragile and that its survival can be guaranteed down through the generations only by a citizenry that is well informed, alert, and active. I tell them about Edmund Burke[1] and assure them that they, too, can create good....

The lives of [the] founders and their characters were indelibly stained by that fact [they owned slaves], though the heinousness of the crime may be relieved a bit by the fact that they were born into an existence anchored in slavery. It might reasonably be asked why I keep returning to the point that these... men were inheritors of a slave society and were shaped from birth by its culture. The answer is that I, like many others who share my views, feel that culture should be a major factor in informing contemporary public policies regarding

---

[1]Edmund Burke, an English contemporary of the founders of the United States, observed, "The only thing necessary for evil to prevail is for good men to remain silent."

poor Americans. That is, I deeply believe that we need to take into account the damage done by the deprivations and humiliations we have inflicted over the generations on poor people, limiting their capacity to cope with our society. And I believe that we need to craft compensatory programs to open paths of opportunity for them. But surely I cannot on the one hand argue that cultural forces can injure people for whom I have ethnic empathy, and on the other refuse to recognize and make allowances for just such cultural injuries in the lives of the founders. To paraphrase the wonderful truism that Walt Kelly put into Pogo's mouth: I have met the founders, and they are us.

I say *us* as a deeply committed American. One famous African American has been quoted recently as saying, "At no time have I ever felt like an American." Well, *I* have—all my life. When I was a child rooting for Jesse Owens and Joe Louis, I was an American kid rooting for genuine American heroes. When I was twelve and dreamed of flying a P-51 Mustang against the Luftwaffe, I was a fantasy American warrior. And when the white adolescents in Grand Rapids spat on my bike seat and threw stones and apple cores at me, I was having a deeply American experience.

Those kids were attempting to define me as something other than and smaller than American: a Nigger. That was not their privilege. Nor was it the privilege of the odd white teacher or two who suggested that my mind was limited and my aspirations should be as well. Down through the decades, there were others who tried to make my blackness constricting. But they didn't have the privilege, either.

The privilege of defining me rests with my African ancestors, who had the fortitude to survive the Middle Passage and the "seasoning" meted out by their new American jailers. It rests with those Enlightenment philosophers who inserted the idea of human equality into the ideology of the West—and that would surely include the founders of America, notably including Thomas Jefferson, that quintessential man of ambiguity. It rests with Abraham Lincoln, who redefined the meaning of the founding, and with the Radical Republicans who put those ideas into the Constitution in the Thirteenth, Fourteenth, and Fifteenth Amendments. It rests with Crispus Attucks and all the other blacks who fought in the Revolution and in every American war after that. It rests with the slaves whose stolen lives built so much of the strength and wealth of this country. It rests with the abolitionists both white and black who would not let their idea die. It rests with every American of whatever color or political persuasion who carried the fight down to my generation so that my mentors, colleagues, and friends could carry it on. And of course, it rests with my grandparents and my parents.

But, most of all, the privilege of defining me rests with my slave ancestors, most prominently, Mound and _____ Jeffries and Emma and Asberry Wilkins. To cede the definition of what an American is or what I am to pigment patriots who attach Confederate flags to the grilles of the tractors pulling their huge highway rigs and who wear American-flag tattoos, or to bigoted legislators who take from the poor to give to the rich, is to give up the entire lives of my slave ancestors and all of the other decent people who contributed to the fight for American justice.

That is not my privilege.

I accept the possibility that my understanding of America may be skewed by the extraordinary advances made in my lifetime, which is, after all, only a snippet in the long sweep of almost four hundred years from the Jamestown landing down to our globalized, cyperspace era. I have seen and participated in a remarkable enlargement of American opportunity and justice over the course of my life. From the one-room segregated schoolhouse in Missouri where I started school, through a lifelong apprenticeship and friendship with Thurgood Marshall and a rich variety of struggles for justice, I have had the great fortune to see and participate in an astonishing American effort to adjust life as it is lived to the ideals proclaimed by the founders. While the transformation is far from complete, the change has nevertheless been so dramatic that my belief in American possibilities remains profound. It could be argued that I have lived through an aberrant period in American history, and therefore my modest optimism is misplaced. Perhaps, but I still believe in the power of citizen action harnessed to our founding ideals to improve American life and even to transform some American hearts. I have seen the process work.

From Jefferson's Pillow: The Founding Fathers and the Dilemma of Black Patriotism *(Boston: Beacon Press, 2001), pages 143-146.*

ROGER WILKINS *is a professor of history at George Mason University. He is the author of the acclaimed* A Man's Life: An Autobiography.

Long Walk to Freedom
BY NELSON ROLIHLAHLA MANDELA

It was during those long and lonely years that my hunger for the freedom of my own people became a hunger for the freedom of all people, black and white. I knew as well as I knew anything that the oppressor must be liberated just as surely as the oppressed. I am not truly free if I am taking away someone else's freedom, just as surely as I am not free when my freedom is taken away from me. The oppressed and the oppressor alike are robbed of their humanity.

From the book by the same name, published by Little, Brown and Company, 1994.

∞

The Montesinos Virus
BY ADAM MICHNIK

I call it the Montesinos virus—a newly discovered cancerous disease found most commonly in contemporary democratic states. It is almost identical to the Milosevic virus, a cancer to which young post-communist democracies seem particularly vulnerable. Let me try to explain what I mean.

The peaceful dismantling of dictatorships by way of negotiation and compromise is rightly regarded as the finest political invention in recent decades. Thanks to negotiations, Spain avoided a bloody slaughterhouse after Franco's death and created a practical model for negotiated and evolutionary transformation that was later applied spontaneously in the Philippines, in Chile, and in Poland and Hungary.

Traditionally, battles against dictatorship took the form of reconquest: A rebellious opposition conquered the Bastille, whereupon, in vengeance, they locked up the people of the *ancien regime*. On the other hand, peaceful dismantling takes the form of reconciliation and national accord, without revenge and hatred.

One should therefore greet with joy the project of national reconciliation in Peru announced by President Fujimori. And yet this very project provokes disgust and revulsion. It assumes amnesty for the military and the police despite major human rights abuses. Only if the democratic opposition consents to this amnesty will President Fujimori schedule new elections. But if the amnesty is declared, it would even spare Vladimir Montesinos, head of the secret political police, who is accused of being responsible for murders and torture, corruption, and drug trafficking. But Montesinos was more than just head of the political police: He was head of a political criminal mafia that included generals and ministers, parliamentarians, prosecutors, and judges. This mafia had entwined the whole country in its spider web. And Montesinos has—tucked away in his files—compromising materials concocted by agents and provocateurs on every major actor in Peruvian political life. Amnesty for him would mean the murder of Peruvian democracy the day after it was born. Alejandro Toledo, candidate of the democratic opposition in the rigged presidential elections, said correctly, "Peru needs reconciliation, but not that kind. We cannot be hostages of the military and negotiate with a gun to our head."

It is obvious that Fujimori and Montesinos are trying to save their own hides, but I suspect they will not succeed. And in my opinion they do not deserve any compassion whatsoever.

Only when I look at Peru—and also Serbia, which is struggling with the problem of Milosevic and his cohorts, who wanted to retain power at all costs— am I able to appreciate the meaning and the real value of Poland's peaceful transformation. How was it possible? It was preceded by an almost two-decades effort to build institutions of civil society. Political thought within the democratic opposition in Poland took as its main objective the creation of alternative structures in politics, labor, culture, media, and publishing. In this way there emerged a complex network of communities independent of the state. Those communities developed alternative practices of thinking and acting, taught intellectual independence and a new kind of resourcefulness, self-reliant decision-making, and a spirit of creativity. We, the people of the democratic opposition, were left to our own devices. We only demanded of the state that it stop putting us into prison.

Looking now at Peru and Serbia, I see that Poland was lucky. The Polish path from dictatorship to freedom led us through the roundtable negotiations in 1989. The opposition, centered around underground Solidarity and its leader, Lech Walesa, negotiated the so-called "contracted elections." Their main provision was that two-thirds of the seats in the lower house of Parliament, the Sejm, were guaranteed for people of the old regime, while the elections to the Senate were completely free. The Solidarity camp won an overwhelming victory. We won all available seats in the Sejm and all Senate seats but one....

In Peru and in Serbia it was different. The dictatorships rigged the elections and began to negotiate transfers of power only because of huge mass protests. In those countries negotiations were not enough, and the ballot box was not enough either. It took streets filled with crowds disgusted by the mendacity of the dictatorships. It was the huge street demonstrations in Belgrade that forced Milosevic to acknowledge his electoral defeat. When mass street protests took place in Peru, Fujimori accused the demonstrators of setting fire to the Parliament building. This primitive propaganda trick made the whole world realize what Peruvians had known for a long time—that the Fujimori regime was drawing upon Hitler's strategies. The signal that launched the Nazi dictatorship was the Reichstag fire....

Vladimir Montesinos, the true chief of the mafia ruling Peru, was publicly accused of corruption and secret killings. It was he who shamelessly tried to corrupt an oppositional member of parliament for $15,000—the price he put on the dignity of Peruvian democracy—which was captured by a hidden video camera. Only then did Fujimori begin to feel threatened. He announced he would give up power and promised elections in which he would not be running. The omnipotent Montesinos left Peru and fled to Panama, asking for political asylum.

Mario Vargas Llosa, the great Peruvian writer, has said, "The country was ruled by a bandit mafia directed by Montesinos—a murderer, thief, and drug dealer." Indeed, Montesinos, a Latin American combination of Rasputin (the Chaplinesque charlatan of the last Czarist family) and Beria (chief of the secret police under Stalin), recalls various dark figures from old Peruvian dictatorships portrayed in Vargas Llosa's brilliant novel, *Conversation in the Cathedral.*

When Montesinos was refused asylum in Panama, he returned to Peru, where the government had just proposed an amnesty for murderers that was given the absurd name, "A Bill on National Reconciliation." In dictatorships, language is always subjected to Orwellian transformations, and the meaning of words is constantly being distorted. No one has any doubt that the proposed bill was dictated from Panama by Montesinos himself so that he could secure impunity for himself.

How has all of that been possible? Why has Fujimori, who won democratic elections ten years ago, introduced several constructive changes in the economy, and confronted terrorists, leftists, and the cruel guerillas of the Shining Path—and who even did quite a lot for equal rights for women, which brought him respect in the world—why is he ending up today as a tyrant, a con-man, and a Montesinos marionette?

Fujimori's regime has transformed itself in ten years from a feeble democracy into a special kind of dictatorship. The army does not openly function as a dictatorial power. Montesinos—behind the constitutional facade of Fujimori—has created a police/military regime that maintains democratic illusions: pluralism, elections, and freedom of the press. The core of this regime has been Montesinos' mafia that rules from behind the scenes. Many years ago, in describing Communism, Orwell wrote of the existence of an inner party; in Peru one can speak of the rules of the inner mafia. This is what I mean by the "Montesinos virus." In a state ruled by an inner mafia, elections are rigged, the rules of the state of law are trampled, and the institutions of a democratic society are sentenced to death. The mafia does not respect the democratic rules of the game. That is why the mafia must be removed from influence, and that is why a reconciliation with the mafia is not possible....

Similarly unhappy reflections are stirred by the situation in Serbia. Serbia was not a classic dictatorship either. The democratic façade of a state with pluralism, elections, and a free press was maintained there as well. But also in Serbia, behind this façade, power was in the hands of the inner mafia of Slobodan Milosevic. The collapse of Milosevic was met with euphoria throughout the world and in Serbia itself, which was racked with poverty and a succession of defeats that Milosevic had brought upon his country. "Welcome to Free Serbia," announced the headlines in Belgrade. "Finally we are returning to normality," said overjoyed Serbian democrats.

Only those with the most incisive minds, like Nebojsa Popov, gave warning: Milosevic has left, but the Milosevic people remain. In the Serbian parliament they still have the majority. They run the administration, the police, the banks, and the economy. In Serbian prisons, there are still political prisoners, and Milosevic still moves about freely and promises an active participation in political life. None of those accused of war crimes was turned over to the Hague Tribunal, and most probably none will be. Slobodan Milosevic will see to that—the Communist apparatchik transformed into the Greater Serbia chauvinist, the real leader of Serbia's inner mafia.

The new President, Vojislav Kostunica, declares that he wants to observe existing law, which is why many people imprisoned and sentenced by the Milosevic regime are still in prison. Kostunica is still, no doubt, the big hope for Serbian democracy. He is a Serbian democrat/nationalist, which benefited him in the election campaign but which will inevitably complicate the normalization of relations with Bosnia, Kosovo, and the other countries of former Yugoslavia. Serbia has only taken the first steps toward democracy. Could this democracy survive coexistence with the inner mafia of Milosevic, who is accused of war crimes? Will not Serbian democracy always be threatened with this man around who created the dictatorship of the corrupt and cynical mafia nomenklatura, with its demagogic language of Greater Serbia accompanied by the rattling of sabers?

In Poland we used to read the novels of Vargas Llosa and Ivo Andric as variations on Polish history. The Peru of Vargas and the Bosnia of Andric were for us great metaphors of nations pushed into the hell of unchained history, into the stinking reality of second-rate dictatorships bordering on horror and the grotesque.

Today we understand that from such dictatorships, hybrids of democracy often emerge, so-called "delegating democracies" with a hyper-presidential system in which the elected president believes that he can conduct his own policies without taking into account the opinions of the opposition or even Parliament....Serbia and Peru are extreme examples of democracies hollowed out from within by a complicated combination of mafia, corruption, and secret police. The Peruvian disease—the Montesinos virus—and the Serbian disease—the Milosevic virus—are exceptional cases of malignant tumors that can infect contemporary democracies....

One can, however, believe in a different way of being involved in politics: namely, by building the institutions of civil society. For us, the people of Central and Eastern Europe, who are struggling with milder forms of the Peruvian and Serbian diseases, Thomas Jefferson's observations should strike a chord. After the unrest in Boston in 1786 known as Shay's Uprising, Jefferson wrote in a letter to Edward Carrington, of Virginia:

> The people are the only censors of their governors; and even their errors will tend to keep these to the true principles of their institution. To punish these errors too severely would be to suppress the only safeguard of the public liberty. The way to prevent these irregular interpositions of the people, is to give them full information of their affairs through the channel of the public papers, and to

contrive that those papers should penetrate the whole mass of the people. The basis of our governments being the opinion of the people, the very first object should be to keep that right; and were it left to me to decide whether we should have a government without newspapers, or newspapers without a government, I should not hesitate a moment to prefer the latter.

Jefferson was wise indeed. He said, after all, that if the government is a symbol of the state, then a free press is the symbol of a civil society. A democratically elected government cannot be truly democratic if its existence is not accompanied by a free press, or if, in other words, the institutions of civil society are not a durable element of this democratic state....

This was explained perfectly by the Hungarian philosopher, Janos Kis, whose thought I would like to recall here. Civil society, in Kis's opinion, is separated from the state by a barrier of human rights. Human rights provided a defense from the state, and gave a particular form to civil society. A respect for human rights requires the same of any state as it requires of any institution and any individual. A society of human rights has to be pluralistic, and everyone decides about his or her own worldview and way of life, about cultural preferences and economic undertakings.

Janos Kis talks about two interpretations of the rule of law. According to the German idea of *Rechtsstaat*, the state can demand of its citizens that they observe only those laws which are unambiguous and known. One cannot limit anyone's freedom on the basis of articles of law that are as flexible as rubber, articles kept in secret, or issue regulations that are retroactively effective. In essence, that is what the *Rechtsstaat* amounts to. If a regulation is clear, it is obligatory, regardless of its content. Such law has nothing to do with moral norms.

But in the constitutional concept of the rule of law, as Kis points out, what is most important is that democratic constitutions refer to the 18th century doctrine of natural rights. Constitutions do not claim to give a person any rights, but they state that those rights belong to that person by nature, regardless of existing laws. The activities of the democratic opposition introduced to Central and Eastern Europe a constitutional understanding of law.

This excellent outline of our work at that time by Kis is at the same time a valuable guide on how to build a space for resistance *vis-a-vis* the corruption that gives birth to hollowed-out people in hollowed-out barren democracies. In those days the international context was our ally: In the 1975 Helsinki Accords, all European countries signed an agreement to respect human rights. For a long time it was possible to apply it only in the countries of the western democracies, and the constant abuse of law by dictatorships did not move international organizations to intervene.

It was the democratic opposition in Central and Eastern Europe that first noticed it need not be that way. We found a way to move western European public opinion. Thanks to that, we were able to pressure the governments of democratic states not to watch passively the abuses of human rights in the east, and by trying to exercise our own human rights in the most demonstrative way, we finally confronted the west with hard evidence. The western governments had to notice that to react by applying pressure was not pointless, and that the communist authorities could be forced to make concessions. Our experience in the '70s and '80s proved that if democratic countries defend human rights when social conflict is relatively limited, that is, when government suppression has not yet provoked uncontrollable social unrest, then diplomatic means are enough to manage it. As it turned out, the defense of human rights could become an institutionalized element of national policy, and could play an essential role in limiting dictatorships and eliminating them peacefully.

However—and this is Kis's conclusion, with which I wholeheartedly agree— the democratic opposition in Central Europe, and along with them the whole community of democratic countries, was particularly fortunate that the communist system collapsed on its own under the influence of both internal and external forces. The example of Yugoslavia reminds us, nevertheless, that it *can* happen differently. Also the crisis in the Soviet empire could have taken a different course, and then one would have had to confront force with force.

Today in Peru and Serbia dramatic conflicts between corrupt mafia-dictatorships and a rickety and chaotic freedom are taking place. The Montesinos virus is still attacking the Peruvian organism, and the Milosevic virus is still weakening Serbia. Persuasion and negotiation are not enough in those countries. There, the power of con men and assassins had to be confronted by the power of the street. The peaceful power of the crowds on the streets of Belgrade and Lima has slightly tipped the scales in favor of freedom. But nothing is final yet. Will they take the path of Pinochet, who gave up his power peacefully, and as a consequence removed himself from Chilean politics, or will they defend their power to the very end, as Ceaucescu did? That is the choice faced by Fujimori and Milosevic. And the outcome of their choice is clear: retirement, as in the case of the Chilean general, or the firing squad, as in the case of the Romanian "Genius of the Carpathians." Which will they choose?

(Translated by Elzbieta Matynia)

Postscript: This essay was written in the early fall of 2000. Since then, immense political changes have occurred both in Peru and in Yugoslavia. Fujimori ran away to Japan, Montesinos is incarcerated, the supporters of the mafia, including high political officers, are in prison. Importantly, as the result of an exemplary electoral process, Peru is now governed by democratically elected bodies, and a Truth Commission has been established to examine the crimes of the past. And Slobodan Milosevic, after a dramatic stand-off at his villa in Belgrade, was put into prison in the spring of 2001. Transferred to the Hague, he was accused of crimes against humanity and violations of the laws of war by the United Nations War Crimes Tribunal in the fall of 2001. Nevertheless, the Montesinos virus as such is not yet dead.—

Adapted from the keynote address delivered at the Transregional Center for Democratic Studies conference "Revisiting Civil Society" on November 2, 2000.

ADAM MICHNIK *is an author and editor-in-chief of Poland's largest daily newspaper,* Gazeta Wyborcza, *and was a leader of the Solidarity movement. His most recent book is* Letters from Freedom: Post-Cold War Realities and Perspectives.

ELZBIETA MATYNIA *is the director of the Transregional Center for Democractic Studies at the New School University, New York.*

∞

FROM
"What Kind of Justice?"
BY DAVID C. ANDERSON

On the first day of testimony before South Africa's Truth and Reconciliation Commission, Nomonde Calata appeared to tell her story. "She was the widow of Fort Calata," writes Alex Boraine, then deputy chairperson of the commission, "one of the so-called Cradock Four who had been brutally murdered in the Eastern Cape in 1984. In the middle of her evidence, she broke down, and the primeval and spontaneous wail from the depths of her soul was carried live on radio and television not only throughout South Africa, but to many other parts of the world. It was that cry from the soul that transformed the hearings from a litany of sufferings and pain to an even deeper level. It caught up in a single howl all the darkness and horror of the apartheid years. It was as if she enshrined in the throwing back of her body and letting out the cry the collective horror of the thousands of people who had been trapped in racism and oppression for so long."

Antjie Krog, a reporter for the South African Broadcasting Corporation, would remember the moment as "the beginning of the Truth Commission, the signature tune, the definitive moment, the ultimate sound of what the process is about."

It might also serve as an anchor for discussion of the South African commission and others like it. As more countries emerge from episodes of human rights abuse, their need to manage legacies of suffering—on a scale incomprehensible to much of the world—becomes ever more obvious. The processes they choose and the institutions they create to promote healing engage strong feelings and inevitably stir controversy. But the need to which they respond remains as compelling and deeply disturbing as Nomonde Calata's cry.

Boraine now serves as president of a newly created International Center for Transitional Justice; working with him as a program director is Priscilla Hayner, who has spent several years studying the work of truth commissions around the world. Both have recently written books—Boraine's *A Country Unmasked: Inside South Africa's Truth and Reconciliation Commission* was published in South Africa last year and in the United States this spring. Hayner's *Unspeakable Truths: Confronting State Terror and Atrocity* was published early this year in the United States and Britain. The books explore the issues—often tormenting—for people who would create truth commissions and the communities they intend to help.

"Expectations for truth commissions are almost always greater than what these bodies can ever reasonably hope to achieve," cautions Hayner, who examined the work of 21 commissions convened since 1974 and offers practical advice about ways to enhance their chances for success. The commissions, she asserts, can only work if they reflect a nation's desire to heal itself; attempts by outsiders to impose them on reluctant societies aren't likely to succeed. Assuming such genuine impetus, legal and budgetary authorization and the availability of respected commissioners and capable staff—hardly givens in severely wounded societies—managers of the process face sensitive decisions early on....

Should the commission take testimony in public? Private hearings may engage the whole population in a potentially constructive process. Should the commission name names? Publishing identities of perpetrators satisfies a sense of justice, but truth commission testimony doesn't have to meet the standards of admiss-ability in a court of law. How to protect the innocent from being implicated?

And should perpetrators testify along with victims? If so, how can officials of the old oppressive regime be compelled to do so—and what risk does that entail if the new government rests on a fragile political base?

However technical, such questions quickly raise large issues of policy, ethics and raw emotion. Indeed, the uncertainties and ambiguities of truth commis-sions lead some to dismiss the idea out of hand: Why not just put known per-petrators on trial and punish those proven guilty according to established law?

Boraine and Hayner acknowledge the value of legal prosecution and observe that the search for truth and reconciliation need not eclipse the possibility of prosecution and punishment. But they argue cogently that calls for prosecution are often glib, especially in the places where the need to address the past is great-est. "Whom do you prosecute?" Boraine asks, when the number of political criminals is in the tens of thousands or more? Trials on a large scale were attempted in the wake of the Nazi holocaust, and courts heard more than 85,000 cases. Yet many times that number were surely implicated—and the tri-als yielded only 7,000 convictions.

The more currently germane case is Rwanda, where government-incited genocide resulted in deaths of some 800,000 people in three months. Nearly all were individual homicides rather than casualties of bombing or other mecha-nized warfare. Therefore, Boraine points out, "more than half a million people ought to have been arrested. More than 100,000 people have been incarcerated in very crude and inadequate conditions, and have been awaiting trial for more than five years. It is clearly going to be impossible to have a fair, meaningful trial for every one of them."

As for South Africa, how to identify prosecutable "perpetrators" of apartheid, a pervasive culture as well as official policy that prevailed for decades? The number would surely run into the hundreds of thousands; even if the criminal justice system had the capacity, what would trying all of them cost, and would that be the most beneficial use of limited government resources in a new democracy?…

The question of amnesty joins the issue of truth versus justice most direct-ly. Should the potential healing power of truth sanction impunity for political crime? The very idea generates revulsion among some in the human rights community, and they can point to dismaying examples. Hayner describes how

El Salvador's parliament granted sweeping amnesty to anyone who participated in "political crimes"—rushing to enact the law just five days after publication of a truth commission report that named more than 40 high-level officials.

But Boraine makes a strong case for the amnesty that became part of the South Africa T.R.C. proceedings. So far, it is the only commission empowered to grant amnesty. It did so in a determinedly limited way: the commission allowed individuals to apply for immunity from future prosecution for offenses "associated with a political objective" rather than personal gain or malice. To gain the immunity, they had to tell the full truth about their crimes and demonstrate their political nature to an amnesty committee of the commission. More than 7,000 applied; they included police officials, members of hit squads and even some members of the African National Congress government now in power. The application flow swelled as prosecutors continued to investigate cases of political violence. A senior investigator in a prosecutor's office told Hayner that his team "chased all the sheep into the corral of the truth commission....Without us, a lot wouldn't have come out."

And in fact the amnestied provided a wealth of information. Boraine tells the story of Almond Nofemela; in 1989, he confessed to involvement in a death squad set up to assassinate A.N.C. insurgents. When Dirk Coetzee came forward to confirm existence of the squad, the government then in power ordered an investigation by a commission that declared the allegations unfounded. When Nofemela and Coetzee applied for amnesty some years later, they filled their applications with details of squad killings, abductions and torture that were hard to refute.

Boraine observes that the amnesty process...reflected fundamental terms of the settlement between the African National Congress and the National Party that created the new South Africa. The postamble to the 1994 interim constitution called for an amnesty to promote "reconciliation and reconstruction." South Africa, he says, has made a choice between retributive justice and restorative justice, which considers punishment [to be] only one possible response.

"The T.R.C.," Boraine writes, "...should not be seen as a necessary evil, a second-best choice, when prosecution and general amnesty are politically problematic. It provided the only justice available in the context of a traumatic transition. The South African model is not an abdication of justice, it is a form of justice particularly suited to the uniqueness of the transitional context...."

Boraine observes that in the new South Africa, the need to come to terms with history remains imbedded in a society beset by crime, corruption, economic disparity and other troubles. In such a context, "reconciliation...is not a sure-fire escalator which takes one consistently and steadily to new heights. It is a process of fits and starts, of going forward and going back, of reaching heights and plumbing depths."

Boraine writes that "the truth that emerged in the stories told by victims and perpetrators challenged the myths, the lies, and the half-truths conveyed and distributed at every level by the former regime. I am unashamed in my belief that, in the South African context, history has to be rewritten and the T.R.C. has made a significant contribution to this end....In trying to come to terms with genocide, crimes against humanity, and other massive atrocities, not only does our moral discourse appear to reach its limit, but ordinary measures that usually apply in the field of criminal justice become inadequate....Abnormal atrocities demand abnormal measures."

From an article of the same title published in the Ford Foundation Report, *Summer 2001, pages 26–29.*

DAVID C. ANDERSON *is the director of communications for the Ford Foundation.*

✑

"Nomonde Calata"

BY ALEX BORAINE

At the [Truth and Reconciliation Commission] hearing, one witness followed after another. The day seemed to be full of trauma, drama, occasional flashes of humour, evidence of great pain, intense anger, and yet a remarkable and wonderful spirit of generosity. Throughout it I sat on the edge of my seat, my body stiff with anxiety and my heart filled with great sadness as I listened to ordinary people telling their extraordinary stories of sorrow and loss.

The second day was in many ways even more moving than the first. This was especially true of the story told by Nomonde Calata. She was the widow of Fort Calata, one of the so-called Cradock Four who had been brutally murdered in the Eastern Cape in 1984.[1] In the middle of her evidence she broke down and the primeval and spontaneous wail from the depths of her soul was carried live on radio and television, not only throughout South Africa but to many other parts of the world. It was that cry from the soul that transformed the hearings from a litany of suffering and pain to an even deeper level. It caught up in a single howl all the darkness and horror of the apartheid years. It was as if she enshrined in the throwing back of her body and letting out the cry the collective horror of the thousands of people who had been trapped in racism and oppression for so long.

From A Country Unmasked, *(Cape Town: Oxford University Press Southern Africa, 2000), page 102.*

ALEX BORAINE *is director of the International Center for Transitional Justice. He served as deputy chairperson of the Truth and Reconciliation Commission in South Africa and founded Justice in Transition to help South Africa address the legacy of the apartheid past.*

☙

Make Justice a Reality
BY MICHAEL F. THURMAN

It is baffling that we humans have still not learned the "simple" art of co-existing on this planet even though we can now explore the deepest recesses of worlds far, far away. September 11th drove that point home. Despite revolutionary advances in information and communication technologies, which make our world truly interconnected *and* interdependent, we have not learned to live together in peace. The viciousness that lurks within the human spirit must be defeated—through education and a clear understanding of the civic values that are the essence of a democratic society. And we must not allow religion to become the instrument by which humanity is annihilated; it can and must be an institution for building bridges linking all humankind.

These dark moments call to mind Dr. Martin Luther King, Jr., my esteemed predecessor in the Dexter Avenue Baptist Church pulpit, who, in 1963, had a dream "to make justice a reality for all God's children."[1] We have not gone nearly far enough in fulfilling Dr. King's dream. In this democratic nation, we have the right and the responsibility to change our society for the better—but do we, I wonder, have the will?

---

[1] The other three were Matthew Goniwe, Sparrow Mkonto, and Sicelo Mhlaui.
[1] "I Have a Dream," speech delivered August 28, 1963, at the Lincoln Memorial, Washington, DC.

The terrorist acts of September 11th, perpetrated in the name of a misguided faith, call for a rededication to Dr. King's dream and a renewal of our own faith, whatever its origin. Surely the widely held religious belief in doing unto others as we would have them do unto us, and our civic commitment to "liberty and justice for all," speak to us in these difficult times. They require us to respond to these crimes against humanity by mounting a vigorous new campaign for freedom and justice for all the world's people.

MICHAEL F. THURMAN *is the pastor at Dexter Avenue King Memorial Baptist Church in Montgomery, Alabama.*

∞

Eleanor Roosevelt's Call to Action

BY ALLIDA BLACK

Democracy was not easy for Eleanor Roosevelt. It was a lifelong struggle marked by both painful disappointment and tempered joy. Yet once she understood democracy, she embraced it with courage and a determined heart. When pundits urged her "to mind her own business," she rebuffed their criticism, responding "we are all on trial to show what democracy means."

It took years for her to reach this position. Although she was Theodore Roosevelt's favorite niece and headmistress Marie Souvestre's[1] favorite pupil, it took years for Eleanor to transcend the spirit of noblesse oblige that permeated her uncle's progressivism and follow her teacher's advice to think and act for herself. In the process, she challenged her family's social customs, the dictates of her party, and her husband's politics to find her own voice and her own vision of what democracy means. That was arduous—and painful. As her quest became known publicly, many of her family and the public mocked her interest. As threats against her escalated, her fears increased. However, committed to doing "the thing you think you cannot do," she put her fears aside.

In the midst of the anti-Communist frenzy of the McCarthy era, the student council of Columbia University invited Eleanor Roosevelt (ER) to address a conference they organized to address the timidity they saw undermining

---

[1]Marie Souvestre was a charismatic Frenchwoman who directed Allenswood, the boarding school outside London where ER was sent at the age of fifteen. Mlle. Souvestre was committed to social and political causes and taught from a feminist and progressive philosophy.

democracy. She quickly accepted their invitation and in late March 1954 urged students to remember that each acquiescent act undercuts democracy. Speaking without notes in a crowded auditorium, she recounted the occasions when international reporters and students questioned the threat to American democracy posed by the anti-communist investigators. They asked, "Are you not permitted to read what you wish in your country?" With sadness she replied that in the past it was considered "almost necessary" to read material with which one disagreed, but now she had "friends who would be frightened if they were seen holding anything that *touched* a leftist or Communist paper."

She challenged the students to rise above this fear-ridden mentality, bluntly telling them that "our freedom will be in jeopardy [if] the young people and the older people of today in this country do not get over their…fear of speaking out. It will cripple, if not destroy, our democracy."

She used herself as an example, telling the students how she sometimes had to force herself to be a responsible citizen. "I read in the paper, not so long ago, that…an ex-communist had accused Aubrey Williams [and] Mr. and Mrs. Clifford Durr…of being Communists. Now, I haven't the remotest idea, naturally, as far as proof that you could present in court, but I worked closely with Aubrey Williams when he was head of the Youth Administration. I know very well that like many others among us he had times of feeling that if certain things could happen to people under our democracy something was wrong and changes needed to occur. But that he was a Communist never would have crossed my mind." ER knew that she should speak out about her experience, even though it would cause her trouble. "I'm sure I'll get an avalanche of letters.…Perhaps I'll even be called down to Washington before the Un-American Activities Committee; and while I wouldn't mind at all, it would be a nuisance." After hesitating briefly, she wrote a column on the subject[2] because, she confessed, "I thought I was getting to be afraid!"

ER challenged the students to follow her lead. She insisted that all who believe in democracy must "take the responsibility of being citizens" and understand that democratic freedoms entail "absolute responsibilities that nobody can shirk." Democracy must find the balance between faith and fear. "We cannot be afraid. We must believe that what we are doing is right but we must not

---

[2]ER wrote "My Day," a six-day-a-week nationally syndicated newspaper column, from December 1935 until October 1962. Although the column initially began as her daily diary, by the 1940s she increasingly used it to urge public support for social justice and human rights issues.

kill the power to explore, to experiment, to think on a wide scale. It will not hurt us half so much as to be closed into a pattern which constantly narrows and does not let us roam throughout the world of the mind and the soul."

After answering questions, ER left the auditorium. But she went on to carry her message to campuses and public meetings around the world. The call to action was her mantra, and she dared the world to embrace it. As she lay dying in New York in 1962, in a frail, sketchy hand she wrote, "Staying aloof is not a solution; it is a cowardly evasion."

ALLIDA BLACK *is the director and editor of* The Eleanor Roosevelt and Human Rights proj- *ect at the George Washington University. She is also research professor of history and inter- national affairs.*

Bold Moves

"What the Protesters in Genoa Want"
BY MICHAEL HARDT AND ANTONIO NEGRI

Genoa, that Renaissance city known for both openness and shrewd political sophistication, is in crisis this weekend. It should have thrown its gates wide for the celebration of this summit of the world's most powerful leaders. But instead Genoa has been transformed into a medieval fortress of barricades with high-tech controls. The ruling ideology about the present form of globalization is that there is no alternative. And strangely, this restricts both the rulers and the ruled.

Leaders of the Group of Eight have no choice but to attempt a show of polit- ical shrewdness. They try to appear charitable and transparent in their goals. They promise to aid the world's poor, and they genuflect to Pope John Paul II and his interests. But the real agenda is to renegotiate relations among the pow- erful on issues like the construction of missile defense systems.

The leaders, however, seem detached somehow from the transformations around them, as though they were following the stage directions from a dated play. We can see the photo already, though it has not yet been taken: President George W. Bush as an unlikely king, bolstered by lesser monarchs. This is not quite an image of the future. It resembles more an archival photo, pre-1914, of superannuated royal potentates.

Those demonstrating against the summit in Genoa, however, are not distracted by these old-fashioned symbols of power. They know that a fundamentally new global system is being formed. The world can no longer be understood in terms of British, French, Russian, or even American imperialism.

The many protests that have led up to Genoa were based on the recognition that no national power is in control of the present global order. Consequently, protests must be directed at international and supranational organizations like the G-8, the World Trade Organization, the World Bank, and the International Monetary Fund. The movements are not anti-American, as they often appear, but are aimed at a different, larger power structure.

If it is not national but supranational powers that rule today's globalization, however, we must recognize that this new order has no democratic institutional mechanisms for representation, as nation-states do: no elections, no public forum for debate.

The rulers are effectively blind and deaf to the ruled. The protesters take to the streets because this is the form of expression available to them. The lack of other venues and social mechanisms is not their creation.

Antiglobalization is not an adequate characterization of the protesters in Genoa (or Goteborg, Quebec, Prague, or Seattle). The globalization debate will remain hopelessly confused, in fact, unless we insist on qualifying the term globalization. The protesters are indeed united against the present form of capitalist globalization, but the vast majority of them are not against globalizing currents and forces as such; they are not isolationist, separatist, or even nationalist.

The protests themselves have become global movements, and one of their clearest objectives is the democratization of globalizing processes. This should not be called an antiglobalization movement. It is pro-globalization, or rather it is an alternative globalization movement—one that seeks to eliminate inequalities between rich and poor and between the powerful and the powerless, and to expand the possibilities of self-determination.

If we understand one thing from the multitude of voices in Genoa this weekend, it should be that a different and better future is possible. When one recognizes the tremendous power of the international and supranational forces that support our present form of globalization, one could conclude that resistance is futile.

But those in the streets today are foolish enough to believe that alternatives are possible—that "inevitability" should not be the last word in politics. A new species of political activist has been born with a spirit that is reminiscent of the paradoxical idealism of the 1960s—the realistic course of action today is to demand what is seemingly impossible, that is, something new.

Protest movements are an integral part of a democratic society, and for this reason alone we should all thank those in the streets in Genoa, whether we agree with them or not. Protest movements, however, do not provide a practical blueprint for how to solve problems, and we should not expect that of them. They seek rather to transform the public agenda by creating political desires for a better future.

We see seeds of that future already in the sea of faces that stretches from the streets of Seattle to those of Genoa. One of the most remarkable characteristics of these movements is their diversity: trade unionists together with ecologists together with priests and communists. We are beginning to see a multitude emerge that is not defined by any single identity, but can discover commonality in its multiplicity.

These movements are what link Genoa this weekend most clearly to the openness—toward new kinds of exchange and new ideas—of its Renaissance past.

Reprinted from The New York Times, *July 20, 2001.*

Michael Hardt *and* Antonio Negri *are co-authors of* Empire. *Hardt is an associate professor in the literature program at Duke University; Negri was a lecturer in political science at the University of Paris and professor of political science at the University of Padua.*

Peter Eigen's Crusade Against Corruption
by Miklos Marschall

Transparency International's roots as the world's first politically non-partisan NGO dedicated to curbing corruption took hold around the table of a World Bank meeting in Swaziland in 1990. Under discussion was the fact that, at a time of large-scale upheaval in many countries, it had become increasingly clear that unfettered corruption constituted a major threat to the development of sustainable political, social, and economic structures in every part of the world. During the meeting, Peter Eigen decided that something had to be done to address an untenable situation. Then World Bank director for East Africa, he spearheaded an initiative to develop an anti-corruption agenda for the Bank and its partners in response to African leaders' calls for World Bank support for improved regional governance.

Eigen had seen firsthand, through 20 years of experience at the Bank, the devastating impact of corruption on development. Corruption, however, was judged to be too much of a political "hot potato" for the Bank, and all efforts to address it were stifled. Undaunted, Eigen boldly decided to take early retirement from the Bank so that he could mobilize support for the cause elsewhere. A number of his friends and colleagues backed his idea of creating an NGO dedicated to increasing government accountability. So, in 1991, with help from the German technical assistance agency (GTZ), Eigen began to travel around the world to drum up support for the initiative, holding discussions with business executives, development officials, journalists, academics, and political leaders. These meetings were invaluable in helping to determine the key principles necessary to an effective coalition against corruption. It became clear to Eigen, too, that the fight against corruption had to be fought at the systemic level; that it had to involve governments, intergovernmental organizations, private businesses, and engaged citizens.

Transparency International was launched officially in May 1993. Among the international notables who attended the launching event were Nobel Peace Laureate Oscar Arias Sanchez, Kamal Hossain (a prominent human rights lawyer and former justice minister of Bangladesh), Ahmedou Ould Abdallah (former foreign minister of Mauritania), and Olusegun Obasanjo of the African Leadership Forum (now the democratically elected president of Nigeria).

At first Eigen worked out of his Berlin home, not certain his crusade would catch fire. Today, just eight years after its founding, Transparency International is a truly global network with more than 80 national chapters—independent civil society organisations working to fight corruption in their own countries. New and creative approaches to fighting corruption have proliferated through the experiences of the TI national chapters, and their work demonstrates the impact that civil society organizations can have on governments. In many parts of the world, TI has broken the taboo of speaking out against corruption. From Mexico to Nigeria, governments are introducing comprehensive anti-corruption programs using guidelines and methodologies developed by TI.

TI works with businesses and government to introduce preventive measures called "Integrity Pacts." Under an Integrity Pact, competitors bidding for the supply of goods and services to governments provide a binding assurance that they have not and will not pay bribes in order to obtain the contract, and accept the condition that sanctions will be applied if the commitment is breached.

TI has helped put corruption on the global agenda. When the organization was founded, it was legal in Peter Eigen's native Germany and many other Western countries for companies to bribe abroad; in fact, it was even a tax-deductible expense at home! TI was instrumental in lobbying for an international instrument to make bribery a criminal act. The OECD Anti-Bribery Convention[1] came into force in 1999.

The Anti-Bribery Convention represents a landmark in the fight against corruption in international business and a success for civil society, which was largely responsible for the drive to get companies to clean up their act. TI has also been credited with influencing the culture of multilateral institutions. In contrast to the silence of the early 1990s, the World Bank, the European Bank for Reconstruction and Development, the United Nations Development Program, and many other global development players are now declaring war on corruption.

In its eight years of existence, Transparency International has succeeded in convincing significant players in development that corruption is not a necessary evil to be tolerated, but a devastating strike at the world's poor and a frontal attack on the democratic rule of law. Thanks to Peter Eigen, it is no longer naïve to crusade against corruption.

MIKLOS MARSCHALL *is executive director of Transparency International for Central and Eastern Europe. He was the founding executive director of CIVICUS: World Alliance for Citizen Participation and served as deputy mayor of Budapest, Hungary, between 1991 and 1994.*

Coming of Age as a Citizen in Tajikistan
BY ZAMIRA DJABAROVA

Democratizing a country is a goal of heroic proportion, but a reachable goal when ordinary people feel and behave like citizens.

---

[1]Organization for Economic Co-Operation and Development Convention on Combating Bribery of Foreign Public Officials in International Business Transactions.

That was our thought and motto when my fellow students, friends, and I decided to organize the Discussion Club. First it was just a club where we gathered to discuss our problems—largely the problems of youth. But as time went on, we chose to discuss serious issues regarding our lives, justice, people, etc. Then we decided to plan our discussions around the subject of democracy. We became a Democracy Club. We tried to find materials—books, newspapers, and journals—that addressed such issues as the history of democracy, the process of democratizing in other countries, and how to build civil society, but it appeared to be impossible.

Then one day we had a guest from Kazakhstan at one of our meetings. She brought with her the handbook, *Democracy is a Discussion II: The Challenges and Promise of a New Democratic Era.* We were delighted! At last we had found a point of entry to the subject of democracy.

Soon after, through *Democracy is a Discussion* editor Sondra Myers, we were able to acquire the handbook, *Democracy is a Discussion: Civic Engagement in Old and New Democracies,* as well as other books, including Benjamin Barber's *Jihad vs. McWorld* and Adam Michnik's *Letters from Prison.* Receiving literature on democracy has been a great influence on the life of our club. It literally started us on the path to civic awareness—and, ultimately, civic power.

Meantime, other doors began to open. The Organization of Security and Cooperation in Europe (OSCE) announced the opening of a Civic Camp. To compete for entrance, we had to write an essay on the themes of democracy and civil society, drugs, ecology, and gender. Some members of our club were selected to participate, and we attended the camp and studied one of the essay themes everyday. After graduating from the camp, we divided into working groups and tackled a specific theme. We decided to broaden the activity of the club, and with the help of new members that we met at camp, we organized a new group, "Youth for an Open Society."

With the support of the National Association of Business Women of Tajikistan, we published the first issue of the group's newsletter. There were five articles on different themes, written by members of the group. We each researched our topic in depth, and spoke with ordinary people, asking their opinions regarding issues of public concern.

In addition, our group participated in an informational campaign, "Sixteen Days Without Violence," sponsored by the organization and supported by the Open Society Institute. We created several programs and presented them at universities and schools. We tried to make people aware of the problem of violence in our society and the role they could play in putting an end to it. It is important in Tajikistan to make people aware of their rights and responsibilities as citizens if we are to evolve into a democratic nation.

We are fortunate to be a group of young people prepared to be agents for change—democratic change—in Tajikistan. But we also recognize how important, in fact, essential, is the help from abroad, from the literature on democracy we received, and from such organizations as the OSCE, the National Association of Business Women, and the Open Society Institute, which offer programs that broaden and deepen our understanding of what it means to be a citizen.

We know that no one can create democracy for us—but at the same time, we know we cannot do it alone!

ZAMIRA DJABAROVA *is a student at Khujand State University in Tajikistan and currently in an exchange program at Marymount College, Tarrytown, New York, for academic year 2001–2002.*

FROM
"Who Really Brought Down Milosevic?"
BY ROGER COHEN

The south of Serbia is known for plum brandy and gracious monasteries but scarcely for places like the Zulu Café in the small town of Vladicin Han, where the décor features African statuary and a favorite number is Lou Reed's "Perfect Day." The sultry song wafts over this sleepy place, as unlikely as a rainbow, and abruptly everything does seem perfect enough: the sun is shining, the well-known police informer in the corner is showing scant interest in a stranger and Slobodan Milosevic is history, ousted in Europe's last democratic revolution. It is possible to taste freedom, just as it is possible to taste murder, and this Serbian air no longer acrid with blood is little short of intoxicating.

Davorin Popovic, 20, savors the light air laced with Reed's voice as he sips a grainy coffee. This establishment opened in June. At the time, before Serbia's October Revolution, a small-town bar with an African name was tantamount to sedition. Davorin compares his childhood here under Milosevic's 13-year rule to that of a "hostage"; he talks of building Serbian democracy "from the roots up"; he exudes a fresh-faced determination that seems almost miraculous in a country so warped by war, so lulled by lies. But I am interested less in the dreams of this young revolutionary than in his fresh scars. For they tell the hard stories of how power really changed hands in this country and of what a necessarily scarred Serbian future holds.

I have traveled southward from Belgrade, over bridges now repaired after NATO's 1999 bombing, because it was not the capital that toppled Milosevic, for all the stirring images of the federal Parliament in flames on Oct. 5. Rather, his overthrow came through a provincial uprising stirred in large measure by Serbian youth acting through a grassroots movement called Otpor ("Resistance"). The provinces and the young turned on Milosevic with a venom that the dithering, protest-by-news-conference political dilettantes of the capital could never muster. And nowhere did popular anger arise more suddenly than in Vladicin Han.

For many years, the town of 9,000 was a typical bastion of the regime. Its setting in a fertile valley of fruit trees is seductive, but little of the charm has rubbed off on the dismal collection of buildings bisected by a railroad track. Here, the apparatchiks of Milosevic's Socialist Party instructed people how to vote if they wanted to keep their jobs in the timber and paper and fruit-juice factories. Serbian television used its monopoly to ram home a simple message: Milosevic or mayhem.

Few rose above the resulting fear to resist; those who did had to answer to Radivoje Stojimenovic, the burly chief of police. Davorin, a student of physical education, knew Stojimenovic because the top cop shopped for groceries at his father's store. Davorin also felt another connection—his 25-year-old brother, Daniel, had joined the police in Belgrade. That sort of career choice earned families respect in Vladicin Han.

So, Davorin recalls, it was doubly shocking for him when, back in early September, he felt Stojimenovic's hands tighten on his throat as the police chief threatened to strangle him. "Are you a terrorist?" the policeman screamed, his breath thick with alcohol. "Who is your leader? Where does your money come from?"

Davorin felt terror and rage rising in equal measure, but recalled the message of his Otpor training. Do not respond to violence. Overcome your fear, because when fear disappears the regime loses a central pillar of its power. Remember that violence is the last sanctuary of the weak.

He answered that his movement had no leader, that he knew nothing of its financing and that it strived only for a better future for Serbia. This was too much for the police chief. "You should be ashamed of your betrayal of Daniel," he yelled, squeezing Davorin's neck hard enough to leave bruises before accusing him of belonging to a "murderous organization for killing the Serbian people."

Such was the official image of Otpor during the months leading up to the September 24 election in which Vojilsav Kostunica would defeat Milosevic, opening the way for the Oct. 5 uprising that at last unseated the Serbian strongman. Against the warnings of his brother and the wishes of his parents, Davorin joined the movement early this year, soon after its local branch opened in a makeshift fitness center. Founded in Belgrade on Oct. 10, 1998, by a half-dozen survivors of the inconclusive student protests of 1996, Otpor had chosen a provocative symbol of defiance; a clenched fist, black-on-white or white-on-black, that riffed off the communist imagery (red fist) dear to Milosevic and his wife.

This uncompromising stance attracted Davorin. Like much of Serbian youth, after 13 years under Milosevic he could see no prospects for himself. No chance to travel, to earn a decent wage, to see an international rock group, to have a say in the governance of the country. Otpor, part political movement, part social club, offered hope. Joining up was a hard decision, in that it involved taming his fears, and an easy one, in that the movement seemed the only way out. Where once there was nowhere to go and nothing to do, now there was Otpor's headquarters and later, the Zulu. On weekends, when the fitness machines were removed, parties raged. There was the heady feeling of belonging—to one another and to some promise, however dim, of changing the world.

Thousands of young Serbs—more than 70,000 in all—followed Davorin's path into activism. Backed by extensive financing from the United States, Otpor steadily coaxed them from the inertia and introspective desperation of the 1990's, when the most decisive act of the best and the brightest was emigration or draft evasion. Through marches and mockery, physical courage and mental agility, Otpor grew into the mass underground movement that stood at the disciplined core of the hidden revolution that really changed Serbia. No other opposition force was as unsettling to the regime or as critical to its overthrow.

Just how unsettling became clear to Davorin and several fellow activists in the early hours of Sept. 8. Under cover of night, they were out spray-painting Otpor fists and election slogans—"Gotov Je" ("He's Finished") and "Vreme Je" ("It's Time"). Briefly detained by the police they were called back the next afternoon to be photographed and fingerprinted. But a routine, if disagreeable, session abruptly veered into a traumatic ordeal when Stojimenovic and two of his police cronies lurched back drunk from a long lunch.

The trigger was a T-shirt worn by Vladica Mircic, 22, a friend of Davorin, that proclaimed a truly terrible and terrifying thing: "Promene"—"Changes." What changes? the three policemen snarled, as they ripped the shirt off him. Who did he think he was? Mircic was pushed into an office where his ankles and wrists were tied before he was beaten to the brink of unconsciousness.

Another of Davorin's colleagues, Marko Pejakovic, 20, was sporting something almost as disturbing to the police as the T-shirt: an earring. Stojimenovic yanked at it, declaring the earring to be proof that Pejakovic was "a decadent Muslim and a hater of Serbs." Shades of Bosnia. A fourth Otpor activist, Aca Radic, 23, endured a mock strangulation similar to Davorin. All of them were threatened with "liquidation" on the nearby Kosovo border.

But in a small town, the disappearance for several hours of six youths will not long go unnoticed. By late evening, about 300 people had gathered outside the police headquarters. Davorin's father, Zoran, was on the phone demanding to know what had happened. "I'm glad I found out relatively late, or I might have done something I regret with my hunting rifle," he says.

As it was, by the time Zoran and Daniel Popovic reached the police station, Davorin and his friends had already been released and were at the local health clinic. When Daniel who was on leave from his police duties in Belgrade, saw his brother's wounds, he felt "disappointed and ashamed." He had not supported Davorin's joining Otpor, but neither could he tolerate such action by the police.

His disillusionment was widely shared. Parents, relatives and friends of the students turned away from a regime that they had grudgingly supported but that had now indulged, before their eyes, in gratuitous violence against unarmed kids. In other provincial towns, similar, if usually less dramatic, incidents also moved people into a new courage, as more than 2,000 Otpor activists were detained. "Nobody could ever convince me that Milosevic would go," says Davorin's mother, Dragica Popovic. "But this beating changed my ides."

Otpor's founding principles were straightforward, refined by the failure of earlier agitation: remove Milosevic because otherwise nothing will change; spread resistance to the provinces; galvanize a cowed population by providing examples of individual bravery; be hip, funny where possible, in order to create a contemporary message; avoid a hierarchy because the regime will co-opt any leader. "The idea was, cut off one Otpor head, and another 15 heads would instantly appear," says Jovan Ratkovic, an early member....

Outrage over Serbian war crimes in Bosnia or Kosovo had little to do with the movement, but the fierce frustration of an Internet generation condemned under Milosevic to the status of international pariah had a lot to do with it. "We wanted to be normal," Homen says, "to be able to raise our own children here."...

From an article of the same title from The New York Times Magazine, *November 26, 2000, pages 43–148.*

ROGER COHEN *is acting foreign editor at* The New York Times.

∞

Dissent at the University: Azerbaijan 2000
BY RUFAT GARAGEZLI

After the considerable success of the democratic opposition in the 2000 parliamentary elections, the authorities, in an effort to do away with dissent at Baku State University, launched a campaign of "witch-hunting" within the ranks of the pedagogical staff. A list was compiled of lecturers who were either members of opposition parties or supported them. Each of them was invited to the rector's office, where he or she was confronted with a choice: Either discontinue your membership in opposition parties and stop criticizing the authorities, or leave the University.

"They told me openly that I had to leave my position as editor-in-chief of *Mukhalifat*[1] or lose my job at the University," according to Nasir Ahmadli, professor of the chair of journalism.

Of the approximately 50 lecturers who had to go through this procedure, none relinquished their convictions. In fact, many started openly protesting such persecution in some of the independent media that appeared in the country after the collapse of the communist regime. The developments stirred a public outcry as stories defending the persecuted lecturers appeared in various independent mass media. Foreign radio stations broadcasting to Azerbaijan also reported on the developments. Political parties and human rights organizations stood up to defend the dissident teachers.

---

[1]An "opposition-minded" newspaper in Baku.

"We felt the support of students. They were ready to start protest actions to defend their teachers," University professor Zeynal Mamedli recalls. "We were not alone; people supported us. I was particularly inspired by the solidarity we witnessed on the part of the people I had not known before. There was a special warmth in their voices when they expressed their support by phone or while shaking hands in the corridors or in the street."

It was this solidarity that enabled the University lecturers to survive the pressure of the authorities. Athough very few were fired, some were accused, allegedly on grounds of "administrative violations." Those who remain in the University have suffered; they are not promoted according to the established process, nor are they invited to attend scientific conferences or to join delegations for foreign trips. Still, the overwhelming majority of the lecturers have remained in their positions. They have not changed their political views and have not dropped out of their political parties. Their ability to dissent without harsher punishment marks a step forward.

Is it possible to say that we have finally formed a rather stable civil society and that freedom of thought has at last become irreversible in our society? Probably not. We have still been unable to hold free presidential and parliamentary elections and to establish an independent judiciary. And the freedom that we do have must be fought for every day. We are beginning to realize that this is the case even in developed democratic societies. But one thing is clear: People have started to appreciate their dignity, believe in themselves, and recognize the importance of civil solidarity. That's progress!

Baku, October 8, 2001

RUFAT GARAGEZLI *is the director of the ADAM Center for Social Research in Baku, Azerbaijan.*

Thinking and Learning

from "Richer Than Rockefeller"
BY EARL SHORRIS

In autumn of 1999, more than four hundred students attended the Clemente Course, a rigorous, university-level course in the humanities. It was not what the world had expected of them, nor what they had expected for themselves. They were all poor, most worked at low-paying jobs, some collected welfare, some were homeless, some had been to prison, more than a few were single parents. Many had not completed high school.

The majority of the students lived in cities: New York, Seattle, Anchorage, Philadelphia, Tampa, Vancouver, Los Angeles, Poughkeepsie, New Brunswick, and Holyoke. Others lived in remote villages in the Yucatán and the Yukon/Kuskokwim Delta. The students were mainly young adults, most of them in their twenties, and even though they were poor, untrained and uneducated, they now entertained the possibility that their lives were not over....

Although the course had expanded to seventeen sites from the original experiment on the Lower East Side of New York, its aims had remained the same: through the humanities to enable poor people to make the journey into the public world, the political life as Pericles had defined it, beginning with family, and going on to neighborhood, community, and state. To do this successfully required an entirely different view of poverty and poor people. The old ideas about the poor had been proved wrong, or if not wrong, at least not very useful in assisting people out of multigenerational poverty. In truth, the poor had often lifted themselves out of poverty, but other than immigration and such obvious factors as equal justice before the law, how they did it was not well known.

The Clemente Course originated in a single idea: Force and power are not synonymous in a democratic society. The idea led to years of traveling across the United States, listening to the poor, trying to understand whether the distinction between force and power worked in practice as it did in theory, and if it worked in practice, what else might be learned about poverty from the poor themselves? If they were not understood as cases to be managed, if one could sit at the feet of the poor, and listen; if one could be a student in the school of their lives, of what had befallen them, was there not something more to be learned?

Starling Lawrence, with whom I first raised the question of force and power, added still another issue to the project: What was to be done?

Of itself, the Clemente Course does not answer the question. It is only a manifestation of the answer. The course is the Greek answer, and even though it operates in Maya and Cup'ik as well as Western/European culture, its Athenian roots are old and very deep. If any one person can be singled out as its founder, it must be Socrates, for he not only gave the course a method, he was the first to exemplify the connection between the political world and the humanities.

Behind the façade of the great ironist, Socrates lived the engaged life. As a young man, he put on the armor of a hoplite and went to war in defense of Athens. Later, in the role of teacher, he explored the question of what a person ought to do, although never in the sense of developing a doctrinal position as in a religion. The gods and the rules for living attributed to them were of no interest to him; he was above all a political man, a humanist, one who held human beings responsible for human thoughts and actions, which as we know may have been part of the reason or rationalization for his death sentence.

The deep connection he made between the humanities and politics was his own life: He did not, as we say, *do* philosophy, he *was* a philosopher. For Socrates, who upon consideration of his imminent death was comforted by the thought that he would either sleep or spend his afterlife in the company of such people as the poet Homer, the humanities and political life were of a piece.

Although there is no bald statement of the relation of the humanities to politics that we can attribute to Socrates, no one who thinks about him can fail to comprehend the importance of the connection. Moreover, the connection did not arise from the mind of Socrates alone; it is bound up in the development of the Greek *polis*, intimately connected to the democratic conduct of the city-state. While the Platonic notion of a philosopher-king was never realized, something even more astonishing occurred in ancient Athens, the philosopher-citizen; that is, the person who thought reflectively about the management of the internal and external affairs of state....

The loss to students and to society that comes of failing to teach the humanities in high schools and colleges merits not one book but many books of diagnosis and prescription. How long a country that forsakes the ethical and intellectual strength of reflective thinking can continue to prosper is open to question. Whether such a nation can maintain a position of leadership is doubtful.

Before the general abandonment of the humanities and the downgrading of post-secondary schooling from education to "preparation," education and more specifically the study of the humanities was thought to be the province of the rich. The children of the Rockefellers (or currently the [Gateses]) would have been expected to know something about history, art, literature, and philosophy. Even today their schooling tends toward the more complex, less repetitive kind of work. The poor, on the other hand, have always been trained to perform simpler tasks, usually less cognitively demanding and consequently less remunerative than the trades.

Whenever the nation becomes interested, for whatever reason, in alleviating the suffering of the poor, the method is always the same: training. Some programs also attempt to teach the poor to wear more appropriate clothing, others to give them the habit of rising early, and so on. In most such programs, including those suggested by the Welfare Reform Act of 1996, both promise and punishment have a role. These policies result from the idea that the poor are different from the rest of the people, either less able or less deserving or both.

If one holds to that view, the idea of educating poor people is absurd. They should be trained, if they are capable even of that. Such a policy has certain obvious advantages for the rest of the society: it enables them to use the poor to do…whatever the non-poor want to avoid and to pay them very little for their labor.

The other, less obvious, advantage involves power: the uneducated poor have neither the economic nor the intellectual resources to take and hold their fair share of power in a democratic society.

By training the poor while keeping education in the humanities beyond their reach, the rich and the middle classes maintain the poor in the role of the meek. The poor may rob or even kill someone now and then, usually each other, but the uneducated poor pose no economic or political threat to those who hold power.

From Riches for the Poor: The Clemente Course in the Humanities. *(New York: W.W. Norton & Company, 2000), pages 3-8.*

EARL SHORRIS *is the author of* New American Blues: A Journey Through Poverty to Democracy *and founder of the Clemente Course in the Humanities.*

Parent Education of the Civic Kind

BY ELAINE ZIMMERMAN

Children thrive when their parents provide them with nurture, love, and the motivation to learn. But it also helps to see their parents having an impact on their own communities; it offers children hope that change is possible. It is that hope, in fact, which *makes* change possible.

Often parents in disadvantaged circumstances lack the know-how to exert their influence as citizens and, indeed, don't realize that they have the right to make their concerns known. In 1992, the Connecticut Commission on Children decided to address the "civics deficit" in parent education by creating the Parent Leadership Training Institute. The Commission also developed an all-in-one, do-it-yourself "democracy tool kit" for the parents. They found that once parents understand how to navigate civic space, they are inclined to enter civic life.

Parents have a lot to worry about. They worry about who will take care of their children while they work, about lost time and missed opportunities with their children as they work one, two, or even three shifts a day to make a decent family wage. They often fear that the public schools won't offer their children the "competitive edge" they need to succeed, and looming large is the knowledge that gangs and drugs are an ever-present temptation to the children, in stiff competition with family influences. In many neighborhoods the children's safety is their primary consideration.

During an intensive 20-week course on democracy, parents learn how to interact with their communities' power structure as advocates and citizens— with savvy and, most important, with positive outcomes for their children.

The curriculum includes a wide range of topics, including how to work with and embrace diversity; how federal, state and local government works; what public policy is; understanding budgets and fiscal allocations; the role of different constituencies in effecting change; how to reach and engage local, and state elected leaders; why voting matters; how to use the media as a vehicle in public dialogue; seeing neighborhood and groups as assets; cultivating the skills to listen, lead and cull ideas in group discussions; ways to strengthen and motivate community; and how to measure outcomes.

Democracy practicums offer parents the opportunity to practice civics during the training period. Each spring parent leaders graduate in the State Capitol, packed with proud children, parents and extended kin. One member of each regional graduating class gives a speech in the State Assembly, and the Secretary of State awards diplomas embossed with the state seal.

The Parent Leader Training Institute is a different kind of parent education—with a powerful civic dimension. The skills it offers are essential to parents, to the well being of their children and to the progress of our democracy.

Graduate success stories abound. One parent graduate stopped a children's library in her neighborhood from closing. Another, in collaboration with the public library system, created a neighborhood library offering books in Spanish as well as English. A group of parents collected new clothes for children who were moving from foster care to adoption. One grandmother created a program for grandparents raising their grandchildren, who then began to influence state policy on extended family support. One father generated an entire municipal parent network to influence public policy for the next generation. Several graduates have run successfully for public office, becoming city council and school board members themselves.

Good parents in a democracy must be good citizens too. Connecticut's Commission on Children recognized that fact and did something about it. Parent Leadership Training Institutes now exist in 14 cities and towns in the rural, urban, and suburban sectors of Connecticut and have been replicated in nine other states as well. Parents need an education for democracy if we are to have an enlightened family policy in the future. And children need nurture from parents who have the will and the skills to make the world a better place.

ELAINE ZIMMERMAN *is executive director of the Connecticut Commission on Children and is affiliated with the Transregional Center for Democratic Studies at the New School for Social Research.*

FROM
"Three Skills That Students Need To Become Citizen-Leaders"
BY MICHAEL S. MCPHERSON

Editor's Note: Michael S. McPherson, president of Macalester College in St. Paul, MN, spent a three-month sabbatical at Tulane University in New Orleans in the spring of 2001 examining relations between democracy and higher education.

How [can we] help students become better citizens? This shouldn't be a matter of preaching at them about citizenly virtue or enforcing certain patterns of thought. Indoctrination is out of place in college and anyway probably counterproductive. We should never tell our students what to think, but it is very much our job to help determine what they think *about*. In fact, it's no exaggeration to say that influencing what students think about is a large fraction of what a college education is. To help students become better citizens, the main thing we can do is help them develop their capacity for deliberation. I find it helpful to think of that deliberative capacity as having at least three components:

- skill at reasoning and argumentation;
- a capacity for empathetic understanding that the classicist and philosopher Martha Nussbaum calls "narrative imagination";
- a capacity for practical deliberation.

The first of these—skill at reasoning and argument—doesn't require much comment. But clearly citizenship does require the ability to spot a logical fallacy or a hidden assumption. Increasingly…it also requires a basic understanding of and comfort with statistical inference. (If you want to be a citizen, you have to do the math!)

The term "narrative imagination" points to a vital—and sometimes neglected—contribution that literature and the arts make to developing a person's deliberative capacities. Nussbaum quotes the constitutional scholar Alexander Meiklejohn: "There are many forms of thought and expression within the range of human communications from which the voter derives the knowledge, intelligence, sensitivity to human values: the capacity for sane and objective judgment which, so far as possible, a ballot should express. People do need novels and dramas and paintings and poems 'because they will be called upon to vote.'"

To deliberate with others requires an ability and willingness to see the world from their point of view. Learning to read a novel, or to act in a play, or to express oneself in a painting or to grasp another's expression—all these are activities that can enlarge a person's imagination and capacity for understanding. It's far too naive to say that reading literature will make you a better person, but it's quite plausible to say that a knowledge of literature and the arts can enable you to inhabit a morally richer world.

There is, finally, the matter of practical deliberation. Aristotle distinguished theoretical reason, which results in establishing true propositions, from practical reason, which results in right action. Traditional academic work connects most naturally to theoretical reason. Democratic deliberation, obviously, is a species of practical reasoning, of reflection that results in action.

Providing students with opportunities to develop skill at such "reflection in action," as the philosopher and psychologist Donald Schon terms it, is a major challenge for American Colleges. Schon has written insightfully about the need to integrate more practical experience into the education of professionals, like lawyers and architects. "In this view of professional knowing, technical problem solving occupies a limited place within the inquirer's reflective conversation with the situation. In the professional's problem setting, means and ends are framed interdependently. And the professional's inquiry is a transaction with the situation in which knowing and doing are inseparable."

But of course, just this is true of problems of democratic decision, where we come upon the interplay of means and ends, of values and facts as well as the need for reasoning to end in action. Indeed, we might think of liberal education as, in important measure, preparation for the "profession" of citizen-leader.

To foster skill at practical deliberation, we need to think about fashioning structured opportunities for students to participate in real-world problem solving, both on campus and in the community. This is perhaps the aspect of education for democracy that colleges have thought least about. How do we embed students in situations that have real deliberative weight, while at the same time preserving the space for reflection and criticism that is essential to learning?

I find the potential enormously exciting, and…some of that potential is being realized…at Macalester, in service learning, action research and allied efforts. To be sure, there are real difficulties. When we engage with our surrounding communities, we need to view them as democratic partners, not as experimental subjects. And we must ensure that student engagement is always deliberative as well as practical: it is in structured reflection on the practical work that real learning takes place.

From an article of the same title from Macalester Today, *Summer 2001*

MICHAEL S. MCPHERSON *is president of Macalester College in St. Paul, Minnesota.*

∞

You Can Create a New School

by Alicja Derkowska

What do you do if the school your child attends is oppressive, uninteresting, and unpleasant? You can change schools. But what if *all* the schools are similarly passive and authoritarian? You can create a new school. Before the change of political systems in Poland over a decade ago, that idea was unthinkable. Even within the new system it was highly improbable. But the idea became a reality.

A mathematician and teacher of higher education by profession and politically aligned with Solidarity, I was a member of the underground national board of education from 1982 to 1989. In 1988 we decided that the first step in making a change in the educational system of communist Poland was to create local education associations. Their mission would be to create non-state schools. The Educational Society of Malopolska was officially registered in that year, just before the birth of the democratic Poland. It is an NGO consisting of parents, teachers and others. We were dedicated to change and eager to move ahead. We moved rapidly once we were given the green light. As a result, 20 independent schools were opened that first year.

How do you start a school with no money, no teachers, and no place? Parents! We put up posters around town. "Are you looking for something different in education? Do the current schools meet your children's needs? Do you want to make a change? Come to my apartment on Friday at 5 p.m." Some 25 parents and teachers showed up. We asked, "What do you want in a school? What will make our school different from the state schools?" Their responses were: smaller classes, more personal attention to students' needs, more foreign languages—especially English, more relevant curriculum, and opportunities for students to have contact with their peers in other places.

And so it came to pass. Fourteen students formed the 9th grade in September 1989. A parent offered to let us rent his two-room apartment. The rent was paid with a gift from Polish Solidarity members in exile in Norway. We borrowed 15 desks and chairs and bought only a blackboard and a box of chalk. Parents recommended teachers who might be willing to teach at the new school. It was a risk, as no one knew whether the experiment would last. The teacher-student ratio was 1:1, which was the subject of jokes—not always friendly ones. Salaries were covered by tuition and the financial supplement mandated and paid by the government. The first 14 students felt that they *were* the school. When, after one month, an authoritarian physics teacher informed the students that if they did not do as they were told he would not teach them, they replied, "So be it." And I had to look for another teacher!

The next year brought rapid growth, which called for changes. We had one hundred candidates, which meant there would have to be entrance exams and a careful selection process. We accepted three classes of 15 each. Since there was an interest in business, one class followed an economic curriculum; the other two were college preparatory. Thus "Splot," meaning "interwoven," became the name of the school. We rented the floor of a building until we outgrew that as well.

Today we own our building, which was formerly a nursery school. We are still in the process of converting it into a modern school with appropriate facilities. We have 120 students in grades 7 through 12. Classes are still small, ranging from 8 to 18, with an occasional group as small as 4 or as large as 24. Emphasis is still put on languages, foreign exchanges and positive teacher-student relations.

But those aspects of education, while important, are not enough to make a difference. From the very beginning our mission was to enable our students to become active and responsible citizens of the new democratic Poland. So we sought to give them as many opportunities as possible to develop skills that would allow them to reach these goals. Classes were active and engaging. Students were encouraged to voice their opinions, and their suggestions and initiatives were often followed. A committee of students and teachers was elected to write a school constitution which, in effect, created a school parliament. The constitution won a prize in a national competition. A program was introduced called "My Five Minutes," requiring each student to speak publicly about something that mattered to her or him. In order to graduate, students had to perform 60 hours of community service and submit a journal that not only described what they had done but also what they had gotten out of the experience. While these ideas may seem commonplace to American readers, they were totally novel to the Polish and Eastern European models of education.

The changes we sought to make were far-reaching. Our goal was to create a better society; to do that we had to reach more than just our own students. In 1990, in cooperation with Educators for Social Responsibility in Cambridge, Massachusetts, we began summer institutes for teaching democracy. Initially they were for teachers throughout Poland, but we soon realized that real change required involving at least three teachers from a given school along with the principal, without whom no changes could be implemented. So our focus shifted to the region of Nowy Sacz—including our school and rural schools in the area.

When our students expressed the desire to look to peers abroad, we began an international project. We started with Polish-Slovak teacher training workshops and seminars. We now work with teachers from the Czech Republic, Serbia, Kosova, Bulgaria, and Romania as well.

The original impetus for the project was the desire to create a student-centered approach to education in Poland. The number of non-state schools has increased exponentially in the past 11 years. They serve all levels from nursery to university and focus on all subject areas. But an important and interesting phenomenon has occurred. The Ministry of Education has watched this expansion with interest, observing the practices that are successful in these innovative schools, and has slowly begun to integrate them into the state system. Instead of a trickle-down effect there has been a trickle-up effect. These grassroots initiatives have slowly become part of the mainstream.

We know that education is a key element in a true democracy and that our schools are playing an important role in ensuring that the next generation is prepared to meet the democratic challenge. But we also know that there is a long road ahead of us. We are definitely ready for the longer journey.

ALICJA DERKOWSKA *is president of the Educational Society for Malopolska in Poland.*

Choosing the Future

"Iranian Village Shapes a Model of Democracy"
BY JOHN WARD ANDERSON

Lazoor, Iran—There are no battles between reformers and conservatives, mullahs and secularists in this small, mountainous farming community south of the Caspian Sea.

Here, in contrast to most other places in Iran, grass-roots democracy is flourishing. Young and old, men and women decide together how to run their affairs, and no one overrules them.

Three hours and 75 miles west, in Iran's capital, Tehran, reformist politicians and religious conservatives are battling over how to govern the country—as an authoritarian theocracy, a liberal democracy, or some combination of the two. Youths testing the limits of social freedoms are being flogged in public, political dissidents are being jailed, and liberal newspapers are being closed.

But in Lazoor, the people run the show, and ideology has yielded to practicality and the common craving for a better life. Two years after winning permission to form a local government, and after participating in classes to encourage local decision-making, success here is measured not only in how the town looks—and the changes are substantial—but in how the residents feel.

"The most important impact is that people are really self-confident, and they have started to believe in themselves," said community leader Ali Esfandiar. "We are capable of finding solutions for every problem."

That approach has infected the entire town, transforming Lazoor's system of government, the local economy, long-standing social customs and personal attitudes, and the management and protection of the environment, which is critical in any farming community. Private aid officials say that the way Lazoor has solidified local democracy and decision-making, boosted the influence and self-esteem of women, empowered the young, and created job opportunities could be a model for developing and managing three-quarters of Iran's rural areas—helping stem the flight of young people to cities.

"The [central] government does not know its own role and level of participation in Lazoor, and the people still do not know what authority they have," said Zia Eddin Almassi, a community development consultant who began working in Lazoor four years ago, when Iran's Agriculture Ministry and the U.N. Development Program launched a joint effort to encourage citizen participation in managing natural resources. "But this project has proven that people are capable of making their own decisions," he said, "and that the government believes people can manage their own affairs."

The results are concrete. The 3,000 residents elect their leaders and tax themselves. In the last two years, they have analyzed their problems, from the low status of women to seasonal flooding, and they have devised and implemented solutions, from sensitivity exercises for men to the construction of mountainside terraces to control erosion. More than 1,000 townspeople labored nine months to build 42 dams to control floods that regularly devastated the village.

They planted 6,700 fruit trees on hillsides overlooking the town, watered by a new spring-fed containment pond, and they plan to create a large community garden for medicinal plants. They reseeded about 40 acres denuded by generations of overgrazing. They built a new mortuary, town dump, and community bath. They began weekly courses in weaving and chicken breeding, with an animal expert provided by the central government. They upgraded the heating and water systems of the town's main mosque. They recently began rebuilding about 18 miles of irrigation canals that are the lifeline of Lazoor's agrarian economy.

Most extraordinary was the change in attitude between men and women, as symbolized by mixed-group organizational meetings in the local mosque, where women previously were required to sit separately behind a screen, said Khadija Catherine Razavi, an activist from Tehran who helped mobilize the community to start doing things for itself.

"Up until then, the only thing a man had to say to a woman in a mosque was, 'Shut your kid up,'" she said. But men were encouraged to consider the role of women in Lazoor and to write down the challenges they faced, "and suddenly there was a very new tone. Then men were saying: 'Women are wonderful. If all the men leave Lazoor, nothing will happen, but if even one woman leaves, we will go into a deep winter's sleep.'"

Many residents say women still need greater representation on local councils that make the most crucial decisions. "In my opinion, 80 percent of the work here is done by women, and those who work must be fully empowered," said Alireza Shoja. He was surrounded by a group of 10 men who shouted "Yes!" in chorus.

State banking officials were so impressed with the town's industriousness— and so swayed by the lobbying of local leaders—that they recently opened Lazoor's first bank branch, so people no longer had to travel 30 miles to pay their utility bills. In less than a month, the bank manager said, residents had opened about 300 personal savings accounts, and he had approved several hundred small loans, ranging from $600 to $1,200.

This was how the leaders of Iran envisioned the country would work when they wrote the new constitution 22 years ago in the aftermath of the 1979 Islamic revolution, political analysts say. The constitution called for layering of elected local, regional, and provincial governments that would concentrate power in the hands of the people. It was to be a model of bottom-up decision-making.

That concept got lost, analysts say, during two decades of legislative inertia that began with Iran's 1980-88 war with Iraq. People accustomed to having the central government provide for them did not demand the local elections that were due them.

But the government began a decentralization drive in the mid-1990s, and after his landslide election in 1997, Mohammad Khatami ushered in Iran's first local elections in February 1999. Voters in 730 cities and 40,000 villages elected about 200,000 local council members, including more than 500 women.

Today, analysts agree that Lazoor's success is an exception. They say that most local councils have yet to realize the dream of making their communities masters of their own destinies.

Laws establishing the councils do not give the bodies enough power, experts say. Because they have little taxing authority, councils still rely on the central government for funding and lack money for their own priorities. Their links to agencies in Tehran and the provincial capitals are weak, and many government bureaucrats have refused to relinquish their planning and decision-making authority. In rural areas, many villages simply elected their traditional elders as councilmen, and they lack experience, education, and management skills.

Some urban councils, particularly the reformist-dominated Tehran city council, have been plagued by factional battles with other institutions controlled by religious conservatives. In fact, the chairman of the Tehran council was gravely wounded in an assassination attempt, and another popular member was jailed for five years.

The battles are similar to ones being fought at a higher level between the elected, administrative side of Iran's state, which is dominated by reformers, and the appointed, Islamic side, which is controlled by religious conservatives. Some analysts indicate that future legislation to grant more power to local councils may be vetoed by hard-liners, who favor a strict, hierarchical Islamic government unencumbered by elections.

But in Lazoor, there is a sort of fairy-tale quality to what has occurred—as if the patient who a few years ago couldn't walk has suddenly become an Olympic track star.

It began four years ago when two people in the town, a young man and woman designated Lazoor's "animators," were selected to attend a two-month training program for people from eight villages—a crash course in how to make decisions, particularly in crafting solutions to local problems.

It was a skill, residents here said, that had been lost in the generations during which first Iran's monarchy and then the national government had assumed full responsibility for addressing community needs. As a result, they said, people forgot how to provide for themselves and communities became dysfunctional, while the central government typically ignored local problems or, when flush with oil money, mandated solutions that were inappropriate because the community was not consulted.

The animators returned home and organized local workshops and training seminars. They formed a 75-person steering committee, including 15 women, to tap more closely into community concerns. They mapped the surrounding area and, with the help of government engineers, analyzed water runoff and flood trends. Week after week, the entire town was urged to attend nightly meetings and air grievances. Sometimes hundreds of people showed up.

"It used to be that the government imposed programs from above, and now the people had a chance to design programs to suit their own needs," said Shokat Esfandiar, Lazoor's 24-year-old female animator. "Women in particular heard, 'The men will take care of it,' but now it is women who are proposing changes. They are much better at figuring out what to do with their own lives."

After months of discussion, the community drew up a list of 81 problems— enshrined on three posters—including the lack of a library, senior high school, women's clinic, and women's sports facility.

But many of the grievances sought to change the traditions and attitudes typically found in rural Islamic communities. Youths demanded more support from their elders. Women deserved more say in the town's affairs, the posters declared, and traditional conventions that prevented them from speaking their minds needed to be eased.

"Traditionally, all of the decisions were made by a small group of elders, so the youth went to them and asked for permission to participate in our own destiny and decisions," said the male animator, community leader Ali Esfandiar, also 24, who shares the same last name as his female counterpart but is not closely related. "This was our greatest success."

Two and a half years ago, as Lazoor was ending the planning phase, the community elected its first five-man local council, which gave the village additional legal authority and a more streamlined process to begin implementing changes. Since then, it has started tackling the 81 most pressing problems systematically and completed work on perhaps half a dozen, as well as several related issues, said Zakaria Shoja, a soft-spoken school administrator who heads the village council.

"There's a lot yet that needs to be done and a lot of awareness that needs to be brought about, but the mood of true democracy is going to be realized here in its entirety," he said. "We plan to create a new world, relying on our own power and capabilities."

The Washington Post, *September 2, 2001, page A24. © 2001, **The Washington Post**. Reprinted with permission.*

JOHN WARD ANDERSON *is a journalist for the* Washington Post *Foreign Service.*

⚭

Sicily Says "Enough!"

BY LEOLUCA ORLANDO

Some time ago, I happened to be talking with a friend, an entrepreneur who had been extraordinarily successful and enjoyed the greatest respect and prestige in all circles of his country. At a certain point we came to talk about tax evasion and he began to say: "I never want to forego my right to pay taxes, because..." "Right?" I interrupted him. "Perhaps you wanted to say duty. The duty we all have to contribute to the functioning of the state."

"No, no", he exclaimed. "I really did mean to say right. And do you want to know why? If it were only a duty for me, I would tell you that I pay my taxes because I think it right to comply with my civic obligation, or because I prefer to be at peace with my conscience, or even because I fear the consequences of being discovered. Now, it is quite right that I pay my taxes for all these reasons. But, aside from that, I do it above all because I find it convenient. In my business, you see, confidence is a fundamental component of success. If I were a tax dodger...I would not be surrounded by the confidence that people have in me today. They would think that if I defraud the inland revenue, I could also try to swindle them....That is why I claim to have the *right* to respect the law."

While my friend was talking, I could not help feeling that, quite apart from his hyperbolic use of the term ["right"] in place of the more proper ["interest"], the concept was of somewhat limited validity on the general level.

∞

Mayor Orlando made a point of involving Palermo's teachers and students. One of his initiatives was a "curriculum of lawfulness"—like one of our civics courses but with a special urgency. The children of Palermo needed to learn that the Mafia was responsible for the violence that permeated the city and that those who informed on them were heroes, not traitors. They needed to learn that obeying the law is the right thing to do and that flouting it destroys a society at its roots. (Something America's teachers want all our students to understand as well.)...In a real sense, the citizens of Palermo were engaged in a war against totalitarianism and terror. Their story can and should be an inspiration to everyone who believes in the basic right of men and women to organize and associate freely. Corruption and organized crime are grave, pernicious threats to democracy. But with determination, leadership, and a citizenry prepared to fight for the values of a free society, democracy can overcome.

— SANDRA FELDMAN
President, American Federation of Teachers

From "Lessons in Courage: Palermo's Battle Against the Mafia Became a Real-Life Civics Course" in "A Culture of Lawlessness to an Economy of Legality," Creating a Culture of Lawfulness: The Palermo, Sicily Renaissance, *proceedings from an international symposium, "The Role of Civil Society in Countering Organized Crime: Global Implication of the Palermo, Sicily, Renaissance," held in Palermo, December 14–15, 2000.*

∞

And yet, the very moment in which [he] finished explaining the theory of his right (more properly, interest) to respect the law, I suddenly realized just how perfectly it fitted the situation in which an entire population, an entire island, namely my Sicily, had come to find itself.

For more than a century Sicily had cohabited with the Mafia, a criminal organization that, as it became stronger and stronger, had come to pervade and condition the entire structure of society. Among the other harm caused by the Mafia, the local economy had remained hostage of a predominant illegality that, quite apart from distorting the free-market rules, suffocated all local entrepreneurial initiatives, deviated public financing from its ultimate ends of general interest, and discouraged private investments from outside the island.

At the same time, the name of Sicily—and more particularly that of Palermo—had become synonymous with Mafia all over the world and therefore also synonymous with a congenital and irredeemable social and cultural backwardness. Outside the island—and even among Sicilians themselves, albeit for different reasons—there had thus developed a total and converging lack of confidence in local society's capacity [to get] under way a healthy development process. And it was precisely this lack of confidence that constituted one of the greatest obstacles to the island's economic growth.

In short, Sicilians had come to find themselves in a situation in which their cultural need [to live] in a society respectful of the rules and their civic duty of complying with the law had become supplemented by a fundamental interest in lawfulness, an interest of a purely economic nature. And, let me add, an interest of which many people were probably not even aware and which not all succeed in fully appreciating even today.

Indeed, when civil society in Palermo and many other Sicilian towns reacted forcefully to the Mafia in 1992 and said "Enough!" it was above all their need of lawfulness that drove the citizens to come out into the streets in large numbers. The cultural revolution that—after maturing slowly for about a decade—burst out after the massacres of Judges Falcone and Borsellino[1] had its ultimate roots in the need the population felt for freeing itself of the violence, the intimidations, the corruption and the material and psychological oppression exercised by organized crime. The economic convenience factor was certainly not in great evidence among the motivations of the citizens who were saying "Enough!" at the time.

Similarly, the efforts to change things that have been made since then by the various components of civil society have had as their principal and most immediate objective the cultural and civic renewal of the citizenry. To all intents and purposes, there was brought into being a permanent educational process that aimed at spreading a culture of lawfulness fundamentally inspired by ethical values among ever larger parts of the population and, above all, among the new generations....

I am very happy to say that, as far as the rest of the world is concerned, the common perception of Sicily and its association with the Mafia have at long last

---

[1]In the summer of 1992, Judge Giovanni Falcone and Judge Paolo Borsellino, both Palermo magistrates, were murdered for their roles in the investigations into and crackdown on the Mafia. These investigations ultimately led to the indictment and prison terms of several hundred mafiosi.

changed. Indeed, Sicily and Palermo are today seen as a laboratory in which there is now being implemented an innovative and valid project of standing up to organized crime that could well serve as a model for other countries....

The key of this success is undoubtedly that civil society took its place by the side of law enforcement. While the latter concentrated on uprooting the Mafia structures in a manner that has no precedents in the island's history, numerous components of society (school, church, associations, local government, press) made their contribution, albeit in various ways, to the formation and spreading of a civic spirit that turned a community dominated by the Mafia into a community in which today there prevails a culture of legality.

Over and above this, civil society has also performed—and continues to perform—other and no less important tasks. The mere fact that it stood behind the policemen and the judges gave these men and women the indispensable moral support they need for carrying out their difficult work and avoided a repetition of the conditions of "isolation" that so often in the past rendered those in the front line of the fight against organized crime particularly exposed to the Mafia's reaction. Lastly, civil society is now committed to keeping an unceasing vigil and to denounce any sign of tiredness or relaxation in the fight against crime and corruption.

The last of these commitments is absolutely essential, for even though the Mafia has been dealt really devastating blows, it has not yet been defeated once

∞

After Liberia, after Rwanda, after Somalia, after Congo-Zaire, after Sierra Leone…after this numbing cycle of the negation of humanity and decay of community that seem resolved to pursue us into a new millennium, a continent in search of models for renewal could do worse than look towards the miracle of an ancient island community [Sicily] that has leapt out of the Dark Ages, regained its obscured identity and lit up the beacon of hope in the eyes and hearts of a new generation.
— WOLE SOYINKA
    Nobel Laureate and Professor, Emory University

From a speech delivered to the Annual Meeting of the Board of Governors, International Monetary Fund, in Washington, DC, September 27, 1999.

∞

and for all. Its remaining parts are still active and dangerous. Its members not yet in the hands of justice have changed strategy. Foregoing all striking and clamorous crimes, they have withdrawn into the shadows and are undoubtedly trying to reorganize themselves. That is why it is so essential that the fight should be continued—both at the level of law enforcement and at that of spreading the culture of lawfulness—with the same intensity that has characterized these last few years, without yielding to the temptation of believing that the battle is finished....

December 2000

From "A Culture of Lawlessness to an Economy of Legality," Creating a Culture of Lawfulness: The Palermo, Sicily Renaissance, *proceedings from an international symposium, "The Role of Civil Society in Countering Organized Crime: Global Implication of the Palermo, Sicily, Renaissance," held in Palermo, December 14–15, 2000.*

LEOLUCA ORLANDO *was mayor of Palermo, Sicily, for twelve years between 1985 and 2000. He currently serves as leader of the minority party in the Sicilian Regional Assembly.*

❧

Bogotá

BY MARK SCHAPIRO

One Friday night last March in Bogotá, I walked past a Fernando Botero statue of a gargantuan woman on horseback at the entrance to the Parque del Renacimiento—a tiny island of calm, containing a number of reflecting pools, in a grimy working-class district of the city. I flashed an official card certifying me as a male with good intentions at a National Policewoman stationed at the gate, and crossed into one of the city zones that had been declared temporarily all-female.

It was March 9, dubbed La Noche de las Mujeres—an occasion on which a city famous for its machismo was turned over to its female inhabitants. Men without a city-issued pass like the one I carried—essentially a signed pact indicating the holder's willingness to learn something from experience—were asked to stay at home. If they ventured out nonetheless, they were blocked from many of the city's plazas and thoroughfares. A female lieutenant colonel in the National Police was made commander of the city for the night, assisted by a mostly female force of police officers and citizen monitors.

According to pollsters, nearly a quarter of the city's 3.3 million women were out that night—an enormous showing that cut across class lines. In the southern barrios grandmothers and their granddaughters trooped into the Parque del Renacimiento to hear a storyteller. In the city's affluent north sophisticated young women, for whom going out with their girlfriends was hardly a revolutionary act, listened to a female band at a tidy little park and coyly threw handfuls of flour at the few males seated self-consciously at an adjacent outdoor café.

La Noche des las Mujeres was the creation of Bogotá's mayor, Antanas Mockus, who has a penchant for freewheeling social experiments to combat the violence and alienation that have corroded Bogotá's social fabric. La Noche was prompted, he told me, by Bogotá's unique combination of social conditions. Men are not only far more likely than women to commit violence but also forty times as likely to be its victims. At the same time, women have improved their status in Colombia—which has one of the highest levels of political participation by women in all of Latin America—through a wholly nonviolent struggle. La Noche would provide an opportunity to see what might be learned from women's forms of social organization and would also serve as an experiment in protecting men from themselves. As it turned out, violence on La Noche was 40 percent lower than on ordinary Friday nights.

The day before La Noche, I visited Mockus in his office at city hall. Seated under a huge portrait of Simon Bolivar signing Colombia's declaration of independence from Spain, he hunched over a scrap of paper and sketched three boxes. The first he labeled "legal power"—something one would expect of a big-city mayor. What marked him as an unusual politician was the other two boxes: "moral power" and "cultural power," which he defines as power derived from one's own standards and power derived from the shared values of the citizenry.

"At first," Mockus told me, "I had the illusion that if I wrote new laws, those words would become reality. But it soon became clear that if you want to change society's habits, law is only one of the means. Most people prefer internal mechanisms for determining for themselves what is right and what is wrong, but perceive other people as needing to be regulated by laws. The question I asked was how to reduce the difference between the laws and cultural and moral means of self-regulation." A governing style that could fairly be summed up as theater-as-politics was the result.

Indeed, Bogotá has been transformed in the past six years by Mockus's combination of street-level politics and symbolic acts. During his first term, he set into motion policies that added substantially to the city's public parks, established a modern bus system and built schools in the city's poorest neighborhoods. These initiatives were largely completed and expanded upon by Mockus's successor, Enrique Peñalosa, who also was responsible for the construction of four new large modern libraries in Bogotá's poorest districts. Mockus has retained many of Peñalosa's appointees in his administration, as Peñalosa had done when he took office, lending a powerful sense of continuity to the governing of Bogotá over the past six years. In part because of Mockus's imposition of a 1:00 A.M. closing for bars (proclaimed Carrot Hour, from the Colombian slang for someone who is uncool) and his unconventional but effective gun-exchange program (those who turned in weapons received small gifts of appreciation, such as flowers or food, and a certificate commending their act), Bogotá's murder rate has plummeted. Some 4,200 murders were committed in the city in 1993; the figure for last year is 2,200.

Bicyclists pedal along newly designated bike lanes; strangers relate to one another with small acts of civility. In 1996 the city government distributed tens of thousands of plastic cards depicting thumbs. When someone engaged in uncivil behavior, the thumb was to be pointed down; for a genial act it was to be pointed up. The thumb cards have disappeared for the most part, but the habit took hold, and it is not unusual for the real thing to flash upward after the observation of an unexpected act of courtesy or kindness.

The humble sidewalk is an early example of Mockus's attentiveness to the interplay between municipal governance and civic responsibility and pride. Until the mid-1990s visitors to Bogotá would have noticed the lack of sidewalks. Cars would park right up against storefronts, and walking down the street involved a perilous zigzag through an obstacle course of bumpers and swinging car doors. Six years ago Mockus initiated a sidewalk-construction program. Now people stroll down the sidewalks, and at intersections they cross in an orderly fashion on the neatly painted white stripes known as zebras. Taxi drivers who attended new city-sponsored classes in driver etiquette (the classes taught, among other things, the principle of yielding to pedestrians) were awarded windshield stickers proclaiming them "gentlemen of the zebras."

Such measures carry both practical and symbolic punch. "The lack of a sense of citizenship in Bogotá was reflected in our lack of sidewalks," Salomon Kalmanovitz, an economist and a director of Colombia's National Bank, told me. "There is a dignity that comes from not walking on the dirt or being forced to walk on the street. Building those sidewalks was an acknowledgment that eighty-five percent of the people in Bogotá do not own cars. You are telling drivers that they are no better than the pedestrians, which people from the car-owning class are not accustomed to hearing."

Similarly, in 1996, rather than hire more traffic cops, Mockus hired dozens of mimes, who stood at major intersections and, with slyly comic, extravagant gestures, admonished drivers who ran red lights, veered in front of pedestrians, or committed other violations. The city experienced an immediate decline in traffic accidents—proof of his theory that power can be wielded with a sense of humor. In the face of Bogotáns' deep distrust of traditional authority, Mockus told me, "sometimes you need a little cognitive dissonance."

Mockus, who is forty-nine and the son of Lithuanian immigrants, spent eighteen years as a professor of mathematics and philosophy and then rector at Colombia's National University—a background that helps to account for his pedagogical approach to governing. "Antanas sees the city as a huge classroom," Alicia Eugenia Silva, his deputy mayor, says. Mockus was elected mayor in 1995. He resigned two years later and ran, unsuccessfully, for Vice President; he regained his office in a resounding victory last October.

In a country long dominated by the Liberal and Conservative Parties, Mockus is an independent, a founding member of the Visionario Party. Although his social policies tend toward the left, a legacy of his years in Bogotá's radical university culture, his economic policies are largely neo-conservative: for example, during his first term he engineered a number of privatizations and municipal cutbacks.

In spite of his successes, Mockus faces formidable challenges. Twenty percent of the city's residents are unemployed, and more than half live in poverty or near poverty. Last year alone some 150,000 people flocked to Bogotá to escape the civil war in the countryside; slums sprawl ever upward into the hills around the city. At the same time, FOR RENT and FOR SALE signs abound in the better neighborhoods, as upper-and middle-class residents, tired of paying the "war taxes" extorted from business owners by the guerrillas, leave the country, often for the United States.

Not surprisingly, Mockus has his critics. One of the most vocal is Maria Emma Mejia, a member of the Liberal Party who served as Foreign Minister under President Ernesto Samper and who ran against Mockus last October. "Mockus's whole approach is to shock people out of their reality," Mejia says,

"But reality in Colombia now is enough to shock people out of their reality. We have real problems in Bogotá, and his symbols do nothing to address them."

Mockus, of course, is quick to counter this assessment. "We live in a world of symbols," he says. He showed me his wedding ring, explaining that it is a sort of talisman for his administration. The ring is a gold Mobius strip—a continuous one-sided band in the shape of a twisting circle. The Mobius strip—large-scale models of which served as backdrops during many of his campaign appearances—is a symbol, Mockus says, of the fact that "we share conflicts in the country, but we are all deeply linked." He continued, "Whenever I get involved in strong conflicts, I look at my finger and try to remember in the end we are all on the same side."

Adapted by the author from an article by the same title in The Atlantic Monthly, *September 2001. Copyright by Mark Schapiro.*

MARK SCHAPIRO *is a New York writer specializing in foreign affairs. His writing appears in* The New York Times Magazine, Harpers, The Nation, *and numerous other magazines.*

∝∾

Newark Confronts Its Past—and Chooses Its Future
BY CLEMENT A. PRICE

We have known for a long time the transformative powers of certain academic rituals on the intellectual life of the college campus. Such rituals, imaginatively mounted and graced with contributions from gifted scholars and civic activists, can also have a deep and enduring impact on local communities. When academic and civic leaders gather together to discuss matters of resonating importance to local identity and purpose, civic energies can be unleashed and spirits reinvigorated. In the fertile ground of such an occasion, the seeds were sown for the Newark Renaissance.

On November 8, 1997, the Rutgers Institute on Ethnicity, Culture, and the Modern Experience organized a half-day conference titled *Memory and Newark, July 1967*. It was a free and fervently public exploration into the various and divergent ways that Newark's infamous racial discord of July 1967 was remembered by individuals from all segments of the community over the past generation. A wide cross-section of citizens from one of the nation's most emotionally damaged cities talked and listened to each other, sharing their memories of a uniquely painful period in the city's life. Held at Rutgers-Newark's Paul Robeson Campus Center in Newark during an afternoon of steady rain, the discussion was unlike anything I have witnessed in my academic career that started in 1968, the year after Newark's infamous near rendezvous with disaster.

The program was risky. After all, America's racial disorders usually occur on contested ground, and they *always* foster contested memories. In Newark the riots were constructed along the variegated lines of race, ethnicity, neighborhood and generation. For some they were not riots at all, but rather a political upheaval by poor African Americans in a city hardly known for interracial harmony and discourse. For white ethnics, especially those in the Jewish and Italian neighborhoods, the riots were a betrayal of the civic order, the near death of a once-vibrant town.

During the long afternoon's deliberations, we were reminded that civic culture is deeply indebted to memoir. Dr. Robert Curvin (formerly vice president of communications with the Ford Foundation) gave the keynote memoir, a stunning narrative that located him as a young activist in a city divided by race and class. With photographs of Newark before and during the riots serving as the visual backdrop to his memoir, Dr. Curvin helped the audience consider anew the odd juxtaposition of optimism and despair in Newark in the 1960s and the devastating emotional impact of seeing one's hometown implode. Other speakers followed with their own unique takes on what it was like to be in Newark during those five days in which race and place really mattered. They remembered the breakdown of trust between elected officials and black leaders and the competing irrationality of the law enforcement officials and the law breakers. One woman, drawing from her memory as a ten-year-old in July 1967, recalled the odd sight of men and women darting through the darkened streets with mattresses. "I thought there was a mattress sale going on."

Mostly people spoke of the enduring emotional pain of witnessing their city nearly unravel. That the riots occurred during the near twilight of the civil rights movement and were followed by years of benign neglect of matters racial, made July 1967 a metaphor for the city's lost innocence.

Newark has had a long and agonizingly slow recovery. But recover it has! Newark in 2001 is a city revived. *Memory and Newark, July 1967* was a cathartic event. It was, in some sense, necessary to the mobilization of a comprehensive civic effort to recreate Newark—not from the ruins of its past, but from the creative ingenuity of its present. Newark is young again—a city poised for the 21st century!

The life-altering national tragedies of the 1960s, including the assassinations of Martin Luther King, Jr., and the Kennedys—John and Robert—America's war in Southeast Asia, and the rise of counter-cultural expressions of identity left deep imprints on the collective memory of the nation. But such local upheavals as the Newark riots had a resonance at least as profound. This was trouble on the ground—at home—to be recalled, mourned and fixed. In a quiet way, the scholars and community citizens who gathered to bring their memories of the riots to a public discussion cleared the air, making way for the Newark of tomorrow.

CLEMENT A. PRICE *is professor of history and director of the Rutgers Institute on Ethnicity, Culture, and the Modern Experience. He was the 2000-2001 scholar-in-residence at the Woodrow Wilson National Fellow Foundation and the author of* Many Voices, Many Opportunities: Cultural Pluralism and American Arts Policy.

Newark Now

BY WAYNE WINBORNE

Recalling its days of glory as New Jersey's capital of business, finance, shipping, and manufacturing, Newark is charting its 21st century renaissance, adding amenities that make it an attractive place to work *and* live in.

The catalyst for much of Newark's renewal was the fall 1997 opening of the $180 million New Jersey Performing Arts Center, which helped spur an unprecedented boom in commercial office leasing. Newcomers are attracted to Newark by convenient rail access to Manhattan, the excitement surrounding the Performing Arts Center, plans by the YankeeNets to build a new $275 million downtown arena, and by other encouraging signs that life is returning to the city. Affordable rents for solidly constructed, pre-war office buildings are attracting small and mid-sized companies seeking to escape higher lease rates elsewhere.

The city is by no means starting from scratch. Over the years, Newark has continued to be home to some of the state's and nation's largest corporations—Prudential, which was founded in the city 125 years ago; Public Service Enterprise Group, Horizon Blue Cross Blue Shield, and Verizon, formerly Bell

Atlantic of New Jersey, which is headquartered in a historic building on Broad Street. New Jersey Transit headquarters are also in Newark, as is the state's largest newspaper, *The Star-Ledger*.

Newark's new ranking as one of the most wired cities in America is attracting technology companies requiring significant bandwidth, led by IDT, the long distance telephone company and Internet service provider, and Net2Phone, a low-cost long distance Internet service spin-off from IDT. The company's move brought 1300 new workers to Newark's Washington Park neighborhood. Other dot.com companies moving to the city include Connect.com, and Broadview Networks.

Bamberger's Department store, which closed its doors at the corner of Market and Halsey Streets in 1992, has been quietly converted into a $1 billion technology center—an Internet "hotel." And a $66 million headquarters is under construction for The Public Health Research Institute, which is relocating from New York. The institute will be a major part of a Central Ward neighborhood known as University Heights Science Park, which rises just west of Broad Street, and includes Rutgers and New Jersey Institute of Technology, Essex County College and the University of Medicine and Dentistry (UMDNJ).

Here are more of Newark's features that spell "renaissance."
- Newark Airport has become one of the nation's busiest and most important international air centers.
- Newark's universities and colleges are expanding in size and quality, bringing national recognition.
- The newly refurbished Newark Museum is proving to be a major cultural asset.
- The Newark Public Library, in its second century of service, has greatly improved its facilities and opened an Information Technology Center for state-of-the-art public training and use.
- The New Community Corporation, the largest community development corporation in the United States, along with the Newark Housing Authority, has started replacing outdated high-rise buildings of the '50s and '60s with attractive, affordable, low-rise units.
- Developers and landowners are spending millions to improve existing landmark office towers, adding air-conditioning, new elevators, and high-speed data lines, to turn them into first-class office space.

- Newark has always been known for its beautiful cherry trees in Branch Brook Park, which extends into neighboring Belleville. Now the city's Passaic River waterfront is being reclaimed and turned into an esplanade.
- In 1999, nearly 50 years after minor league baseball was played in the city, the first pitch was thrown out in the new $35 million, 6,000-seat Riverfront Stadium, home to the independent Atlantic League's Newark Bears.

And on the drawing board are these major projects:

- Construction of a $325 million arena to be home of the NBA's New Jersey Nets and the NHL's New Jersey Devils.
- A new $150 million light rail system to link key downtown neighborhoods with New Jersey Transit's Broad Street station, Penn Station, and Newark Airport.
- Redevelopment of the long-vacant Broad Street retail and commercial strip into a vibrant residential, commercial and retail neighborhood.
- The creation of a new community just a short stroll from the city's colleges, the Newark Museum and Library, and the performing arts center by The New Newark Foundation, backed by Raymond Chambers and the Prudential Foundation.
- New restaurants opening downtown, providing competition to the long-established and well-known Portuguese, Spanish, and Brazilian restaurants in the Ironbound neighborhood. A glowing September *New York Times* review described Maize, the new restaurant at the Robert Treat Hotel, as "a high-end restaurant that is a vote of confidence in Newark's revival." For those with simpler tastes, a Starbucks is now open at 744 Broad Street.

The new Newark is solidly grounded in a vision that is as civic and cultural as it is economic, reflecting not only its entrepreneurship but also its strong commitment to provide a healthy social environment for all its people.

WAYNE WINBORNE *is vice president, business diversity outreach, at Prudential Financial in Newark, New Jersey.*

Togliatti, a Russian Town on the Move

BY SVETLANA PUSHKAREVA

A Russian town called Togliatti? Everyone asks me if I've got that right. But I do. Let me explain, because there's lots of meaning in a name. Togliatti, as we know it now, was founded in 1737 as Stavropol-on-Volga as a small fortress town. Then, in the 1950s the town started to grow. First there were built a large hydro-electric power plant and several chemical enterprises. Then a giant automobile factory was built with the assistance of Italian Fiat, which is why the city was renamed after an Italian Communist leader—and the boom was on. Togliatti became a magnet for young, well-educated specialists, adventurous people who saw it as a place where they could use their energies and ingenuity to build something new. They were provided with free housing and other incentives to come and be part of the development of a new place.

Fast forward to the 1990s. Togliatti is still on the move. Its mindset is positive, its mood is hopeful, its economy is getting stronger. Togliatti accounts for a major part of the growth of the Samara, one of Russia's richest regions. Because of its unique vitality, Togliatti was chosen to become the birthplace of the first community foundation in Russia. Representatives of several foundations from the U.S. and the U.K., e.g. Mott, Ford, Charities Aid Foundation, and EURASIA, came to Togliatti to decide whether to give start-up funds for a community foundation to Moscow or Togliatti. They chose Togliatti for its great sense of community and leadership, and for its potential for strong collaboration among the governmental, business, and non-profit sectors. I was fortunate to join the Foundation team built by Boris Tcirulnikov, executive director at that time.

The challenge of creating a foundation and a culture of philanthropy in Russia is somewhat daunting. Though there were some philanthropists in the days of the czars, in the days of the commissars, the concept of philanthropy was "perverted." Today local business and individuals are relearning what charity really is. Though we have had a great deal of support, both financial and intellectual, from foundations and organizations in the U.S. and the U.K., we know that it ultimately depends on us, the people of Togliatti, to create the new culture of civic responsibility. We've been fortunate to develop good relations with many local businesses and we are working on increasing the individual and public support of the foundation. We see a steady tendency for improvement in understanding what corporate social responsibility is and we continue to educate people about charity giving. Though we still need the support of foreign partners, we keep in mind that we must rely on ourselves to develop the financial capacity and the psychological will to be in charge of our own personal and collective destinies.

The Togliatti Community Foundation, we are proud to say, has funded 111 projects in its first three years, for a sum of two million rubles—$124,250! We have a long way to go, and every step we take is revolutionary. We now need to work on building a solid endowment. Other communities look to us for leadership, and we provide support for emerging community foundations in Russia. We have conducted a series of seminars and conferences for them, provided all the materials and documents that we have developed, and shared every single successful practice that we learned from abroad and adapted to the Russian environment. There are now 12 community foundations in Russia and we hope this number will grow.

After graduating from the International Academy of Business and Banking I participated in the Young Leadership Fellows for Public Service Program 1999-2000, which was administered by International Research & Exchanges Board (IREX). I studied International Relations and Communications at Miami University in Oxford, Ohio, volunteered at the Oxford Community Foundation and had my internship in Chicago at a non-profit organization called Urban Gateways: Center for Arts in Education. I focused on obtaining skills and knowledge that I could apply when I go back to the community foundation in my hometown. I returned to Togliatti and offered my services to the Togliatti Community Foundation. Today I am the Foundation's Public Relations and Cross Cultural Communication Manager. We have a strong beginning and the potential to build on our strength. Because of my foreign experience, I have many ideas about how to navigate the long road ahead.

I want to keep going. Although I've had attractive work opportunities in the U.S. and Moscow, I chose to give back to my community. Perhaps some day I will move on. But for now, I feel it quite rewarding to be with the Togliatti Community Foundation and pioneer together with my colleagues in creating a people-based, new-Russian-style philanthropy in my town. If democracy is to be a global project, it must start at the local level, in communities like mine.

Svetlana Pushkareva *is the public relations and cross-cultural communication manager of the Togliatti Community Foundation in Togliatti, Russia.*

Reflections After the Terror

A Letter of Sympathy
BY ALEXANDRA MITREA

Once more I realize that the history of humankind has been nothing but an alternation of light and darkness. Or perhaps in reverse order, since darkness seems to have had a longer hegemony than light. Do we need darkness in order to be able to appreciate light? Do we need oppression in order to appreciate freedom? Do we need times of suffering in order to fully enjoy times of happiness?

Most of my still-short life has been dominated by darkness. I grew up in a country in which communism and totalitarianism took extreme forms—no freedom, no rights, just standing in line and keeping silent. But every now and then light pierced the darkness and left me with a nostalgia that I could not escape. Even when there was no light in sight, I instinctively felt that it must be there somewhere. I instinctively felt that one day communism would collapse, that it was bound to come to an end simply because it was against the order of things—because it perverted all values and transformed us all into slaves.

Then, when few still believed in it, communism collapsed like a castle of sand, and we set out on the road to democracy. It has not been an easy journey, though I think it should be. Every now and then we stumble against obstacles, not only external but internal, too. As Adam Michnik said in *Letters from Prison*, "we still carry in us the seeds of captivity, the manacles of old-fashioned mentalities." Still, we felt reassured whenever we looked at the beacon [of the United States] and glimpsed its reassuring light. We felt strengthened when we looked at the country which, as early as the 18th century, held "these truths to be self-evident, that all men are created equal, that they are endowed by their Creator with certain unalienable rights, that among these are life, liberty and the pursuit of happiness."[1]

Now the beacon has been struck and for a moment we lost our bearings. For a minute we were engulfed in darkness, but only for a minute. Because we understood instantly that buildings can be leveled to the ground and people can be killed, but that the light of the democratic ideals of "liberty and justice for

---

[1] The United States Declaration of Independence

all" cannot be dimmed in our minds. And we understood something else: that we are all together in the struggle for democracy. The bell has tolled for all of us, as we have all been attacked. Our values have been attacked, our belief in a world of peace, reconciliation, and understanding among all nations.

To paraphrase Ecclesiastes, there is a time for cries and there is a time for action, for proactive solidarity. We believe the time for action has already come and are confident in the victory of the united forces of democracy. In this catastrophe we realized that freedom and democracy must not be lost, whatever effort it takes. More than ever, we are fully committed to the cause of democracy and are determined to pursue it, irrespective of the price. The terrorist attack on the United States is a catastrophic blow to freedom. All of us who love freedom must rise up and proclaim that love and secure that freedom.

ALEXANDRA MITREA *is professor of American Studies at Lucan Blaga University in Sibiu, Romania.*

ALEXANDRA MITREA *is professor of American Studies at Lucan Blaga University in Sibiu, Romania.*

FROM
"Notes on Prejudice"
BY ISAIAH BERLIN

Isaiah Berlin liked to allude to a passage in Bertrand Russell's History of Western Philosophy *where Russell says that, if we are to understand a philosopher's views, we must "apprehend their imaginative background,"[1] or the philosopher's "inner citadel," as Berlin calls it.[2] The character of one of the main rooms in Berlin's own citadel is vividly expressed in some hurried notes Berlin wrote for a friend (who does not wish to be identified) in 1981. His friend was due to give a lecture, and wrote to Berlin to ask for suggestions about how he might treat his theme. Berlin had to go abroad early on the day after he received the request, and wrote the notes quickly, in his own hand, without time for revision or expansion. The result is somewhat breathless and telegraphic, no doubt, but it conveys with great immediacy Berlin's opposition to intolerance and prejudice, especially fanatical monism, stereotypes, and aggressive nationalism. Its relevance to the events of September 11, 2001, hardly needs stressing.*

Berlin's manuscript is reproduced here in a direct transcript, with only a few adjustments to make it easier to read. I have omitted material relevant only to the specific occasion. —Henry Hardy

---

[1] *History of Western Philosophy* (Simon and Schuster, 1945), p. 226.
[2] For example, in *Four Essays on Liberty* (Oxford University Press, 1969), p. 135

1.

Few things have done more harm than the belief on the part of individuals or groups (or tribes or states or nations or churches) that he or she or they are in *sole* possession of the truth: especially about how to live, what to be & do—& that those who differ from them are not merely mistaken, but wicked or mad; & need restraining or suppressing. It is a terrible and dangerous arrogance to believe that you alone are right; have a magical eye which sees the truth; & that others cannot be right if they disagree.

This makes one certain that there is one goal & one only for one's nation or church or the whole of humanity, & that it is worth any amount of suffering (particularly on the part of other people) if only the goal is attained—"through an ocean of blood to the Kingdom of Love" (or something like this) said Robespierre[3]: & Hitler, Lenin, Stalin, & I daresay leaders in the religious wars of Christian v. Moslem or Catholics v. Protestants sincerely believed this: they believe that there is one & only one true answer to the central questions which have agonized mankind & that one has it oneself—or one's leader has it—was responsible for the oceans of blood: but no Kingdom of Love sprang from it— or could: there are many ways of living, believing, behaving: mere *knowledge* provided by history, anthropology, literature, art, law makes clear that the differences of cultures & characters are as deep as the similarities (which make men human) & that we are none the poorer for this rich variety: knowledge of it opens the windows of the mind (and soul) and makes people wiser, nicer, & more civilized: absence of it breeds irrational prejudice, hatreds, ghastly extermination of heretics and those who are different: if the two great wars plus Hitler's genocides haven't taught us that, we are incurable.

The most valuable—or one of the most valuable—elements in the British tradition is precisely the relative freedom from political, racial, religious fanaticism & monomania. Compromising with people with whom you don't sympathize or altogether understand is indispensable to any decent society: nothing is more destructive than a happy sense of one's own—or one's nation's—infallibility, which lets you destroy others with a quiet conscience because you are doing God's

---

[3]Berlin may be referring to the passage where Robespierre writes that *«en scellant notre ouvrage de notre sang, nous puissons voir au moins briller l'aurore de la félicité universelle»* "(by sealing our work with our blood, we may see at least the bright dawn of universal happiness)." *Rapport sur les principes de morale politique qui doivent guider la Convention nationale dans l'administration intérieure de la République* [Paris, 1794], p. 4.

(e.g. the Spanish Inquisition or the Ayatollas) or the superior race's (e.g. Hitler) or History's (e.g. Lenin-Stalin) work.

The only cure is understanding how other societies—in space or time—live: and that it is possible to lead lives different from one's own, & yet to be fully human, worthy of love, respect or at least curiosity. Jesus, Socrates, John Hus of Bohemia, the great chemist Lavoisier, socialists and liberals (as well as conservatives) in Russia, Jews in Germany, all perished at the hands of "infallible" ideologues: intuitive certainty is no substitute for carefully tested empirical knowledge based on observation and experiment and free discussion between men: the first people totalitarians destroy or silence are men of ideas & free minds.

2.

Another source of avoidable conflict is stereotypes. Tribes have neighbouring tribes by whom they feel threatened, & then rationalize their fears by representing them as wicked or inferior, or absurd or despicable in some way. Yet these stereotypes alter sometimes quite rapidly. Take the nineteenth century alone: in say, 1840 the French are thought of as swashbuckling, gallant, immoral, militarized, men with curly moustachios, dangerous to women, likely to invade England in revenge for Waterloo; & the Germans are beer drinking, rather ludicrous provincials, musical, full of misty metaphysics, harmless but somewhat absurd. By 1871 the Germans are Uhlans storming through France, invited by the terrible Bismarck—terrifying Prussian militarists filled with national pride etc. France is a poor, crushed, civilized land, in need of protection from all good men, lest its art & literature are crushed underheel by the terrible invaders.

The Russians in the nineteenth century are crushed serfs, darkly brooding semi-religious Slav mystics who write deep novels, a huge horde of cossacks loyal to the Tsar, who sing beautifully. In our times all this has dramatically altered: crushed population, yes, but technology, tanks, godless materialism, crusade against capitalism, etc. The English are ruthless imperialists lording it over fuzzy wuzzies, looking down their long noses at the rest of the world—& then impoverished, liberal, decent welfare state beneficiaries in need of allies. And so on. All these stereotypes are substitutes for real knowledge—which is never of anything so simple or permanent as a particular generalized image of foreigners—and are stimuli to national self satisfaction & disdain of other nations. It is a prop to nationalism.

3.

Nationalism—which everybody in the nineteenth century thought was ebbing—is the strongest & most dangerous force at large today. It is usually the product of a wound inflicted by one nation on the pride or territory of another....If the Russians...had not been treated as a barbarous mass by the West in the nineteenth century, or the Chinese had not been humiliated by opium wars or general exploitation, neither would have fallen so easily to a doctrine which promises they would inherit the earth after they had, with the help of historic force which none may stop, crushed all the capitalist unbelievers. If the Indians had not been patronized, etc., etc.

Conquest, enslavement of people, imperialism etc. are not fed just by greed or desire for glory, but have to justify themselves to themselves by some central idea: French as the only true culture; the white man's burden, communism: & the stereotypes of others as inferior or wicked. Only knowledge, carefully acquired & not by short cuts, can dispel this: even that won't dispel human aggressiveness or dislike for the dissimilar (in skin, culture, religion) by itself: still, education in history, anthropology, law (especially if they are "comparative" & not just of one's own country as they usually are) helps.

From an article of the same title printed in The New York Review of Books, *October 18, 2001.*

Isaiah Berlin *(1909–1997), an Oxford fellow, was a political theorist and public intellect. He wrote on many topics, including free will and determinism.* Henry Hardy, *a fellow of Wolfson College, Oxford, is Berlin's editor and literary trustee. Two new books by Berlin will be published in 2002:* Liberty, *an expanded edition of* Four Essays on Liberty, *and* Freedom and Its Betrayal.

"What Terror Keeps Teaching Us"
by Richard Rhodes

To a 4-year-old boy, as I was on Dec. 7, 1941, the carnage at Pearl Harbor was invisible, as the carnage at the World Trade Center and the Pentagon was largely invisible on the September day of the terror attacks, before crews began to sift the wreckage. The news came by radio rather than by television, in the early evening, in the gathering dark, but it was no less vivid and portentous: "The Japanese have bombed Pearl Harbor!" My family lived in a boarding house in a neighborhood of large older houses on the east side of Kansas City, Mo. Awed and uncomprehending, my older brother and I were sent door to door to rouse our neighbors.

Lights came on, voices relayed word back into the depths of houses, radios blared, people came out of doors and strangers talked to strangers as if they had known one another for years. I went to bed that night, as all of us did on the night of Sept. 11, with a sense that the world was irrevocably changed.

The final casualty toll at Pearl Harbor was smaller than the toll of the terror attacks: 2,403 military and civilians killed, 1,178 wounded. But both were surprise attacks, unprovoked; both were heinous; both brought home a conflict that was raging elsewhere and drew us in.

What possessed the Japanese? They meant to demonstrate the strength of their convictions and hoped by destroying our fleet to buy time to win access to Asian oil and iron ore to replace supplies the United States had embargoed. What possessed the terrorists? They meant to punish us and to show us our vulnerability, of course, but they also meant to demonstrate the strength of their convictions. The terrorists meant to show us up, but also to force us to take them seriously.

One lesson we took from Pearl Harbor was the necessity of being prepared; after the war, we maintained standing armies and arsenals as we had never done before. But we learned a greater lesson than readiness from the Second World War, with its 60 million dead. We learned that violence originates in suffering—in poverty and disorder that bows to fanaticism when the world turns its back. The suffering find their champions, and they are not all Gandhis.

We had been isolationists before Pearl Harbor, secure in Fortress America. After Pearl Harbor, we had first to fight a war, just as we have to extirpate the terrorist organization that organized the September attack. From Pearl Harbor and the war emerged our commitment to the United Nations and, a few years later, when we understood the consequences of continuing disorder in devastated Europe, to the Marshall Plan. The war refuted our policy of disengagement and isolation; Fortress America let down its moat. Today, Germany and Japan are our allies, prepared to settle disputes with us nonviolently.

Since the end of the cold war, we have been retreating into isolation again, doubting diplomacy, dodging treaties, abandoning Africa, fantasizing a missile shield, dismissing the Middle East. Neighbors got together with neighbors after Pearl Harbor and again after the terror attacks. The piracy of terrorism must certainly be outlawed, but against the murderous altruism of surprise attacks by suicide squads the only long-term resolution is the affirming altruism of international community.

From an article of the same title printed in The New York Times Magazine, *September 23, 2001.*

RICHARD RHODES *is a writer for* The New York Times Magazine *and the author of* Why They Kill, *an examination of the roots of violence.*

"Nowhere Man"

BY FOUAD AJAMI

Islam alone didn't produce Mohamed Atta. He was born of his country's struggle to reconcile modernity with tradition.

I almost know Mohamed Atta, the Egyptian who may have been at the controls of the jet that crashed into the north tower of the World Trade Center. I can almost make him out. I have known Egypt for nearly three decades, and so much of Atta's life falls neatly in place for me. I can make out the life of the 33-year-old man, one of a vast generation of younger Egyptians making their claims on a crowded land, picking their way through the cultural confusion that has settled upon the country in recent years.

Atta's father, a well-off but strict lawyer, has given foreign reporters fragments of the life. He has done it in an angry way, outraged as much by claims that his son is a hijacker as by the reports that his son may have been drinking vodka and playing video games days before he boarded American Airlines Flight 11. "We keep our doors closed," the elder Atta said, "and that is why my two daughters and my son are academically and morally excellent."

The father was giving voice to the Egyptian bourgeoisie's discipline and anxieties, to its desire to keep its world and its norms intact. From the father still: "He was so gentle. I used to tell him, 'Toughen up, boy.'" So much of the world of younger Egyptians is given away in that admonition.

There had come to Egypt great ruptures in the years when the younger Atta came into his own. A drab, austere society had suddenly been plunged into a more competitive, glamorized world in the 1970's and 1980's. The old pieties of Egypt were at war with new temptations. There must have been great yearning and repression in Mohamed Atta's life; it is the torment of Atta's generation. They were placed perilously close to modernity, but they could not partake of it.

The place affected an unaccustomed hipness—big new hotels, the cultural clutter of Europe and America, the steady traffic of foreign tourists throwing in the air intimations of more emancipated ways in less constricted, repressed lands. But the sons and daughters were to be chaste, and the old prohibitions were to be asserted with increasing stridency.

An easy secularism had once been the way of Egypt, and a measure of banter between men and women. Never as tranquil as its legend, but a gentle and soft country all the same, Egypt knew a cultural wholeness and prided itself on a fairly vibrant cultural life. This had given way by the time young Atta, born in 1968, made his way to the university.

On the crowded campuses where Atta and his peers received an education— an education that put off the moment of reckoning with a country that had little if any room for them, little if any hope—there emerged an anxious, belligerent piety. Growing numbers of young women took to conservative Islamic dress—at times the veil, more often the head cover. While the secularists sneered, it became a powerful trend, a fashion in its own right. It was a way of marking a zone of privacy, a declaration of moral limits. Young men picked up the faith as well, growing their beards long and finding their way into Islamist political movements and religious cells. A cultural war erupted in the land of Egypt. A stranger who knew the ways of this land could see the stresses of the place growing more acute by the day.

The sermons of the country—religious and political, the words of those who monitored and dominated its cultural life—insisted on a false harmony, held on to the image of the good, stable society that kept the troubles and the "perversions" of the world at bay. But the outwardly obedient sons and daughters were in the throes of a seething rebellion. In an earlier age, Egyptians had been known as a people who dreaded quitting their native soil. In more recent years, younger Egyptians gave up on the place, came to dream of fulfillment— economic, personal, political—in foreign lands. Mohamed Atta, who left for Germany in 1993, was part of that migration, of that rupturing of things on the banks of the Nile.

Religion came to Atta unexpectedly, in Hamburg, where he had gone for a graduate degree in urban planning. In *bilad al kufr* (the countries of unbelief), he needed the faith as consolation, and it was there that he sharpened it as a weapon of war. He styled himself emir, commander, of a religious cell. But the liberties, the temptations, still tugged at him; there were those reports from south Florida of drinking and video games. Mohamed Atta carried the contradictions of his worlds, the new liberties and the medieval theology side by side. The man who willingly flew into a tower of glass and steel for the faith broke one of the canons of the faith.

The modern world unsettled Atta. He exalted the traditional, but it could no longer give him a home. He drifted in "infidel" lands but could never be fully at ease. He led an itinerant life. The magnetic power of the American imperium had fallen across his country. He arrived here with a presumption, and a claim. We had intruded into his world; he would shatter the peace of ours. The glamorized world couldn't be fully had; it might as well be humbled and taken down.

It must have been easy work for the recruiters who gave Atta a sense of mission, a way of doing penance for the liberties he had taken in the West, and the material means to live the plotter's life. A hybrid kind has been forged across that seam between the civilization of Islam and the more emancipated culture of the West. Behold the children, the issue, of this encounter as they flail about and rail against the world in no-man's-land.

The New York Times Magazine, *October 7, 2001.*

FOUAD AJAMI, *professor of Middle Eastern Studies at the School of Advanced International Studies at the Johns Hopkins University, is author, most recently, of* The Dream Palace of the Arabs.

∞

FROM
"This **Is** *a Religious War"*
BY ANDREW SULLIVAN

...**T**he question of religious fundamentalism was not only familiar to the founding fathers. In many ways, it was the central question that led to America's existence. The first American immigrants, after all, were refugees from the religious wars that engulfed England and that intensified under England's Taliban, Oliver Cromwell. One central influence on the founders' political thought was John Locke, the English liberal who wrote the now famous "Letter on Toleration." In it, Locke argued that true salvation could not be a result of coercion, that faith had to be freely chosen to be genuine and that any other interpretation was counter to the Gospels. Following Locke, the founders established as a central element of the new American order a stark separation of church and state, ensuring that no single religion could use political means to enforce its own orthodoxies.

We cite this as a platitude today without absorbing or even realizing its radical nature in human history—and the deep human predicament it was designed to solve. It was an attempt to answer the eternal human question of how to pursue the goal of religious salvation for ourselves and others and yet also maintain civil peace. What the founders and Locke were saying was that the ultimate claims of religion should simply not be allowed to interfere with political and religious freedom. They did this to preserve peace above all—but also to preserve true religion itself.

The security against an American Taliban is therefore relatively simple: it's the Constitution. And the surprising consequence of this separation is not that it led to a collapse of religious faith in America—as weak human beings found themselves unable to believe without social and political reinforcement—but that it led to one of the most vibrantly religious civil societies on earth. No other country has achieved this. And it is this achievement that the Taliban and bin Laden have now decided to challenge. It is a living, tangible rebuke to everything they believe in.

That is why this coming conflict is indeed as momentous and as grave as the last major conflicts, against Nazism and Communism, and why it is not hyperbole to see it in these epic terms. What is at stake is yet another battle against a religion that is succumbing to the temptation Jesus refused in the desert—to rule by force. The difference is that this conflict is against a more formidable enemy than Nazism or Communism. The secular totalitarianisms of the 20th century were, in President Bush's memorable words, "discarded lies." They were fundamentalism built on the very weak intellectual conceits of a master race and a Communist revolution.

But Islamic fundamentalism is based on a glorious civilization and a great faith. It can harness and coopt and corrupt true and good believers if it has a propitious and toxic enough environment. It has a more powerful logic than either Stalin's or Hitler's Godless ideology, and it can serve as a focal point for all the other societies in the world, whose resentment of Western success and civilization comes more easily than the arduous task of accommodation to modernity. We have to somehow defeat this without defeating or even opposing a great religion that is nonetheless extremely inexperienced in the toleration of other ascendant and more powerful faiths. It is hard to underestimate the extreme delicacy and difficulty of this task.

In this sense, the symbol of this conflict should not be Old Glory, however stirring it is. What is really at issue here is the simple but immensely difficult principle of the separation of politics and religion. We are fighting not for our country as such or for our flag. We are fighting for the universal principles of our Constitution—and the possibility of free religious faith it guarantees. We are fighting for religion against one of the deepest strains in religion there is. And not only our lives but our souls are at stake.

From an article of the same title printed in The New York Times Magazine, *October 7, 2001, page 53.*

ANDREW SULLIVAN *is a contributing writer for* The New York Times Magazine *and former editor of* The New Republic. *He is author of* Love Undetectable: Notes on Friendship, Sex, and Survival.

᪥

"Terror's Aftermath: U.S. Strengths Are Terrorist Opportunities"
BY BENJAMIN R. BARBER

The tragic irony of last Tuesday's terror is that America was humbled by its strengths, not its weaknesses. Adept practitioners of strategic jujitsu—the Japanese system of wrestling in which an opponent's strength and weight are used against him—the terrorists leveraged America's technological wizardry and democratic openness to the purposes of destruction.

Imagine the attack succeeding without commercial aviation, architectural modernism, credit cards and car-rental agencies. Terrorism's success was not just the horrendous body count. It was how it forced the nation to abandon modernity: The terrorists hijacked four airliners and turned them into instruments of slaughter, but America itself closed its skies and halted its financial transactions, yielding to a kind of self-paralysis. Jujitsu.

A nation of farmers cannot be terrorized by a blow to the cities. A hard-mail system cannot be interdicted by a single electronic subterfuge. It is the efficient interdependence of our economy, our technology, our communication and transportation systems, and our government that renders them vulnerable. It is the same with our democracy.

Imagine such an attack being successfully organized in a police state, where all rights are suspended, all immigration terminated, identity papers checked on every block, "foreigners" randomly stopped throughout the land. The terrorists turned openness into vulnerability and tolerance into weakness. We could suspend the Bill of Rights, and the war against terrorism would become easier— but the terrorists would then have forced us from the very democratic habits in whose name we make war on terrorism. Jujitsu.

The hard lesson of the war between the forces of fundamentalism—jihad— and the forces of commercial, cultural and technological modernity is that jihad not only detests and combats modernity, it does so jujitsu-style by leveraging its weight and turning its virtues into frailties. For jihadic reaction is not just Islamic, and its enemy is not simply America. Jihadic reaction is still trying to combat the Enlightenment, and the ambiguous Enlightenment values that America embodies: its wealth but also the materialism that accompanies it; its secularism but also the cynicism about religion; its commercial successes but also the hubris with which it flaunts them; its economic globalism but also the inequalities that are spread by it.

America's understandable instinct in this moment of agony is to go it alone, strike hard unilaterally, collaborating with others only to the extent we demand a declaration "for us or against us," only to the degree others do what we want them to. Yet, the age of American independence is over.

We have lived, if hypocritically, with the myth of independence since our founding days, when two oceans were deemed sufficient protection from the torment of world history. Not even the two great wars of the 20th century could alter this dream of independence. Just two weeks ago, a national missile shield was to be our virtual ocean to protect us from evil. No more.

Rudely, bluntly, murderously, the terrorists have taught us that there is no standing against interdependence. Terror is fundamentalist violence globalized. It cannot be defeated by unilateral actions, however forceful or pointed. This is not a moral point but an empirical one. When the terrorists proclaim, "There are no innocents!" and set about their zealous and methodical slaughter, they are saying, "There are no more boundaries between civilian and military, millionaire and proletarian, cynical pol and innocent child; you are all caught up in modernity's web of interdependence; you will all die." Frontlines and civilian sanctuaries are all one in the global jihad of virtual warriors whose tools are not just the plastic knife but the Internet, not just the ideological tract but the pilot's manual. Alone, we can wrestle with anarchy only by surrendering our modernity and giving up our democracy. To preserve them and defeat terror, we have to acknowledge and embrace the reality of our interdependence.

The long-term lesson is as simple to discern as it is hard for Americans, born to independence, to accept: America today can be no blessed island, if ever it was one; it cannot survive alone, if ever it could. We will live together in this new globe, or we will die together.

Jujitsu works only when the powerful try to dominate the weak. When strength is anchored by democracy and weighted by justice, and rules by law rather than by force, it cannot be leveraged by jihad. If in the coming struggle against terrorism we remember that we are engaged, not in a clash of civilizations or a war on fundamentalism, but in a quest to legitimize our interdependence, terror will not win and democracy cannot lose.

The Los Angeles Times, *September 16, 2001.*

BENJAMIN R. BARBER *is the Gershon and Carol Kekst Professor of Civil Society at the University of Maryland and a principal of The Democracy Collaborative. He is the author of numerous books including* Jihad vs. McWorld *and* The Truth of Power: Intellectual Affairs in the Clinton White House.

The Globalization of Justice
BY WOLFGANG ISCHINGER

The special European Union summit has confirmed the solidarity with the United States that German Chancellor Gerhard Schroeder stressed some days ago, ruling out no option. Beyond the short-term measures now required: we need a comprehensive, long-term strategy if we want to get to the root of terrorism. Globalization is not, as some would have it, the cause of this new kind of terrorism. But this new kind of international terrorism demands a global response. In fact, the formation of a global coalition against terrorism means that we are now moving beyond the globalization of the economy to the globalization of politics.

The bloody attacks on New York and Washington force us to accept that America and Europe cannot successfully isolate themselves from tension, conflict and war elsewhere in the world. To ignore instability caused by poverty and underdevelopment, to ignore civil wars in Africa or failing states in other parts of the world places our own security at risk, directly or indirectly. These regions may well be the breeding grounds of the fanatics and extremists whose very swamp we are trying to dry out.

Therefore, we must urgently address regional conflicts not only in the Balkans and in the Middle East but also in Central Asia and elsewhere—in a much more determined and comprehensive manner than in the past. Developing and implementing a comprehensive strategy for regional conflict prevention and conflict management on the basis of a broad and strong coalition against terrorism and not forgetting the poorest of the poor will be a major element of the common agenda of Europeans and Americans in the years to come.

Finally, the Bush administration deserves praise for the effective way it has worked with the United Nations and NATO during the initial hours of the international coalition-building effort against terrorism. Such efforts will need to be continued, within both the U.N. Security Council and NATO, and possibly also within other international and regional forums. This is multilateralism at its best—helping to create and sustain the broadest possible international legitimacy. But shouldn't this multilateral approach also apply when it comes to bringing terrorists and their leaders to justice? Wouldn't it make sense if terrorists and their sponsors could be brought to justice before an internationally recognized criminal court?

A letter to the editor of The Washington Post, *printed on September 24, 2001.*

WOLFGANG ISCHINGER *is German Ambassador to the United States.*

∞

"My Islam"
BY MONA ELTAHAWY

I am a Muslim. The terrorist attacks on Sept. 11 shook my faith to its foundation. I am angry and ashamed that Muslims will forever be remembered for such horror.

But being angry and ashamed is not enough. Muslims must ask ourselves, how did we get here? We are long overdue for a healthy dose of introspection.

We've heard many times how the U. S. government must reexamine its foreign policy and about the list of corrupt dictators it calls friends. It is just as important for Muslims to do our own soul-searching.

For starters, liberal, moderate and progressive Muslims must speak out. We've been quiet too long, and I blame us for the sad state of affairs of the Muslim Umma (community) as much as I blame the clerics, whom, I must admit, I gave up on long ago.

It is no longer enough for the clerics to issue tired platitudes on how Islam means peace and surrender. Where were they when Osama bin Laden and his coalition of terrorists vowed to target every American man, woman and child?

We have to look inward and ask ourselves what in Islam, what in the way it is practiced today, allowed bin Laden to promote his murderous message? And, please, those of you out there penning letters to tell me Islam is nothing but a bloodthirsty religion of the sword or that the Sept. 11 attacks were a Zionist conspiracy that had nothing to do with Islam—save your ink and close those e-mail messages. I have no time for either camp.

I belong to a third camp that refuses bin Laden's options of being on his side or with the "infidels." I am fed up with the self-pity and self-denial that for too long have paralyzed Muslim thinking. By constantly blaming Western conspiracies for our ills we fuel our own helplessness. Strength is the essence of introspection.

We must make that introspection public. We should not be ashamed to question out loud. Muslims love to remind the world that the Islamic empire at its height stretched from Morocco to China. That we gave the world Avicenna, Averrones and the concept of zero. That at its founding, Islam gave women more rights than any other religion or social system.

All that is true, and I have shared in that pride. But by pointing to our achievement and not to our shortcomings we give in to what I call the Pyramid curse. I am from Egypt, would swell with pride whenever I saw those magnificent structures. But that pride was often tempered with sadness that their magnificence was a reminder of what Egypt used to be. They are three gauntlets thrown down nearly 5,000 years ago by a golden dynasty whose splendor we strain to understand, let alone better.

Some may question who I am to speak for Muslims. My answer is who is bin Laden? He received no formal religious education but took it upon himself to represent us. He does not represent me. I am a Muslim woman who is wrestling with her faith and questioning its meaning for me today. It is equally my right to speak out.

About 10 years ago, I went through a crisis of faith that swept away lazy answers and made me realize how much work it takes to keep my faith viable. For inspiration I turned to Muslim scholars whom I considered revolutionaries. They were reinterpreting Islam by looking at it squarely with modern eyes. They dared to utter the R-word—reformation.

One of these books was *Toward an Islamic Reformation: Civil Liberties, Human Rights, and International Law*, by Abdullahi An-Na'im, an Emory University law professor. I recently turned once more to his book and wrote to Prof. An-Na'im to seek his advice.

He wrote back to tell me that he was about to oversee a new program that includes supporting nine fellows over the next three years to promote human rights in their own communities from an Islamic perspective.

Muslims in America are fortunate because we are free to debate without risking our lives. Prof. An-Na'im's book presents and builds upon ideas of Sudanese Muslim jurist Mahmoud Mohamed Taha. The Sudanese government publicly executed Taha in January 1985. Many Muslims consider Taha's ideas controversial because of their espousal of reform, but they offer a welcome alternative to the fundamentalists, whose ideas too often go unchallenged.

Kevin Hasson pointed out in his Dec. 27 op-ed article how religious freedom in America had influenced the Catholic Church. American Jewish friends have told me how their faith has evolved in America and given birth to the Reconstructionist movement. Muslims in America have the chance to lead the way for the Umma.

From The Washington Post, *January 2, 2002.*

Mona Eltahawy *was a journalist in the Middle East for ten years before moving to the United States.*

The Handbook

A Consolidated and Updated Version of the
Democracy is a Discussion Handbooks

Introduction

In the several years that have passed since the publication of the two *Democracy is a Discussion* handbooks in 1996 and 1998 we have seen new democracies cropping up in every part of the world. The post-Cold War period has been the most fertile ever in spawning democratic governments and civil society organizations; yet at the same time it has been host to some of the most insidious countervailing forces—from crime and corruption to murderous acts of terrorism—putting the fragile seedlings of freedom and social justice at great risk.

Without the bipolar tensions of the Cold War, which were stabilizing if not benign, there is a global asymmetry that causes anxiety, which erupts episodically into hysteria and anger, which we have seen escalate to unbridled and murderous violence. Whether of ethnic, racial, or religious origin, this violence represents the absence or suppression of the will to resolve conflicts through negotiation and compromise. In many places—largely in what we have unfortunately come to characterize as the third world (the geography of which is indeterminate), hopelessness overcomes the energy, skills, and political will needed to build a democratic society. In such places violence and even terrorism can be seen as justifiable responses to the frustrations of victimization by poverty and disease and the facelessness that results from living as a "have-not" in a globalized, economically driven society.

The dramatic changes in the world in the last twenty years have not relieved the plight of the poorest among us. If anything, the globalized economy has made life more difficult for them. Into the void created where totalitarian or authoritarian powers existed before, the forces of the globalized market moved with centrifugal force. Economic power tends to precede and subsume attempts to establish democratic political structures which, in time, put in place the rules and constraints that make the economy a function of, rather than the force behind, a free democratic society. The new "reigning sovereign" is the collective power of transnational corporations, with corporate executives in charge, rather than duly elected, accountable political leaders. The goal of the market, after all, is not building a better society but making larger profits for shareholders. In the context of democracy, that is not necessarily a problem—but lacking the democratic context, the market can have devastating consequences for the poor.

And so, what could have been—and still can be—a new democratic era requires deeper understanding and more informed and bolder civic action.

With more democratic nations in the world than ever before, with the unprecedented effectiveness of telecommunications, and with the dynamic power of ordinary people to become citizens committed to making democracy work, we are well armed to continue the struggle for democracy worldwide.

The Handbook is the new edition of the *Democracy is a Discussion* handbooks, consolidated and revised to include new texts; to delve deeper into the roots of the challenges to democracy; and to cite new strategies and approaches to addressing them. Entirely new is a section on globalization, its dominance in the new era, its many and wide-ranging manifestations, and the dangers and hopes that it offers. While globalization is not new to the world, it is essential to understand and respond to its contemporary incarnation if we are to use it to advance the cause of democracy.

Even before the terrorist attack on the United States on September 11, 2001—the most sobering event in my memory—it had become clear that the struggle for democracy in our time is a long-term, ongoing project—a work perpetually in progress. It requires a heroic effort on the part of people in every corner of the world. But it is a struggle well worth that effort because democracy, with all its imperfections, is the only sustainable antidote we know to tyranny and terror. The twenty-first century can herald in a new democratic era—if we educate ourselves to the culture and the politics of democracy. Free people—citizens—in free societies, through their vigilance, their courage and their creativity, will leave a legacy of freedom to future generations. That is today's dream that can become tomorrow's reality. —Sondra Myers

Basic Elements of Democracy

I

Democratic Imperatives: Trust, Goodwill, Idealism

"There is a point to democracy if we assume that human life is not about accumulating toys but about freedom, justice, and goodwill."
—Erazim Kohák

Introduction by William M. Sullivan

Summing up his decades-long struggle against totalitarianism, Václav Havel has urged that advocates see themselves as "ambassadors of trust" in a fearful world. Yet the word *trust*, like goodwill and idealism, is sometimes dismissed as too vague or too soft to be taken seriously as a central issue in politics. But such apparently tough-minded assumptions are mistaken about what actually makes democracy work.

It is important that advocates of civic democracy recognize the critical value of developing trust, goodwill, and idealism in their societies and the folly of relegating them to the sidelines of politics for fear of being thought naive. Based on the willingness of individuals and groups to abide by common norms of honesty and reciprocity, the civic virtues of trust, goodwill, and idealism are essential sources of social and political power. In today's increasingly interdependent world, the resilience and strength of both individuals and societies depend upon their ability to cooperate for common purposes.

Without the civic virtues of trust, goodwill among citizens, and a strong dedication to the ideals of democracy, individuals and societies lose the capacity to attain their goals. From social conflict to insensitive economic development to environmental degradation, many of our biggest problems arise from conditions in which all parties would be better off if they could cooperate, but where lack of mutual trust and goodwill makes common action impossible. For example, when industrial waste or auto emissions pollute the air or water upon which all, even the polluters themselves, depend, it would clearly benefit all parties to show self-restraint and devote effort to devising a common system of waste-management. In the absence of mutual trust, however, each party actually has an incentive to defect from cooperation, fearing to be played for a "sucker" or left "holding the bag." The consequence of this lack of goodwill is that everyone suffers, victims of a self-imposed inability to act together for a common good.

Trust, goodwill, and democratic idealism, then, are key practical resources. While these civic virtues can be depleted through exploitation, they are also renewable and expandable resources. Trust is one of the benefits produced when citizens come together to discuss and deliberate in common. Goodwill enables citizens to begin a conversation; to listen and to speak, to understand better their differences and agreements. This in turn strengthens civic bonds so that future cooperation is made more likely and more effective. In this way, democratic idealism gradually redeems its promise of a better and more humane form of public life. President Havel is right. In the practice of trust and goodwill, civic idealism becomes the realism that generates the power on which democracy builds.

WILLIAM M. SULLIVAN *is senior scholar at the Carnegie Foundation for the Advancement of Teaching and a professor of philosophy at La Salle University. He is co-author of* Habits of the Heart *and* The Good Society *and author of* Work and Integrity: The Crisis and Promise of Professionalism in America.

Discussion Questions

1. What assumptions about human nature are inherent in the concept of democracy? Do you agree with these assumptions? Why or why not?

2. What is the importance of consensus building in a democracy, and what role do trust, goodwill, and idealism play in this process?

3. Do trust, goodwill and idealism seem old-fashioned or out of date? If so, why, and what problems seem to underlie their decline?

4. How much of what William Sullivan calls "key practical resources" does your country/society/ region have? Have these resources been depleted? If so, how can they be renewed and expanded?

5. Is democracy a *natural* form of government that will arise spontaneously or evolve in time without a specific effort to nurture it? What examples does history provide to support an answer?

Readings

FROM
"The Faces of Democracy– Looking to the Twenty-First Century"
BY ERAZIM KOHÁK

Does democracy have a future in the post-Communist world?

So stated, the question tends to take us by surprise. In spite of democracy's rather dismal record outside northwestern Europe and North America, that is the one thing we never doubted. As we fought one war after another to make the world safe for democracy, we remained confident that once we had at last defeated its enemies, democracy would blossom forth, ushering in an age of peace, justice, and goodwill.

The apocalyptic war with which our century opened was supposed to accomplish all of that. When the weary victors met at Versailles, they showed a great concern to punish Germany and Austria for their war crimes, but surprisingly little concern to create the conditions for democracy. That, they were confident, would take care of itself. Yet it was not democracy that grew on the wreckage of the old order but rather communism, several varieties of fascism, and national socialism that sprouted like weeds among rubble. Barely 20 years after the war to make the world safe for democracy the world was locked in another World War and democracy was on the precarious defensive.

Still, we kept the faith. In retrospect, perhaps the most puzzling aspect of the Second World War was the conviction of the Allies that if only we could defeat Hitler and his clique, democracy would blossom forth, bringing in the promised age. The grand alliance, which included Stalin's Soviet Union as well as the United States and Britain, had no common program beyond defeating "the fascists," and that seemed enough. Given a chance, democracy, we assumed, would emerge spontaneously from the wreckage.

It did not happen that way. "Anti-fascism" proved far more fertile ground for communism than for democracy. Three years after the second war to end all wars, democracy was once again on the defensive, locked in another global war, no less bitter for being mostly of the cold variety. Yet the rhetoric of that Cold War suggests that we learned little from the first two rounds. That rhetoric produced little critical reflection about the conditions that make for democracy, about what democracy is, what makes it work—and what makes it fail. The emphasis was again on defeating the enemies of democracy, this time atheistic communism and its evil empire. Once that was accomplished, democracy would blossom spontaneously, bringing in the promised age of freedom, goodwill, and prosperity at long last.

It was an odd faith. Its foundation was the Enlightenment conviction that all humans are capable of freedom and responsibility and so of sharing the prerogatives and burdens of power. Democracy is possible because all humans are capable of rationality, of grasping and pursuing the common good. But while the thinkers of the Enlightenment believed that this ability must be carefully nurtured, the twentieth century added a much more problematic romantic belief that the maturing of humans and societies to the responsibility of freedom would happen spontaneously, that humans are "naturally good" and therefore also "naturally" democratic, as long as they are not corrupted and/or constrained by democracy's enemies, the Communists, the fascists, the militarists and, perhaps, others like religious fanatics or nationalists. Hence our strategy. While the great philosophers of democracy, T. T. Masaryk or John Dewey, taught us that democracy must be first carefully nurtured in every one of us and in our society at large and only then can be expected to work as a political system, we preferred to believe that we could just fight the enemies of democracy and trust that democracy would simply happen.

After a century of futile triumphs, it is that romantic faith in the spontaneity of democracy that is no longer tenable. Both the Third World and the post-Communist world—Angola, Liberia, Somalia, the former Soviet Union, the former Yugoslavia, the former Czechoslovakia—all testify that, left to their own devices, humans do not prove spontaneously democratic, blossoming forth in freedom, tolerance, goodwill, and responsibility. They are far more likely to go on acting in ways that proved productive in the past, no matter how destructive they may be, now that the warfare is ended and democracy's foes vanquished. With the collapse of Soviet power, the negative ideology of "anticommunism" has become as irrelevant as the Pied Piper after the rats left town, or as the negative ideology of "anticolonialism" once the colonial empires crumbled. Old habits, though, die hard. It will take rather more than defeating the evil empire and leaving it up to the invisible hand to assure the future of democracy in the post-Communist world. Democracy is an achievement, not a spontaneous growth. It takes an active and informed effort....

The troublesome truth is that democracy, as presently understood not only in the post-Communist world but in the entire post-Cold War era, reflects the problems of the twentieth century and is ill-equipped to cope with the problems of the twenty-first. Its cold war model of social interaction is one of triumphing over opponents, not one of seeking a consensus. Typically, in Czechoslovakia, the leaders of the two most powerful parties agreed on a division of the country rather than accept a need to compromise in a united one. Similarly, present-day democracy's model of social organization is not one aimed at compensating the tendency to polarization but one of fostering individual affluence. Perhaps most troublesome, present day democratic societies see the human goal in life not as one of sustainable harmony but one of open-ended economic expansion. We could once more quote the Prime Minister of the Czech lands: "Ecology is the icing on the cake and we can eat our cake without the icing."

Yet, is unrestricted gratification of individual greed what democracy is all about? The embattled farmers at the rude bridge in Concord hardly thought so. In spite of the Stamp Act and the mercantile policies of the British Empire at the time, that Empire offered far more secure opportunities than the uncertainties and sacrifices of a revolution. For them and for their representatives in Congress assembled, democracy was about something else. It was about the conviction that all humans and not only a few are capable of assuming the full stature of free humanity, of accepting responsibility for themselves and for the common weal without a tutor over them, be he benign or otherwise. Democracy was a vision of a voluntary cooperation, of a world without masters and serfs, a world of equals living together in freedom, in responsibility and in mutual respect as citizens, not as subjects.

It was and still is an audacious vision. All through the centuries, all over the globe, the underlying assumption of social organization had always been that humans in their thousands are not capable of maturity, of freedom and responsibility. Only the few are, and it is they that must rule. They are the beautiful people, the many are drudges who must remain perennial adolescents, at times obstreperous, at times charming, at times well-treated and at others abused, but always free both of the privilege of freedom and the burden of responsibility.

The grand vision of the European Enlightenment was one of all humans as potentially capable of full humanity, regardless of race or creed, even the wretched of the earth, capable of making their own decisions and sharing in the care of the common weal. Against the Hobbesian vision of humans as intrinsically egotistic, having to be restrained in their greed by a sovereign, it was the vision of humans as capable voluntarily of subordinating their private ends to a common good and the law of reason.

That, of course, also means that democracy cannot be simply declared or legislated.

So what are the attitudes and habits that democracy presupposes in its citizens? Perhaps the basic is a certain moral maturity. Ralph Waldo Emerson spoke of "self-reliance," but that word has since acquired a whole range of rather unfortunate connotations. Other writers speak of accepting the responsibility of freedom, though that again is less than clear. Perhaps the most helpful distinction may be a Kantian one: the characteristic of adolescence is self-indulgence, that of maturity is self-respect, respect for humanity, whether in my own person or that of another. Democracy builds on respect and self-respect.

Hannah Arendt offers another metaphor. What is characteristic of adolescents—of unfree persons—is the tendency to regard diversity as a threat and to interpret all human relations in adversary terms, as differentiating between friends and enemies. Moral maturity means a perspective of goodwill, a willingness to welcome diversity as an enrichment and to approach others in openness, seeking a common good. It is not simply a matter of being willing to tolerate rather than to fear and crush dissent. It is a matter of perceiving diversity as a valid form of participation. Democracy cannot be built in closed ranks and closed minds. In Karl Popper's metaphor, it requires an open society.

Metaphors abound. Democracy, we could say, is about the willingness to pay taxes, giving up self-indulgence for the sake of all that is needed to make for a free community, from school through communications down to environmental protection. Environmental concerns provide another metaphor: democracy is about the willingness to live simply that others may simply live. Less metaphorically, the justification of authoritarian rule has always been what in recent discussion has been symbolized by the unwillingness of individuals to give up their self-indulgence for the sake of the common good. The familiar metaphor here is the tragedy of the common. For every individual grazing his sheep on the common land, adding just one more sheep represents a significant personal advantage while refraining from so doing offers no visible advantage at all. Yet when all users add just one more sheep each, the flock will overgraze the land and all the sheep will perish. The lord of the manor is said to be needed to save the peasants from their own shortsightedness. Democracy is about the willingness to accept responsibility for the common ourselves.

Democracy is, finally, about a good dose of idealism. Maturity, yes, and a generosity of spirit, but beyond that, democracy cannot get along without idealism. Idealism today has acquired a bad name throughout the lands of the former Soviet empire. The Communists had long and stridently appealed to idealistic motives. Much of the appeal of communism to outside observers was precisely its invocation of high ideals—business for the people, not for profit; liberation of women from household drudgery; the fight for peace. The reality we saw behind that facade was wholly different: the crass corruption in business, the exploitation of women in the lowest-paid menial jobs, the manipulation of the peace movement in the service of Soviet imperialism. Over the years, all idealism became suspect and we learned to trust only the crassest, egotistic motives and to seek or assume them behind every act. Greed, we assume, is honest, altruism fake.

Yet democracy is impossible without a great deal of altruism and idealism. On a strictly realistic basis, it would be hard to avoid starkly Machiavellian conclusions, accepting democracy in the same role as communism before it, that of an ideological smoke screen of crass calculating egotism. There is certainly enough of that all around, and perhaps has always been. The Founding Fathers knew it well: the elaborate system of checks and balances they built into the American Constitution attests as much. They were, though, willing to hope that humans are also capable of responding to ideal motives, of finding self-fulfillment in self-transcendence. Not the brash young graduates making their first million as advisers to post-Communist governments but the young women and men serving in the Peace Corps are the bearers of the democratic ideal.

There is a point to democracy if we assume that human life is not about accumulating toys but about freedom, justice, and goodwill. And that, finally, sums up the problem of democracy in the post-Communist world. It is problematic because the decades of the Cold War have given us an idea of democracy suited to the needs of that time, as an ideology of conflict and an instrument for the advancement of personal greed. So conceived, democracy could contribute little to resolving the pressing problems of the coming age, building up a community of shared cultural heritage, overcoming the global and social polarization of humanity, and reorienting humans from unlimited expansion to a life in harmony. Yet that is not what democracy is all about. At its core, democracy really is about maturity, not pettiness; about goodwill, not about contentiousness; about idealism, not about greed.

This, then, is the global task of democracy in the twenty-first century: to recover the maturity, goodwill, and idealism that democracy was about before the decades of Cold War deformed it in the image of contentious greed. It is a difficult task: everything around us seems to bid us give up the hope and the struggle and accept that contentious greed is the wave of the future, perhaps hoping with Heidegger that some god will take it upon him or herself to save us while we mindlessly follow the momentum of affluence to the ultimate collapse. Still, it is not a hopeless task because from the heritage of democracy there are other voices speaking to us as well, speaking not of contention and greed but of liberty and justice, proposing malice toward none and charity and justice for all, seeking a future not of black or white but of all humans, asking us not what we want from our country but what we can bring to it. Perhaps for all the electronic din, more clamorous even than the class of arms, we shall yet hear those voices in time.

From an article of the same title in Kettering Review, *Fall 1995, 50-52, 60-63, by permission of the author.*

ERAZIM KOHÁK *is professor ordinarius of philosophy at The Charles University in Prague and a professor emeritus at Boston University. He wrote* The Embers and the Stars.

∞

"Black Africa's Open Societies"
BY IBA DER THIAM

Tolerance has always held a preeminent position in the thought of many African peoples. In West Africa, for example, it is the fundamental principle on which the entire social life of the Senegambian region is built, governing the interaction between individuals and ethnic groups as well as international relations.

Nothing illustrates this better than the central place the concept of peace occupies in the region's moral thinking. The Wolof saying, "*Ci Jaam la yeep xeej*," which signifies that peace bears innumerable promises, implies that peace is the necessary precondition for social stability, political equilibrium, economic prosperity and moral and material progress.

Even before the experience of the slave trade and colonial oppression, the aspiration for peace was a deeply felt need in a society exposed for centuries of its long history to the vicissitudes of wars fought in the name of conquest or in defence of local aristocracies. It has left its mark on the most anodyne details of daily life. When two people meet, one says as a greeting, "Are you at peace?" "Nothing but peace," the other replies, as if the harmony born of universal accord, whatever the philosophical, religious or moral starting points or choices of the people involved, could bring an inner calm and sense of hope more valuable than anything else life has to offer.

The same leitmotif of an aspiration for peace and security reappears in the prayer offered by each family to call down God's blessings on its members and on all things. In the words of one traditional Guinean supplication, "Let peace reign in the world! May the pot and the calabash not fall out! Let the beasts live in harmony! May every bad word and unbecoming thought be rooted out and packed off to the back of beyond, to the depths of the virgin forest!"

As the principal element regulating relations between people and between communities, tolerance is the imperative that governs all social life. In some African societies it means refusing to mistrust other people and rejecting both fear and preconceptions in dealing with whatever is new, unknown, unusual or out of the normal pattern.

THE HUMAN DIMENSION
Professor Cheikh Anta Diop suggested that in the Cayor region of Senegal the election of the king was a traditional perquisite of what he called the "governing council." All the social groups that made up the nation were represented in

this institution. The aim was not merely to make the body representative but also to encourage collegial participation and friendly social relations in an atmosphere of mutual tolerance and respect.

Although the *diawerigne m'boul*, the officer presiding over the council, was always chosen from among the *geer* or aristocracy, the *lamane diamatil*, the *bataloupe ndiob* and the *badie gateigne*, all of whom were governors of important provinces as well as council members, had to come from the *gmegno*, the ranks of the people of caste, while the *diawerigne boule* represented the house-slaves.

For traditional societies of this sort, humankind may be one in essence but it is nonetheless diverse in its ways of living and thinking and in the manner in which its constituent groups come to terms with themselves and other peoples. Consequently they made the *nitt*, or human being, their principal frame of reference. This human essence was seen as a generic concept, independent of time and place, the supreme embodiment of the divine presence on Earth. Stripped of all moral, philosophical or political connotations, it became a sublimated ideal to which everyone owed consideration and deference.

It is in this light that the treatment of strangers in some African societies must be considered. Newcomers are welcomed with kindliness and generosity, no matter what language they speak or what their sex, age, religion or social or political condition may be, for they are human beings first and foremost. As such, they have a right to food and shelter. Their person, goods and health will be protected, and they will be given a decent burial if they die.

In some Wolof communities, it is quite common for the head of a family to give up his own house and bed, or that of his wives or children, to strangers, without giving a thought to his own state of health....

Following this logic, the differences between peoples, far from being stressed as barriers separating humankind, are minimized to such an extent that they finally lose much or all of their meaning and their divisiveness, and are blurred and blunted until they become harmless. Integration of this sort involves not a denial of the foreigner's identity—and here I have in mind those insidious processes of assimilation that are really more like mutilation—but a profound and freely accepted awareness of the symbiotic complementarity linking the individual to other people. Unbreakable bonds are forged in this fusing of essences.

RENEWING THE TRADITION

This was the state of mind in which Africa, from the dawn of history, opened itself to the outside world. From the time of Queen Hatshepsut's expedition from her native Egypt to the land of Punt in the years between 1493 and 1490 B.C. until the nineteenth century explorers, there is no lack of witnesses to the African spirit of tolerance and unfailing hospitality.

It was as a result of the prevailing peace that Habib ben Unaïda and al-Fazari, around 800 A.D., were able to compile their chronicles, the first to mention the existence of the empire of Ghana; that Ibn Hawqal was free to visit the lands south of the Sahara; that al-Bakri, alIdrisi, Yakut Ibn Saïd and alUmari, between the eleventh and the fourteenth centuries, could give us precious descriptions of the kingdoms of the so-called Sudanic belt from Senegal to the Nile; that Ibn Battuta could visit Mali and Leo the African Timbuktu. Free of dogmatism and sectarianism, the spirit of tolerance encouraged dialogue and the exchange of ideas.

The same phenomenon was at work on the West African coast. Gomes Eanes Zurara's chronicles of Guinea, and the travel writings of Diogo Gomes, Duarte Pacheco Pereira, João de Barros and of the Venetian Ca'da Mosto all bear witness to the open-mindedness of the peoples of Cayor, Bo and Sine Salem, whose humanity would also be attested to by other Western visitors from the seventeenth to the nineteenth centuries. Tolerance extended to color, language, religion and ethnic and social origin as well as to sex and philosophical or moral views. This atmosphere enabled Christian missionaries to carry out their work without risk wherever traders had set up bases and colonizers had raised their flags.

Despite longheld views to the contrary, these were in effect open societies where freedom and justice reigned. Dare one say that democracy and tolerance flourished there until the slave trade and colonial conquest and all that went with it—native status, taxes, military conscription, land seizure, forced labour—created an endemic state of violence that corrupted social habits and ways of life to the point at which they were no longer recognizable.

So a precious heritage lies buried beneath the still smouldering ruins of colonial imperialism. Contemporary Africa must rediscover it quickly, to create worlds of freedom, peace and social harmony in which all its children can find fulfillment.

Reprinted from the UNESCO Courier, June 1992, 31–33.

IBA DER THIAM, *a Senegalese historian, politician, and diplomat, is co-editor of the two volumes of UNESCO'S* History of Mankind: Cultural and Scientific Development.

2
The Role of Citizens: Rights and Responsibilities

"The only thing necessary for the triumph of evil is for good men (and women) to do nothing."
—Edmund Burke

Introduction by William A. Galston

As the twentieth century draws to a close, the debate over the role of citizens has assumed a new complexity and urgency. In the long-established democracies of western Europe and North America, declining political participation and trust in public institutions have become pervasive concerns. In nations of central Europe and Asia emerging from communism's yoke, the task of citizens is to nurture institutions and practices that are compatible with local conditions and conducive to democratic aspirations. In nations still laboring under the burden of authoritarian regimes, the challenge is to expand the small arenas of liberty that exist within the interstices of oppression.

The basic rights of citizens are reasonably clear. They include freedom of speech and expression, of association and assembly, and of participation; safeguards against state arbitrariness in the administration of law; and protections for personal privacy, individual conscience, faith and worship. Full citizenship also requires the right to marry, to travel freely, and to participate in economic and social life on fair and equal terms. The responsibilities of citizens include, not only compliance with legitimate laws and institutions, but also the willingness to do their fair share to create and sustain them. Perhaps the most important responsibilities of citizens are to make appropriate use of their liberty and to respect the rights of others. For history suggests that the abuse of liberty by some promotes the growth of government authority that can restrict the liberty of all.

The appropriate balance between the rights and responsibilities of citizens will vary in accordance with local circumstances. In the United States, for example, the dramatic expansion of individual rights during the past generation must now be matched by an increased willingness of citizens to take responsibility for one another and for their common life.

Post-communist regimes, by contrast, cannot take liberty for granted. They must construct institutions that defend core individual and political rights. But this task cannot succeed unless individual citizens see themselves as active participants in, not passive recipients of, the nurturance of liberty. At the same time, citizens of these regimes must wrestle with profound issues of moral responsibility for past abuses, a task that will require a sensitive balancing of justice, mercy, democratization and social reconciliation.

One thing is clear: there is no one-size-fits-all account of the rights and responsibilities of citizenship. Each nation must work out for itself the approach that comports best with its history and circumstances. Here as elsewhere, a broad-based dialogue among citizens is the key to progress.

WILLIAM A. GALSTON, *director of the Institute for Philosophy and Public Policy at the University of Maryland, served from 1993 to 1995 as deputy assistant for domestic policy in the Clinton White House. He is the author of five books and many articles.*

Discussion Questions

1. Evaluate the rights granted to you by your political system. Which rights set boundaries and which are entitlements or "affirmative duties to promote actively the well-being" of citizens?
2. What are your responsibilities as a citizen? If the commonwealth is a "partnership for the common good," which of your responsibilities promotes the commonwealth?
3. According to Mary Ann Glendon, an important responsibility is respecting the rights of others, not just in the abstract but often at some cost to us. What costs might be incurred in respecting others' rights, and do you agree that we should have to pay?
4. Why can't we just sit back and let the government take care of things? What are the consequences of the absence of citizen participation in government? Might dictatorial forces fill the vacuum?
5 Václav Havel's "tunnel at the end of the light" is a clever inversion of a common metaphor. What is he driving at?
6. How does your country/society/region compare to the regions identified by Robert Putnam as good examples of democracy in practice? What does your area need to improve?

Readings

FROM
Democracy on Trial
BY JEAN BETHKE ELSHTAIN

Political power does not explode out of the barrel of a gun or flow from the dripping blade of a guillotine. Rather, it comes into being when men and women, acting in common as citizens, get together and find a way to express their collective hopes and possibilities.

A modulated politics whose practitioners open their hands in gestures of anticipated fellowship to all persons of goodwill, white or black, rich or poor, offends those who want a totalistic and revolutionary politics. Hate is easy; arousing the regressive urges of one's fellow men and women requires little more than a capacity for spite. What is difficult, what is the most daunting task of the political imagination is to fight the allure of hate, particularly when it comes to us in the name of revolution....

THE "HORIZONTAL VOICE" OF LAS MADRES

Democratic rights that are encoded in law refer to [the] idea of a dignified indi-vidual....Just about anything anybody wants gets bruited about as a right in America nowadays, and although Americans sometimes grow weary of "rights talk," the fact that rights exist as immunities, as the ways we express what governments are not permitted to do to us because we are persons with political standing and dignity, is both a precious reality and a precarious achievement. "Human rights" is the name the vast majority of the world's people give to a persistent yearning. I learned these lessons, or perhaps better put, came to remember them, as I listened to the powerful and sometimes terrible stories told to me by mothers who have become public citizens—in Argentina, Central America, Israel and the West Bank, the Czech Republic, and the United States. Because the stories of those political mothers, Latin America's Las Madres— "the Mothers of the Disappeared"—jolted me out of my complacency about rights and public freedom, I will recount their saga briefly.

The issues, remember, are democratic possibility and the robustness of democratic yearning in our complex world as it lurches and lumbers toward the end of the twentieth century. Political actors all over the world are busy writing new acts for, and enacting scenes from, an ongoing drama of democracy, often as a form of dissent from and disaffection with an undemocratic order....I turn to the tragedy of the Las Madres of Argentina and how these women took to the public squares, speaking a double language of maternal grief and human rights, advocating justice, and seeking recognition not so much for themselves as for the "disappeared." Las Madres transgressed the boundary between private and public to reaffirm the integrity of that boundary against those who, in the name of the state, had violated it by rounding up, torturing, and killing thousands of persons, most of them young, all of them stripped of dignity and denied political standing and recognition.

The authoritarian, militarist system that Las Madres opposed after it had seized and destroyed their children permitted one sort of politics (or pseudopolitics) only: that of supplication to a high authority. In this system, all political life was constructed vertically, and what was essential to all democratic political life had been virtually wiped out. Some social scientists, following the political theorist Albert Hirschman, have called this the "horizontal voice": the right to address others, to call forth some sort of "we," to make manifest a political identity.[1] Antidemocratic regimes must try to destroy this horizontal voice—the voice Las Madres found in themselves. These women created a "we," forging a group political identity based on their shared experience. Condemned to silence, they repudiated the sentence of the regime and voiced their grief and outrage in the Plaza de Mayo, a great public square in Buenos Aires, by marching weekly around the square in protest of their children who had been imprisoned, tortured, or killed by the state. Having lived a private life of grief, they found strength and political identity by deprivatizing their mourning. By fusing a language of grief with a language of human rights, they not only kept alive the particular realities and identities of individuals, their sons and daughters, tormented and lost to state terror, but issued a call to nonviolent arms to their fellow Argentines and to the wider world: Protect mothers and families, but embrace and protect a democratic constitution as well. To do so, one must honor the dignity of free citizens, young and old.

Recall, if you will, the potent terms that have pervaded this discussion thus far: hope and reality. Hope gives rise to political being and action, for without

---

[1]This is an argument elaborated by Guillermo O'Donnell and based on the concepts of Albert O. Hirschman in his book *Exit, Voice, and Loyalty* (Cambridge, Mass.: Harvard University Press, 1970). O'Donnell's essay appears in "Shifting Involvements: Reflections from the Recent Argentine Experience," Kellogg Institute Working Paper no. 58, February 1986, Notre Dame University.

hope the people, and individuals, perish politically. Concrete attention to particular concerns constitutes reality, not grandiose schemes that require antidemocratic methods to attain some ostensibly better or more perfect democracy down the road, after we have rid ourselves of all counterrevolutionaries who stand in our way. In my conversations with Las Madres over nearly a decade, I was struck by how many of them, especially those who called themselves the Linea Fundadora, understood the language of rights in its fullest and richest embodiment as setting boundaries not only for the politics of the state but for their own politics. "We, too, must behave democratically in our movement, one mother told me, if we are to advocate democracy for our society."

To be sure, human rights language is hardly as ancient a maternal language as that of mourning and loss. Las Madres put these languages together. Human rights was, for them, a way to express the timeless immunities of persons from the depredations of their governments, rather than a vehicle for entitlements, as we Americans more and more see things. Rights gave political form and shape to Las Madres' disobedience, linking the women to an international network of associations. They not only breached the private-public divide of their own society in the interest of protecting the integrity of family life against wholesale destruction and definition by their government; they crossed the boundaries of states as well, astonishing themselves in the process as they gained support and inspired other human rights–based mothers' movements throughout Central and Latin America.

Las Madres made it clear to me that they sought justice, not vengeance. For this reason, they opposed the death penalty. "Human beings are not robots," Renée Epelbaum, mother of three of the "disappeared," told me. "The man or people who killed my children are criminals, those who tortured and those who gave the order to torture. Human beings are responsible for what they do. They destroyed the rights, the lives, of other human beings." Another mother, María Adela Antokoletz, added: "When justice is not fulfilled, when rights are not cherished, democratic possibilities vanish." Renée continued: "You know, we understand that not everyone responsible can be punished—that's utopian. But we must press forward from a sense of hope and reality. We don't want the Mothers' movement changed into a class movement. We demand justice strongly. But we are not utopians." María Adela agreed: "What we want and think is that the Mothers of the Plaza de Mayo must endure forever, much more than in our own lifetimes. It has to do with having a guardian position in society in order to watch so this will not happen again."

These dissident mothers encoded the specifically liberal and constitutional understandings of democracy, which are grounded in human rights construed as immunities and duties, into their political self-definition. Through Las Madres' actions and deeds, the ethical force of an argument for human rights helped to animate quiescent sectors of the moribund and demoralized Argentine civil society. Whatever Argentina's future fate, Las Madres would say, human rights can never again be trampled upon with such impunity. That is their wager—one to which they have devoted their lives in the name of the lost lives of their children....

VÁCLAV HAVEL: "TUNNEL AT THE END OF THE LIGHT"
A remarkable freedom from rancor and the corrosive force of resentment characterizes these brave exemplars. Václav Havel showed as much courage as Las Madres when he found himself, on several occasions, in Communist prisons for his dissident crimes. But even in rebellion, Havel insists, there must be limits. Freedom is not the working out of a foreordained teleology or political prophecy; rather, freedom comes from embracing what one is given to do in one's time and place. Democracy is the political form that enables human beings to work out freedom as responsibility, in service to the notion that there are things worth suffering for.

For Havel, hope, responsibility, freedom and acceptance of paradox are all of a piece. What makes Havel such a fascinating performer of democratic political thought is that he provokes the complacent, mocks the smug, tweaks the arrogant, and suffers without excusing the weak, from a stance of compassion, not sickly pity. In his rejection of the petrified politics deeded by the legacy of the French Revolution and a century of total wars and totalist politics, Havel helps us to move into the future, disillusioned hence paradoxically free. I think he would agree that a central task of political philosophy for our time lies in recognizing what has happened in Europe since 1989 for what it is: the definitive collapse of an attempt to rebuild human society on some overarching Weltanschauung. Europe, Havel notes, has entered the long tunnel at the end of the light. This is a wonderful metaphor for the democratic drama in general. There is the light of public freedom, individual liberty, and political equality, and then we move through that long tunnel, a world of politics without end, guided by these ideals.

Havel argues that the world is possible only because we are grounded. If this world of "personal responsibility," with its characteristic virtues and marks of decency, both public and private (justice, honor, friendship, fidelity), is ruptured or emptied, what rushes in to take its place is politics as a "rational technology of power" whose exemplar is the manager, or apparatchik. When human beings play God, the wreckage grows. In this mode, the human being finds himself in the "rut of totalitarian thought, where he is not his own and where he surrenders his own reason and conscience."[2] He or she lives within a lie as the self is given over to the "social auto-totality"; identity is surrendered and responsibility falters. A totalitarian society counts on this, requires it. A democratic society, in its mass, consumerist forms, may give rise to a similar mentalité, and should this mentalité grow apace, shared responsibility for the civic world will fade there, too.

From Democracy on Trial (New York, 1995), 117–134, by permission of Basic Books a division of HarperCollins Publishers, Inc.

JEAN BETHKE ELSHTAIN *is the Laura Spelman Rockefeller Professor of Social and Political Ethics at the University of Chicago. A noted author and lecturer, her latest book is* Who Are We? Critical Reflections and Hopeful Possibilities.

∝∾

FROM

"The Infrastructure of Democracy: From Civil Society to Civic Community"
BY WILLIAM M. SULLIVAN

The idea of civic culture was first enunciated by classical humanism, as in Cicero's influential definition of a commonwealth or *res publica* as "not any collection of human beings brought together in any sort of way, but an assemblage of people in large numbers associated in an agreement with respect to justice and a partnership for the common good." The citizen is thus defined both as a bearer of rights, as defined by the "agreement with respect to justice," and also as a member of a community, a "partnership for the common good."[1]

Civic membership entails two responsibilities: to maintain the terms of the "agreement" with respect to justice, but also to contribute to the public

---

[2]From "Politics and Conscience" in Václav Havel, *Living in Truth*, (London: Farber and Farber, 1987) p. 151.

partnership. In the case of the United States, the founding documents, the Declaration of Independence and the Federal Constitution, set out the terms of the agreement as well as, in the Constitution's famous Preamble, the goals of the public partnership. It is sobering, however, to note that it required decades, and a destructive civil war, to establish national consensus about the meaning and application of the terms of the agreement on "freedom and justice for all," while the dimensions of the public partnership are still hotly debated.

Today, the importance of the link between civic culture and enduring democratic life is becoming clearer. It has long been argued that democracy requires enough political and social equality to provide all citizens with a sense of dignity and standing. Some have gone further to maintain that civic solidarity needs a relatively egalitarian distribution of at least economic opportunity and security, if not economic rewards. Recent research strongly suggests that both these claims are correct, while filling out with empirical detail the operational meaning and practical consequences of civic culture.

In his landmark study of Italian regional governments, Robert Putnam developed a set of characteristics, as well as empirical measures, of the kind of social space[†] necessary for "making democracy work." Putnam discussed four features of the civic cultures of regions in which democratic government worked well. These were the regions of Italy in which governments were efficient and effective and whose citizens took pride in their governments and identified with them as their own.

The first characteristic of successful regions was civic engagement, the expectation that individuals and groups are "alive to the interests of others." The second was a high degree of political equality, defined as a social context in which "horizontal relationships of reciprocity and cooperation" predominate over "vertical relationships of authority and dependence." Putnam found that in such places leaders "conceive of themselves as responsible to their fellow citizens" rather than functioning narrowly as the representatives of the interests of party or faction, as was true in the less civic regions.

Thirdly, civic regions were characterized by high levels of solidarity, trust, and tolerance. This enabled citizens to cooperate with different others for the

---

[1]Marcus Tullius Cicero, *De Re Publica* (On The Commonwealth), trans. Clinton Walker Keyes, (Cambridge, MA: Harvard University Press, 1988), I. 39, p. 65.

[†]*Editor's note:* Earlier in the article, Sullivan defines social space as "a metaphor for describing the norms and expectations which guide thought and behavior in everyday life, the standards to which persons hold themselves and each other accountable."

sake of developing public goods. Fourth, civic regions were places of dense and overlapping associational life. This developed the skills of cooperation and habits of shared responsibility. The crosscutting membership associations worked to "moderate and expand loyalties and interests," further strengthening bonds of trust and reciprocity.[2]

All four of these characteristics of civic cultures turned out to be present to the same degree as three quantifiable measures: the extent and intensity of associational life, the extent of newspaper readership, and the level of voter participation. In sum, the relative strength of civic norms and expectations determined the extent of social tolerance, trust, and cooperation. Perhaps more surprisingly, the strength of civic culture also turned out to be the best predictor of economic vitality as well.[3]

In sum, civic culture structures the social space of civil society in public-regarding ways, anchoring individual identity and conscience in shared norms of solidarity, trust, and reciprocity. When these are effectively institutionalized, citizens derive a strong sense of standing and purpose through participation in public life. A pluralistic civil society provides opportunities for individuation and creative experiment, but sustaining an open society requires integrative virtues as well, a high level of personal and social discipline. These capacities grow from an individual's willingness to cooperate for the sake of an enlarged sense of identity and purpose. It is in this quite realistic sense that democratic citizenship is a moral project, a historically rare and precarious process of collective moral development.

From an unpublished paper of the same title (1996), 13–16, by permission of the author.

For information about WILLIAM M. SULLIVAN, *see page 110.*

---

[2] Robert D. Putnam, *Making Democracy Work: Civic Traditions in Modern Italy* (Princeton, NJ: Princeton University Press, 1993),87-90.
[3] *Ibid.*, pp. 6-8.

FROM

"Welfare Rights at Home and Abroad: A Learning Process"

BY MARY ANN GLENDON

YOUR RIGHTS AIN'T LIKE MINE

A renowned European legal historian recently compiled a "basic inventory" of rights that have been accepted by most western countries at the present time. The list included, first and foremost, human dignity, then personal freedom, fair procedures to protect against arbitrary governmental action, active political rights (especially the right to vote), equality before the law, and society's responsibility for the social and economic conditions of its members. It is hard to say what would strike most American readers of this list as more strange—the omission of property, or the inclusion (in a catalog of "rights") of affirmative welfare obligations. Yet the list is an accurate one. Welfare rights (or responsibilities) have been accorded a place beside traditional political and civil liberties in the national constitutions of most liberal democracies. It is the eighteenth-century American Constitution that, with the passage of time, has become anomalous in this respect.

The fact that welfare rights have been accorded constitutional status in so many countries cannot be attributed exclusively to the relatively recent vintage of their constitutions. To a great extent, it is a legal manifestation of European attitudes toward the state that are traditionally less suspicious than American attitudes. Continental Europeans today, whether of the Right or the Left, are much more likely than Americans to take for granted that governments have affirmative duties to promote actively the well-being of their citizens. The leading European conservative parties espouse openly and in principle what American conservatives have only accepted grudgingly and sub silentio: a mixed economy and a moderately interventionist state. A broad social consensus in Europe supports the subsidization of child-raising families, and accepts the funding of health, employment, and old age insurance at impressive levels. American politicians of both the Right and the Left, by contrast, find it almost obligatory to profess mistrust of government.

THE INTERNATIONAL STANDARD

Article 25 of the United Nations Universal Declaration of Human Rights, adopted by the General Assembly in 1948, provides that "Everyone has the right to a standard of living adequate for the health and well-being of himself and his family, including food, clothing, housing and medical care and necessary social services, and the right to security in the event of unemployment, sickness, disability, widowhood, old age or other lack of livelihood in circumstances beyond his control." To implement that principle, the UN Covenant on Economic, Social, and Cultural Rights was opened for signature in 1966. The Covenant came into force a decade later after being ratified by nearly 90 countries. The United States is the only one of the liberal democracies that has failed to ratify that instrument or its companion, the UN Covenant on Civil and Political Rights....

WELFARE RIGHTS IN PRACTICE

When considering welfare rights in foreign constitutions, Americans may wonder, "How have these rights worked out in practice? Does the experience of other nations shed any light on what might have happened here if the Supreme Court had accepted arguments made in the late 1960s and early 1970s that welfare rights could and should be made part of our constitutional regime instead of remaining purely legislative creations?"

In practice, interestingly, the contrast between the United States and countries with constitutional welfare rights is much less sharp than it appears on paper. For no liberal democracy has ever placed social and economic rights on precisely the same legal footing as the familiar civil and political liberties....

THE UTILITY OF CROSS-NATIONAL COMPARISONS

...Every country within the democratic world is in its own way grappling with a common set of problems: how to provide humanitarian aid without undermining personal responsibility, how to achieve the optimal mix in a mixed economy, how to preserve a just balance between individual freedom, equality, and social solidarity. The basic problem is nothing less than the great dilemma of how to hold together the two halves of the divided soul of liberalism—our love of individual liberty and our sense of a community for which we accept a common responsibility.

Below the surface of that dilemma lies a long-neglected political problem. It is that neither a strong commitment to individual and minority rights, nor even a modest welfare commitment like the American one can long be sustained without the active support of citizens who are willing to respect the rights of others (not just in the abstract but often at some cost to themselves), who are prepared to accept some responsibility for the poorest and most vulnerable members of society, and who are prepared to take significant responsibility for themselves and their dependents. Liberal democratic welfare states around the world are now asking men and women to possess and practice certain virtues that, even under the best of conditions, are not easy to acquire—self-restraint, self-reliance, compassion, and respect for the dignity and worth of one's fellow human beings.

The question that seldom gets asked, however, is this: Where do such qualities come from? Where do people acquire an internalized willingness to view others with genuine regard for their dignity and concern for their well-being, rather than as objects, means, or obstacles? These qualities cannot be generated by governments or instilled by fear and force. The fact is that both our welfare state and our experiment in democratic government rest to a great extent on habits and practices formed within fragile social structures—families, neighborhoods, religious and workplace associations, and other communities of memory and mutual aid—structures that are being asked to bear great weight just at a time when they themselves do not seem to be in peak condition.

The question then becomes: what, if anything, can be done to create and maintain, or at least to avoid undermining, the social conditions that foster our commitments to the rule of law, individual freedom, and a compassionate welfare state?...

Reflection on our own tradition, moreover, should give us pause concerning the disdain for politics that underlies so much current American thinking about legal and social policy. For one of the most important lessons of 1789 is the same one the world learned anew in 1989: that politics is not only a way of advancing self-interest, but of transcending it. That transformative potential of the art through which we order our lives together represents our best hope for living up to our rights, ideals and our welfare aspirations in coming years.

From an article of the same title in Current, *November 1994, 12–15 by permission of the author.*

MARY ANN GLENDON, *Learned Hand Professor of Law at Harvard University, is co-editor with David Blanenhorn of* Seedbeds of Virtue: Sources of Competence, Character, and Citizenship.

⚭

3

The Free Flow of Ideas: An Independent Press and the Public Sphere

"...citizens have learned by experience that the autonomy of the media and the right to speak freely are not perquisites but guarantees of freedom."
—Gábor Demszky

Introduction by Jay Rosen

"**W**e hold these truths to be self-evident..."wrote the authors of the Declaration of Independence. That democracy requires a free press and free expression is a truth of that kind: self-evident to all who understand. So let us be clear: government cannot control what is written or broadcast, and it cannot throw people into jail for their views. The most obvious sign of an undemocratic regime is the violation of these fundamental rights.

Not as obvious are the conditions that make freedom of the press and the free flow of ideas *matter* in a society where such freedoms are legally established. If ideas flow freely but do not touch people's lives, if the press is independent of government but consumed by trivia, if the public square is open but also empty, then democracy can corrode just as surely as it collapses when fundamental rights are violated. This is important to think about whenever we discuss the need for a free press and free speech. Formal guarantees are essential. But it is the informal and unofficial life of the people that turns essential freedoms into unshakeable facts.

Free expression as a political good requires thinking citizens willing to do the work of democracy: people who will pay attention, participate in public life, argue with each other and, through a thousand small decisions, create the kind of conversation that keeps democracy alert as well as alive. It is the business of culture—a democratic culture—to produce such citizens, for they are the only real guarantee that political freedom will survive.

JAY ROSEN *is a professor of journalism at New York University and was director of the Project on Public Life and the Press from 1993 to 1997. His most recent publication is* What Are Journalists For?

Discussion Questions

1. Freedom of expression and a public sphere where citizens can discuss and debate issues of common concern are highly revered in democratic societies. How important do you think they are?
2. Has the press in your country or region been under the control of any one group? If so, what has been the effect of this control? What changes have occurred in recent years?
3. Do you consider the autonomy of the press a luxury or a necessity? Why?
4. Boutros Boutros-Ghali warns that the power of the press has outstripped our ability to understand it. How powerful is the press in your country or region? What are the liabilities of a too-powerful media?
5. What is the point of an independent press, if it has nothing worthwhile to report? Is your media cluttered with trivia? What are possible remedies?

Readings

FROM
"Opinion—The New Authority"
BY BOUTROS BOUTROS-GHALI

Democracy is perhaps the most ancient form of government, finding its roots in clans and tribes before the age of dictators. Over the centuries democracy came to be seen as an ideal. But all too often it was a fragile plant in those lands where it was allowed to grow. Without question its finest flowering has been, as in Tocqueville's title, *Democracy in America*. In the course of establishing democracy in this country, challenge after challenge to it has been faced, from within and without.

What is new about democracy today? It no longer is an ideal for many but a reality for only a few. Peoples and governments in every part of the globe now are striving to establish the institutions and foster the mentalities which democracy needs in order to flourish. The peoples who now clamor for democratic life are aware that every aspect of human betterment today—social, political, security, environmental, and economic—cannot long endure unless guaranteed by democratic processes.

The media are the second new factor. Thomas Jefferson famously declared that he would prefer newspapers without government to a government without newspapers. Jefferson's advice may still be correct, but the power and prestige of what we call "the media" have outstripped our ability to fully understand this phenomenon. The media today are as important as the branches of government, and have a direct impact on each of them: the executive, the legislature and even the judiciary.

From the keynote address at the Freedom Forum Media Studies Center 10th anniversary conference, adapted for reprinting in the Media Studies Journal, *Summer 1995, 21–22, by permission of the publisher.*

Boutros Boutros-Ghali *was secretary-general of the United Nations from 1992 to 1996. He served as Egypt's minister of state for foreign affairs from October 1977 until May 1991.*

FROM
"Breaking Censorship—Making Peace"
BY Gábor Demszky

We all start life wanting to be autonomous and free persons, members of the order of free thinking that faces censorship the world over. Censorship is the most anachronistic thing in the world. If we look back at history, the censor is seen as a comical, even a despised figure.

New censors, however, appear day by day. They like to mask their activities as the defense of elevated values, the avoidance of unforeseen dangers and the ultimate protection of a brave new world. They refer to God, king or the homeland; always something sublime. They claim that it is for our common good that we not see, read and know everything we are interested in.

Censorship is not on the right or the left. It cuts political families in the middle. I have spent half of my life in a political system where secret policemen could easily walk into your apartment or read your diaries. If they thought that things they saw were not friendly enough for some kind of reason of state, the writings could have been confiscated, their authors imprisoned. In this system agents of the Communist Party decided which books were not to be published, which were harmful to the pure soul of the people. Even questions of literary criticism were decided by party decrees. Fortunately, that system now belongs to history....

Today, looking around as a former underground publisher, I can feel safe. My portable printing machine has become an object in a museum. The old totalitarian regime that sought complete control over information is no more. With it, classic censorship—which wanted power over the whole of culture, the totality of life—perished. I know that in liberal democracies there are power groups which sometimes use indirect forms of censorship. Yet in such democracies there is room for maneuvering between different centers of power. Pluralist democracies are not always ideal, but they cannot establish a total monopoly on discourse. And new media increase communications opportunities for those pushed to the margins of society. The kind of censorship that I knew under communism is not likely to return....

Many in the West speak in disappointment about the new democracies in Eastern Europe. Ethnic conflicts stand behind this disappointment, mainly the war in the Balkans. It is true: what is happening in Bosnia is tragic and unacceptable. It is an outrage of civilization that the community of nations let things go this far. The war in the Balkans, however, is not proof of the fact that the nations of Eastern Europe could not live with possibilities offered by freedom after the collapse of communism. Just the opposite: the war shows where things end if communists stay in power....

In recent years,...we have awakened to the realization that the collapse of state rule does not automatically provoke the triumph of democratic arrangements in all spheres of life. We must develop and adopt new rules of conduct. Tens of millions must unlearn ingrained habits and archaic reflexes. We are collectively enrolled in a vast "Democracy 101" course in Eastern Europe. The role of the press in this is inestimable.

Nevertheless, we learn all too frequently about how politicians in some formerly communist nations attempt to gag newspapers, radio or television. If not so brutally as their predecessors, they too attempt to curtail the freedom of the press. Direct censorship has vanished in the written press, but there are recurring attempts to undermine outspoken newspapers by crippling them economically. An equally pressing concern is that many Eastern European countries are reluctant to liberalize the establishment of radio and television stations, leaving the state monopoly on broadcast media virtually intact. He who fights for the freedom of the press in Eastern Europe today is more than likely engaged in a battle against state monopolies, since monopoly by definition implies inadequate freedom.

Under communism most people thought of the freedom of the press as a kind of luxury—a pleasure to have, but something they could do without. Since then, however, citizens have learned by experience that the autonomy of the media and the right to speak freely are not perquisites but guarantees of freedom. They are the very token of liberty, a liberty won so late and at such a dear price in this part of Europe that people will never surrender it again. Freedom has become one of our most cherished values. I take this as the safest guarantee of the demise of censorship, which is destined to become a phenomenon so irrelevant that in the future it will arouse only the interest of media historians.

From an article of the same title in Media Studies Journal, *Summer 1995, excerpts from 79–85, by permission of the publisher.*

GÁBOR DEMSZKY, *a sociologist, was the first post-Communist mayor of Budapest, Hungary.*

࿐

4
The Democratic Rule of Law

"...it is freedom within the framework of law that constitutes the essence of democratic order."
—Adam Michnik

Introduction by Jean Bethke Elshtain

Democracy without the rule of law is quite literally unthinkable. When Thomas Jefferson penned his brief against King George III and the various insults of the British Empire against the American colonies, his language rang with outrage at illegalities suffered; reasonable expectations and immunities ignored. When Alexis de Tocqueville traveled around America, looked and listened carefully and wrote his classic, *Democracy in America*, one of the things he observed was the centrality of law to Americans and the complex relationship between the laws and the mores. When Václav Havel signed "Charter 77," he and his fellow dissidents did so in the name of law, a law that cannot be abrogated by authoritarian state power. To be a citizen is to be the subject of a range of rights and immunities and it is, as well, to be the responsible bearer and transmitter of those rights.

Let us return to Tocqueville. He noted the extraordinary respect Americans had for the law and for lawyers. He described juries as little laboratories of democracy. He warned that, should the law falter, American democracy would be much troubled. To be sure, the rule of law wasn't the only feature of American life Tocqueville highlighted as central to the operation of democratic life—habits of the heart secured through religious association were even more fundamental, but these habits of the heart helped to nourish the law and the law, in turn, kept civic spiritedness alive and sustained the delicate balance between liberty and equality.

But what do we see when we look at the American democracy as we near century's end? The law is in ill-repute in many quarters, berated as little more than rules put in place to protect the powerful. Whatever truth one may find in such charges, surely the wrong response is to deride the rule of law altogether. Indeed, the response of our great democrats, including those who resorted to civil disobedience, has been that we need more respect for law rather than less; that our civil law and statutes should conform to a higher law that begins with, and must reflect, innate human dignity. The democratic rule of law is, in part, about procedures and the recognition that the law, to be law, cannot be capricious. But it is also substantive, reflecting deep ethical and moral convictions about what is just, fair, decent, right, wrong, unjust, unfair, outrageous. The democratic rule of law is both firm and flexible: it names aspirations and it is open to revision but not infinitely so, or it would no longer be a rule of law. This is clearly honored and understood by citizens in so many emerging democracies who, having been subjected to decades of unchecked power and caprice, look to law, lawyers, judges, and constitutionalists to encode a basic rule of law to which all must conform.

That the law and its exercise has fallen so low in America, both in reputation and, alas, all too often, in practice, is a troubling phenomenon. For without law, there is only a wasteland where power roams freely and caprice is the name of the game. That is why our law, from our fundamental and founding documents on through disputes about these documents and their ongoing renewal and revivication, is central to our democracy. Being subjected to the rule of law may sometimes be a vexation, but it is the only sure and certain protection we have against tyranny, demagogues, and mob rule. Without the rule of law at the end of the day there is, and can be, no democratic life, no democratic learning, no democratic society, no democratic heritage.

For information about JEAN BETHKE ELSHTAIN, *see page 126.*

Discussion Questions

1. According to the authors, how does the idea of utopia get us into trouble? Do you agree? Why or why not?
2. How does the rule of law help to bring about equality?
3. According to Bickel, we must allow a little room for doubt in our formulas for political solutions. Do you agree? Why or why not?
4. Are the laws in your country or region clear? Are they just? Are they applied to all citizens equally?

5. What is the limit of what the law can do for us? According to Jean Bethke Elshtain, what "higher law" should the law reflect? Do you agree? Why or why not?

Readings

FROM
"The Literary Impact of the American and French Revolutions"
BY ADAM MICHNIK

From a uniquely Polish perspective, the American and French Revolutions appear as two distinct ways of experiencing freedom. Through this lens, the American Revolution appears to embody simply an idea of freedom without utopia. Following Thomas Paine, it is based upon the natural right of people to determine their own fate. It consciously relinquishes the utopian vision of a perfect, conflict-free society in favor of one based upon equal opportunity, equality before the law, religious freedom, and the rule of law. From the American Revolution also comes the idea of a plurality of exiles. The Revolution was fought by people who had tasted the bitterness of humiliation and servitude. And it brought about a republic of people who have become conscious creators of their own destinies. We see in America the embodiment of the principle of an open society and an open nation. We must remember, however, that this ideal was long compromised by reality: this republic of free people tolerated slavery for many decades.

The French Revolution, in contrast, has left us an intrinsically ambiguous legacy. It was the embodiment of Montesquieu's notion of a triple division of power and of the rule of law: all that is not forbidden by law is allowed. At the same time, this revolution translated the glorious vision of freedom, equality, and fraternity into a language of utopia in which the cult of reason, guarded by the Jacobin Terror, would replace the dictatorship of church doctrine. Thanks to the Jacobins, the Declaration of the Rights of Man—the monument of Europe's democratic culture—has been forever linked to the shadow of the guillotine, the symbol of revolutionary terror. The French Revolution thus leaves us a dual legacy: it is to us a source of freedom but also represents that first fit of the madness of boundless reason. Because of this madness, the French Revolution and the Terror were followed by Bonapartism and then by the triumphant Restoration. The French Revolution gave birth to both the principles of human rights and the Jacobin Terror of Robespierre and Saint-Just; it gave us Thermidor as well as Bonapartism. It also gave rise to De Maistre, the classic defender of counter-revolutionary terror. The French Revolution declared war on God in the name of freedom. But whoever wishes to destroy God in the name of freedom elevates to power either the devil wearing the mask of a Saint Just or the executioner glorified by De Maistre.

I am a Pole. I look at the tradition of anti-feudal revolution from the perspective of a man who came to spend most of his life rebelling against Communist dictatorship. What was Communism? It was a temptation and an illusion. It was the temptation to participate in the great cause of social justice, and it was the illusion of bringing about a world in which the powerless could control their own fate. Communism was based on the illusory Promethean hope of stealing from the gods the secret of the universe and creating thereby a world based on equality, justice, and true universal values. Communism believed it had deciphered the hidden meaning and the end of history. In practice, it was but an intimate union of violence and lies.

How did the opposition to Communist dictatorship take shape? The first phase of the rebellion against Communism was "revisionism," the critique of Communist practice from within the Communist value system. To paraphrase the Polish philosopher Stanislaw Brzozowski, one might say that this movement was the rebellion of the flower against its roots. The second phase of the anti-Communist opposition was metaphysical critique, which, while attacking Communism's deceptive facade, simultaneously rejected the Communist principle of total control over individuals. The first phase of the opposition saw a struggle of reason against the irrational; the second was founded on a defense of natural law against the claims of boundless reason. Was this rebellion a revolution or a counter-revolution? Whatever it was, it appealed to values rooted in the American rather than the French Revolution. At the same time, there has always existed a small but serious trend which criticized Communism in the name of Communism, best exemplified by Leon Trotsky's *Revolution Betrayed.*

The entire actual anti-Communist opposition, represented by KOR Solidarity, Sakharov, Solzhenitsyn, Charter 77, and the Hungarian intellectual resistance, all appealed to the idea of human rights and to the principle of natural law which was, in turn, rooted in religious tradition. One could say that Poland's leading intellectuals—Gombrowicz and Milosz, Kolakowski and Herbert, Cardinal Wyszynski and Cardinal Wojtyla—consistently articulated their opposition to Communism in anti-utopian terms. While not always agreeing upon the definition of normality, they repudiated the absurd in the name of normality. What was common to the entire opposition? I do not think it was the spirit the French Revolution expressed by the Jacobin principle, "Be my brother or I'll kill you." It was rather the spirit of the American Revolution, the spirit of freedom founded on law, on diversity guaranteed by equality of all religions, and on the deeply rooted right of private property, a right protected against the all-powerful claims of the state.

Today, certain elements of utopian and doctrinal thinking are resurfacing in this strange post-Communist era. This is an era whose sense we can no more grasp than Jonah could comprehend the interior of the whale. But let us try to name some of these new utopias. First, there is the peculiar new syndrome combining populism with an authoritarian temptation, xenophobic nationalism with religious fundamentalism. We have here the ideal of a nationalistic Catholic Polish state. Such a state would be founded on privileges granted to the Catholic Church and on legislating Catholic principles into the law of the land. In such a society only racially pure Poles could obtain citizenship; for only the racially pure Pole could be considered a real Catholic, and only the faithful and obedient Catholic could be a real Pole....

And the issues of ethnic minorities, disputed territories, and contentious futures are likely to constantly reheat passions. The future is still questionable. Fukuyama is wrong when he talks about the end of history. Dahrendorf is right when he says that history is just beginning.

The next few years will be marked by a deep conflict between the religious-nationalist fundamentalists and the proponents of the idea of an open society. But the idea of an open society is not the same as the utopia of liberal capitalism. The utopia of liberal capitalism seeks to combine the principle of the free market with the practice of a strong police state. The police dictatorship of General Pinochet combined with the market economics of Milton Friedman is thus supposed to furnish a new model of the road to prosperity. Currently, we see various attempts to tap into populist moods and rhetoric beginning to dominate our public discourse.

How can one oppose all this? One can and should, as always, oppose this with Jefferson's and Paine's ideas of the natural rights of people to freedom under the rule of law. For it is freedom within the framework of law that constitutes the essence of democratic order. It is not likely that the long debate over the genesis of totalitarian systems will end soon. There will still be those who see in totalitarianism the triumph of the striving for absolute salvation, the victory of irrationalism and mysticism. And there will be those who view totalitarianism as the triumphant march of reason trampling over the sacred. In other words, while some fear the death of the sacred, others fear the dictatorship imposed in the name of the sacred. What can we say? Above all, that any type of dictatorship will certainly destroy the sacred. "Above all" does not mean exclusively. One can reject the sacred by turning one's back on it, but the sacred cannot be successfully defended by police and dictators.

I am a Pole. In the pantheon of Polish heroes, the highest place is taken by Tadeusz Kosciuszko, a hero of the American Revolution and of the Polish struggle for freedom and independence. Kosciuszko loved freedom, without any Jacobin madness; he loved his nation, without hating anyone. Allow me to say that I, along with my friends, hope this tradition within Polish culture will prevail in our time of democratic transition.

From "Intellectuals and Social Change in Central and Eastern Europe," a conference held at Rutgers University on April 9, 10, and 11, 1992, first published in Partisan Review, *Vol. LIX, No. 4, 1992, 621–623, 625–626, by permission of the author.*

ADAM MICHNIK *is editor-in-chief of Poland's largest daily newspaper,* Gazeta Wyborcza, *and was a leader of the Solidarity movement. His most recent work is* Letters from Freedom: Post-Cold War Realities and Perspectives.

FROM
The Haunted Land: Facing Europe's Ghosts after Communism
BY TINA ROSENBERG

Fascism espouses repugnant ideas, but communism's ideas of equality, solidarity, social justice, an end to misery, and power to the oppressed are indeed beautiful. The New Socialist Man—tireless, cheerful, clean, brave, thrifty, and kind to animals—is an ideal all humanity should aspire to reach. The problem, as even believing Communists admit, is that this utopian landscape must be stocked with ordinary people. Communism is lofty and grand, but human beings are flawed creatures, unwilling to pay communism the tribute of sacrifice it demands.

Although committed Communists treat the system's unreality as an incidental flaw, it is a major reason for the system's crimes. Human beings are so petty and scheming that we resist being remade into selfless heroes. Wealthy and powerful people in capitalist societies want to keep their wealth and power. Ordinary people bullheadedly continue to do only those activities they perceive to be in their interest, activities that rarely coincide with the interest of a regime that has been designed to eliminate self-interest as a motivating factor. A socialist regime is soon left with two choices: it can, like Salvador Allende did in Chile, choose to live up to its beautiful, nonrepressive socialist ideals. And, as a result, Allende fell. Or the regime can choose to keep power—which means repression. Simply put, maintaining a system that is resisted by most influential citizens requires unchecked power.

Unchecked power is the evil in communism, what transforms it from Pegasus to Gorgon. This is not particularly startling news, but it is important to repeat when looking at democracy's prospects in eastern Europe. Unchecked power seems to be a necessity to maintain a Communist regime. But the reverse is not true; one does not need to be a Communist to seek unchecked power. Such power in the service of anticommunism is just as dangerous. This is the threat to the former Soviet Bloc today: not communism, but the state's own unchecked power.

This is why many of the attempts to deal with the past in eastern Europe are counterproductive. When the state does not grant its citizens the right to defend themselves from its power, when it withholds from citizens information that concerns them, when it declares itself lord and master of the truth, when it twists the legal system to suit political ends, democracy is threatened. The opposite of communism is not anti-communism, which at times resembles it greatly. The opposite is tolerance and the rule of law. How these new democracies deal with their past is the first test of whether these good things will prevail.

From The Haunted Land *by Tina Rosenberg, copyright © 1995 by Tina Rosenberg. Used by permission of Random House, Inc.*

TINA ROSENBERG *is foreign-policy writer for* The New York Times. *She is a recipient of a MacArthur Fellowship award, and her book* The Haunted Land *won both the National Book Award and the Pulitzer Prize.*

FROM

The Morality of Consent

BY ALEXANDER MORDECAI BICKEL

Burke's pragmatism, strong as it is, did not go to the length of taking mind out of politics. Metaphysics, yes; mind and values, no. But where are a society's values to be found? In theory? Metaphysics, abstract rights, would always clash with men's needs and their natures, and with various unforeseeable contingencies.

Theories were not fit to live with, and any attempt to impose them would breed conflict, not responsive government enjoying the consent of the governed. The rights of man cannot be established by any theoretical definition; they are "in balances between differences of good, in compromises sometimes between good and evil, and sometimes between evil and evil. Political reason is a computing principle: adding, subtracting, multiplying, and dividing, morally and not metaphysically, or mathematically, true moral denominations."[1] The visions of good and evil, the denominations to be computed—these a society draws from its past, and without them it dies....

When bushels of desires and objectives are conceived as moral imperatives, it is natural to seek their achievement by any means. There is no need to fear that the same means will be open to others, because the objectives of those others will be understood to be bad and unacceptable whatever the means used to attain them. One has to believe rather that no amount of opinion can be eternally certain of the moral rightness of its preferences, and that whoever is in power in government is entitled to give effect to his preferences. Then, but only

---

[1]Louis Hartz, *The Liberal Tradition in America,* (New York: Harcourt Brace and Co., 1955), 49.

then, it is crucial that everyone adhere to certain procedures, and that some means be forbidden to all. The fabric is held together by agreement on means, which are equally available or foreclosed to all, and by allegiance to a limited number of broad first principles concerning the ends of government. These first principles are what the law of the Constitution is about. They change over time and develop, and become entrenched as they gather common assent. Beyond them lies policy, and there lie our differences.

If most of the things that politics is about are not seen as existing well this side of moral imperatives, in a middle distance, if they are not seen as subject on both sides of a division of opinion to fallible human choice, then the only thing left to a society is to succumb to or be seized by a dictatorship of the self-righteous. I do not wish to overstate the case, but this seems to me inevitably the conclusion to which disenchanted and embittered simplifiers and moralizers must come. But if we do resist the seductive temptations of moral imperatives and fix our eye on the middle distance where values are provisionally held, are tested, and evolve within the legal order—derived from the morality of process, which is the morality of consent—our moral authority will carry more weight. The computing principle Burke urged upon us can lead us then to an imperfect justice, for there is no other kind.

From The Morality of Consent *(New Haven, Conn., 1975), 23–24, 141–142, by permission of Yale University Press.*

ALEXANDER MORDECAI BICKEL *(1924–1974) was the Oliver Wendell Holmes Lecturer at Harvard Law School until 1969. He authored Part One of* The Judiciary and Responsible Government, 1910-1921.

5
Understanding a Civil Society

> *"Civil society is the domain of citizens: a mediating domain between private markets and big government."*
> —Benjamin R. Barber

Introduction by David Mathews

Public politics is more than volunteering to serve Thanksgiving dinner at a shelter for the homeless. It is not the same as charity or service and goes deeper than voting, obeying laws, and paying taxes. It includes but involves more than serving in advisory bodies and participating in government hearings. Public politics is citizens acting themselves—acting to gain greater control over their future. It is citizens working with citizens for the larger public good. It is organizing a neighborhood watch or creating an ad hoc group to preserve a historic site or joining in a forum on what to do about a community-wide issue such as saving the American family.

Public politics really isn't a secret; it isn't rare or hidden. It just doesn't fit the conventional definition of politics as only those things that politicians or governments do. Public politics contradicts Walter Lippmann when he said that the public was a phantom, a political myth. The public is not the voice of the Almighty, but it is a real (and necessary) political force. And though they don't intend to, the people practicing public politics aren't just "taking the system back"; they are changing the system by redefining politics as something that citizens do.

The conventional wisdom about politics continues to block our view of a public that has a strong sense of civic duty, a public that can do more than vent its anger and voice its cynicism. While the power of citizens to affect politics may be most visible in the support for candidates, public politics is not reducible to popular protests. Citizen organizations collaborate often and happily with governments. However, they usually insist on a different relationship with officeholders, breaking with the conventional wisdom, which would have citizens merely listen to solutions officials had already chosen. Now civic organizations are trying to get officeholders into a prior dialogue on what the issues are and how they should be framed.

We need more public politics. Public politics is a necessary additive. Without a public, politics is not just a contest of "us" versus "them." It is worse: politics degenerates into an endless war of "them" versus "them."

But what turns a mass of people into a body of citizens, a public? How do people become, in the richest sense, political?

Our research at the Kettering Foundation suggests that people who become part of a responsible public start with the doorway into politics—a dialogue of citizens talking to each other eye-to-eye as they struggle to act together on the problems that invade their lives and dim their futures.

Not just any kind of talk will do the job of creating a public. In the Kettering research, we have been asking people what kind of conversations they look for as they are sizing up problems and deciding whether to become involved. They say they want more dialogue than debate. They want to be able to weigh carefully all the options for action as well as the views of others. They want to explore, to test ideas, not just score points. They want to look at the shades of gray in issues that are often presented in extremes of black and white. They want all the emotions to come out—but without the acrimony that characterizes partisan debate. In a word, they want more public deliberation in the political debate. Deliberation is not just talking about issues or understanding one another. It is making decisions together about how to act as a public.

As we have learned from the National Issues Forums, deliberation moves people from first reactions to more reflective and shared public judgments.[1] People who don't inform their opinions by carefully weighing the consequences of possible actions are prone to faulty decisions. All of us, at one time or another, have despaired over popularly applauded decisions that seem unwise and profoundly unjust. Any hope that popular reaction will change into sounder judgments depends, in a large measure, on the way we reason together. Our common sense has to be refined in public deliberation that is inclusive enough, goes on long enough, and probes deep enough for reflective judgment to emerge.

If one is to change the way a system works, the public can't wait to be persuaded. It has to be active in making up its own mind on the issues facing the

---

[1] The National Issues Forums (NIF) are deliberative forums conducted by a large and diverse network of local forums covering the United States.

country. More than the usual partisan debate, there needs to be a public dialogue in which people hold counsel with one another.

DAVID MATHEWS *is president of the Kettering Foundation and former U.S. Secretary of Health, Education, and Welfare. He is the author of* Politics for People: Finding a Responsible Public Voice.

Discussion Questions

1. Is politics only what politicians and governments do? According to David Mathews, what more is it and what value does it have?
2. According to Mathews, what type of information and interaction does the public need to become an engaged citizenry? Do you agree? Why, or why not?
3. Does the "civic space" defined by these authors exist in your region or area? If so, is it growing or shrinking? If not, what, according to these authors, is the way to enter and create the space? What other possibilities are there?
4. Are governments and commercial interests eroding the civic space in your region or country as Benjamin Barber warns? If so, how can this erosion be checked? How can citizens be empowered to work together in common cause?
5. What do you think of Václav Havel's definition of "home?" What "memberships" do you hold and how important are they to you? Does stressing your nationality over all the others seem lopsided, as Havel indicates?

Readings

FROM
"On Civic Society"
BY VÁCLAV HAVEL

I have the honor to receive an honorary doctorate in a town that centuries ago became a refuge to a large group of my countrymen and that today shelters many Czechs and Slovaks who, having found their new home here, still feel their bonds of attachment to their old country. Yet at this time their old country itself is at a historical crossroads; not only is it seeking a new form of its statehood but, having shed its satellite status, it is striving to define its new political home in Europe and in the world. With these two imperatives in mind, I want to use this opportunity to reflect briefly on the notion of home and on the question of what type of a social and political order would most fully respect that which gives human beings their humanity, that is, their home.

The category of home belongs to what modern philosophers call the "natural world." (The Czech philosopher Jan Patocka analyzed this notion before the war.) Home is a fundamental existential experience of everyone. What we perceive as our home, in its philosophical meaning, resembles a set of concentric circles with our "I" occupying the center. My home is the room in which I have lived for a while and am accustomed to and which I have imbued, so to speak, with my invisible patina. (Even my prison cell, I recall, was sort of a home to me and I always felt very much put upon whenever I suddenly had to move to another cell. It may have been identical to, or even better than the previous one, yet I perceived it as something foreign and hostile and felt at first uprooted and estranged. It took me some time to find my place in it and to get used to the new cell so I could stop missing the old one.) My home is the house I live in, the village or town where I was born or where I now live. My home is my family, the world of my friends, my social and intellectual environment, my profession, the enterprise I work for, my work place. Of course, the country in which I live is my home too, and so is the language I speak as well as the spiritual climate of my country embodied in its language. The Czech language, the Czech perception of the world, the Czech historical experience, the Czech sense of courage and cowardice, Czech humor—all of these are inseparable from this level of my home. And so my home is also my being a Czech, meaning my nationality, and I see no reason why I should not show my allegiance to this aspect of my home which is no less essential to my existence than, for instance, that other part of it that I might call my manhood. My home, of course, is not only my being a Czech, but also my being a Czechoslovak, meaning my citizenship. Eventually my home is also Europe and my being a European and, finally, this very planet with its present civilization and of course, the entire universe. Nor is this all: my home is also my education, my upbringing, my habits, the social setting in which I exist and which I accept as mine. If I were a member of a political party that would certainly be my home too.

I believe that each of these aspects of one's home should be recognized and accepted as such. None can be sensibly denied or forcibly excluded from playing its role or interpreted as less important or inferior to others. All of them belong to our natural world and a sound social order must duly respect them all and give all of them a chance for self-fulfillment. This is the only way of opening the space necessary for individuals to exist as human beings and to affirm their identity because all the aspects of our home, together with our entire natural world, are an integral part of ourselves and an integral part of the setting for our human self-identification. A person totally deprived of all the aspects of his home would have been deprived of his essence, his humanness.

I favor a political system based on the citizen with all of his basic civic and human rights in their universal validity and therefore in their basic equality, meaning that a member of this or that race, of one or another nation, sex or religion may not have basic rights different from anybody else's. Thus, I favor what is known as a civic society.

Today, this civic principle is sometimes contrasted with the national principle creating the impression that somehow the nationality aspect of our home is overlooked or suppressed. This I see as a gross misunderstanding. I favor the civic principles precisely because it best enables human beings to realize or identify themselves at all levels of their homes, to enjoy all that belongs to their natural world and not just some of it. To build a state on a foundation other than the civic principle, for instance on ideology, nationality or religion, only means to elevate one aspect of our home above the others and so to limit us as human beings, to limit our natural world. And that usually leads to nothing good; for instance, this one-dimensional conception of the state has been at the root of most wars and revolutions. On the contrary, a state grounded in a civic society, respectful of individuals and their natural world in their entire scope and diversity, is in its very essence a peaceful and humane state.

Thus I am far from seeking to suppress a person's national identification, to deny its legitimacy and the individual's right to self-realization. I simply reject those political concepts which in the name and in the interest of the national principle would suppress other aspects of the human home, other layers of humanness and other human rights than the single right to one's nationality. Also it seems to me that the civic society, the social order toward which modern democratic societies are gradually working, is precisely the kind of society which gives individuals the entire spectrum of choices within their diversified natural worlds and thus their levels of self-identification.

A civic society, founded on the universality of human rights, enables us best to realize ourselves for what we are, as members not only of our nation, but also of our family, our community, our region, our church, our profession, our political party, our state, our international community. This self-fulfillment is possible because a civic society conceives of us, above all, as members of the human family, as real human beings whose individual existence finds it primary, most natural and most universal expression in our status as citizens. This is citizenship in its broadest and deepest meaning.

The sovereignty of the community, of the region, of the nation or of the state, as any higher sovereignty, derives its validity from the truly original sovereignty, that is, from human sovereignty which finds its political expression in civic sovereignty.

From a speech upon receiving an honorary doctorate at Lehigh University, Bethlehem, Pennsylvania, on October 26, 1991, as the sixth Cohen Lecturer on International Relations.

Václav Havel *is president of the Czech Republic. A noted playwright and poet, Havel is a world renowned champion of democracy.*

FROM
Jihad vs. McWorld
by Benjamin R. Barber

Civil society, or civic space, occupies the middle ground between government and the private sector. It is not where we vote and it is not where we buy and sell; it is where we talk with neighbors about a crossing guard, plan a benefit for our community school, discuss how our church or synagogue can shelter the homeless, or organize a summer softball league for our children. In this domain, we are "public" beings and share with government a sense of publicity and a regard for the general good and the commonweal; but unlike government, we make no claim to exercise a monopoly on legitimate coercion. Rather, we work here voluntarily and in this sense inhabit a "private" realm devoted to the cooperative (non-coercive) pursuit of public goods. This neighborly and cooperative domain of civil society shares with the private sector the gift of liberty: it is voluntary and is constituted by freely associated individuals and groups; but unlike the private sector, it aims at common ground and consensual (that is, integrative and collaborative) modes of action. Civil society is thus public without being coercive, voluntary without being privatized. It is in this domain that our traditional civil institutions such as foundations, schools, churches, public interest and other voluntary civic associations properly belong. The media too, where they take their public responsibilities seriously and subordinate their commercial needs to their civic obligations, are part of civil society.

Unhappily, civil society has been eclipsed by government/market bipolarities, and its mediating strengths have been eliminated in favor of the simplistic opposition of state and individual: the command economy versus the free market. This opposition has forced those wishing to occupy noncoercive civic space—whether in traditional democracies, new democracies, or the global civic domain back into the private sector, where they reappear, quite improperly, as special interest advocates supposedly unmarked by common concerns or public norms. We are compelled to be voters or consumers in all we do; if we wish to be citizens, if we want to participate in self-governance rather than just elect those who govern us, there is no place to turn.

Throughout the nineteenth century, in Tocqueville's America and afterwards, American society felt like civil society. Without trying to romanticize the social conditions of that decentralized period, we can see how they allowed liberty a more local and civic aspect, while a modest governmental sphere and an unassuming private sector were overshadowed by an extensive civic network tied together by schools, granges, churches, town halls, village greens, country stores, and voluntary associations of every imaginable sort. It was these municipal institutions that fired Tocqueville's imagination. Government, especially at the federal level, was a modest affair (probably too modest for some of the tasks it needed to accomplish) because the Constitution had left all powers not specifically delegated to it to the states and people. Markets were also modest affairs, regional in nature and dominated by other associations and affections.

It was only when individuals who thought of themselves as citizens began to see themselves as consumers, and groups that were regarded as voluntary associations were supplanted by corporations legitimized as legal persons, that market forces began to encroach on and crush civil society from the private sector side. Once markets began to expand radically, government responded with an aggressive campaign on behalf of the public weal against the new monopolies, inadvertently crushing civil society from the state side. Squeezed between the warring realms of the two expanding monopolies, statist and corporate, civil society lost its preeminent place in American life. By the time of the two Roosevelts it had nearly vanished and its civic denizens had been compelled to find sanctuary under the feudal tutelage of either big government (their protectors and social servants) or the private sector, where schools, churches, unions, foundations, and other associations could assume the identity of corporations and aspire to be no more than special interest groups formed for the particularistic ends of their members. Whether those ends were, say, market profitability or environmental preservation, was irrelevant since by definition all private associations necessarily had private ends. Schools became interest groups for people with children (parents) rather than the forges of a free society; churches became confessional special interest groups pursuing separate agendas rather than sources of moral fiber for the larger society (as Tocqueville had thought they would be); voluntary associations became a variation on private lobbies rather than the free spaces where women and men practiced an apprenticeship of liberty.

Paradoxically, once civil society had been privatized and commercialized, groups organized in desperate defense of the public interest found themselves cast as mere exemplars of plundering private interest lobbies. Unions, for example, though concerned with fair compensation, full employment, and the dignity of work for all became the private sector counterparts of the corporations, and in time learned all too well how to act the part. When they tried to break the stranglehold of corporations over labor, they were deemed another special interest group no better than those against whom they struck, and perhaps worse (since the companies struck were productive contributors to the wealth of America). Environmental groups have undergone the same transmogrification more recently. Although pursuing what for all the world looks like a public agenda of clean air for all including the polluters, they are cast as the polluters mirror-image twin—another special interest group whose interests are to be arbitrated alongside those of toxic-waste dumpers. The media surrendered their responsibility to inform democracy's proprietors and became sellers of gossip and wholly owned subsidiaries of private sector proprietors with no responsibilities at all other than to their profit margins. Under such conditions, the public good could not and did not survive as a reasonable ideal. Its epitaph was written by David B. Truman, who in his influential 1951 primer *The Governmental Process*, a book that helped establish the dominant paradigm in social science throughout the 1960s and 1970s, wrote summarily that in dealing with the pluralist pressure system of private interests that in America, "we do not need to account for a totally inclusive interest, because one does not exist."[1] McWorld has only dropped an exclamation point into Truman's assertion.

We are left stranded by this melancholy history in an era where civil society is in eclipse and where citizens have neither home for their civic institutions nor voice with which to speak, even within nation-states nominally committed to democracy. Be passively serviced (or passively persecuted) by the massive, busy-body, bureaucratic state where the word *citizen* has no resonance; or sign onto the selfishness and radical individualism of the private sector where the word *citizen* has no resonance. Vote the public scoundrels out of public office and/or vote your private interests into office by voting your dollars for the scoundrels willing to work for you: those are the only remaining obligations of the much diminished office of citizen in what are supposed to be the best established democracies.

If these cheerless observations are at all well grounded, and democracy suffers from the polarizing effects of a vanished civil society in America and other Western democracies, surely those looking to create new democracies under the conditions either of Jihad or of McWorld face formidable challenges. Their first priority surely must be the reconstruction of civil society as a framework for the reinvention of democratic citizenship, a mediating third domain between the overgrown but increasingly ineffective state governmental and the metastasizing private market sectors. Our choices need not be limited by the zero-sum game between government and commercial markets in which growth for the one spells encroachment for the other: a massive statist bureaucracy or a massive McWorld. Although that is precisely the choice that has been offered to peoples in Russia and East Germany, we need not opt either for some caricatured Big Brother government that enforces justice but in exchange plays the tyrant, or for some caricatured runaway free market that secures liberty but in exchange fosters inequality and social injustice and doggedly abjures the public weal. For this leaves us only with the choice between McWorld or tyranny. Indeed, as the nation-state loses its sovereignty, it is not so much the choice between tyranny and McWorld but the tyranny *of* McWorld itself that becomes our destiny. Only some versions of a global civil society can hope to counter its inadvertent despotism.

Civil society grounds democracy as a form of government in which not politicians and bureaucrats but an empowered people use legitimate force to put

---

[1]David B. Truman, *The Governmental Process*, first published in 1951, second edition (Berkeley: Institute of Governmental Studies, 1971), p. 51.1.

flesh on the bones of their liberties; and in which liberty carries with it the obligations of social responsibility and citizenship as well as the rights of legal persons. Civil society offers us a single civic identity that, belonging neither to state bureaucrats nor private consumers but to citizens alone, recouples rights and responsibilities and allows us to take control of our governments and our markets. Civil society is the domain of citizens: a mediating domain between private markets and big government. Interposed between the state and the market, it can contain an obtrusive government without ceding public goods to the private sphere. At the same time it can dissipate the atmospherics of solitariness and greed that surround markets without suffocating in an energetic big government's exhaust fumes. In the international domain, where states are weak and markets dominant, civil society can offer an alternative identity to people who otherwise are only clients or consumers or passive spectators to global trends they can do nothing to challenge. It can make internationalism a form of citizenship. Within national states, both government *and* the private sector can be humbled a little by a growing civil society that absorbs some of the public aspirations to self-government, without casting off its liberal character as a noncoercive association of equals. Because they tend to their own affairs and take more responsibility on themselves, citizens inhabiting a vibrant civil society worry less about elections and leaders and term limits and scandals and they simultaneously free themselves from the free markets that otherwise imprison them in a commercial mentality that leaves no room for community or for spirit.

To re-create civil society on this prescription does not entail a novel civic architecture; rather, it means reconceptualizing and repositioning institutions already in place, or finding ways to re-create them in an international setting.[2] In the United States, for example, this suggests turning again to schools, foundations, voluntary associations, churches and temples and mosques, community movements, and the media, as well as myriad other civil associations and removing them from the private sector, repositioning them instead in civil society. It suggests helping citizens to reclaim their rightful public voice and political legitimacy against those who would write them off as representing only hypocritical special interests. In Russia and other transitional societies it means supporting the new civic infrastructure and worrying more about getting people involved in

---

[2]There is a new international organization called *Civicus* dedicated to creating a framework for transnational N.G.O. cooperation. See also Peter J. Spiro, "New Global Communities: Nongovernmental Organizations in International Decision-Making Institutions," *The Washington Quarterly*, 18:1, Winter 1995, pp. 45–46.

local civic associations than about the outcome of elections or the vicissitudes of competing nationalist, socialist, capitalist, and reformist parties playing at parliamentary politics. For McWorld, it means seeking countervailing institutions not in international law and organization but in a new set of transnational civic associations that afford opportunities for nationally based civil societies to link up to one another and for individual citizens of different countries to cooperate across national boundaries in regional and global civil movements. Civil society needs a habitation; it must become a real place that offers the abstract idea of a public voice a palpable geography somewhere other than in the twin atlases of government and markets.

More than anything else, what has been lost in the clash of Jihad and McWorld has been the idea of the *public* as something more than a random collection of consumers or an aggregation of special political interests or a product of identity politics. The public voice turns out to be the voice of civil society, the voice of what we can call variously an American civic forum, a Russian civic forum, or a global civic forum—civil society's own interactive representative assembly. We have noted that the democratic citizen must precede the democratization of government. It now becomes clear that civil society offers conditions for the creation of democratic citizens. A citizen is an individual who has acquired a public voice and understands himself to belong to a wider community, who sees herself as sharing goods with others. Publicity is the key to citizenship. The character of the public voice is thus essential in defining the citizen. For a public voice is not any old voice addressing the public. The divisive rant of talk radio or the staccato crossfire of pundit-TV are in fact perfect models of everything that public talk is *not*.

Much of what passes for journalism is in fact mere titillation or dressed-up gossip or polite prejudice. The media have abandoned civil society for the greater profits of the private sector, where their public responsibilities no longer hobble their taste for commercial success. How long a journey it can be for women and men nurtured in the private sector and used to identifying with one another only via a cash contract on the one hand, or in terms of Jihad's blood fraternity on the other, to find their way to civil society and speak in its measured public voice, particularly if that voice must also have a transnational or international resonance. Public inflects voice in a remarkable fashion that turns out to hold the key to civil society and citizenship. A genuinely public voice— the voice of civil society can empower those who speak far more effectively than either the officially univocal voice of government or the obsessively contrary talk of the private sectors jabbering Babel. The voice of civil society, of citizens in deliberative conversation, challenges the exclusivity and irrationality of Jihad's clamor but is equally antithetical to the claim of McWorld's private markets to represent some aggregative public good. Neither Jihad nor McWorld grasps the meaning of public, and the idea of the public realized offers a powerful remedy to the privatizing and de-democratizing effects of aggressive tribes and aggressive markets.

From Jihad vs. McWorld *(New York, 1995) 281-287, by permission of Time Books.*

For information about Benjamin R. Barber, *see page 101.*

☙

FROM
"In Pursuit of Global Civic Virtues"
BY Claire L. Gaudiani

Why focus on a pluralistic democracy? Though it has problems, that is the only model available. Given the apparent demise of the Marxist-Communist system, some form of democracy appears to offer the best opportunity for people to experience a high-quality life—a life with personal liberty, self-governance, and opportunity.

On the other hand, democracy and the rights of citizens are increasingly endangered by the rise of intercultural conflicts. Most modern nation-states face or will face the challenge of conflicts among diverse cultures within their borders. Those who would advance democratic values need to explore the virtues that will make this diverse world livable for all.

The concept of the nation-state is a relatively recent phenomenon in the scope of human history. Even in Europe, the unification of Italy dates only from the nineteenth century, and the Soviet Union is a twentieth-century phenomenon that may not outlast the century. In the Middle East and in Eastern Europe, current crises can be understood only in the context of borders and politics that have been imposed on lands, tribes, and families to whom secular nationhood is an alien concept.

In the last decade, moreover, peoples' allegiance to nations has weakened in favor of their attachment to cultural subgroups. The increase in incidents of racism and interethnic conflict and the rise of fundamentalism can be documented in many parts of the world. The voices of individuals as citizens tend to be submerged, and group mentality dominates. To define themselves, subgroups demand that members hold rigidly defined values that tend to describe "the other" as the enemy; they refuse to learn about the other or admit commonality with other individuals or subgroups, much less the possibility that the other has something of value to teach. The identification of subgroups' concept of "chosenness" or "entitlement" often is a justification for hatred, persecution, and violence. Virtues like tolerance often are in peril; compassion is equated with weakness.

Democratic nations make different demands on citizens and subcultures. Laws protect individuals against incursions by the government, groups, or other individuals to personal freedom: to pursue life, liberty, and happiness. As the founders of this country understood, pluralistic democracies must assume civic virtues in their citizens. Jefferson, Madison, Adams, Federalists and antifederalists: All were concerned with the role and definition of civic virtues in designing and maintaining a form of government that respected each person's self-interest and still promoted and secured the common good. Now we have lost sight of civic virtues: both how to value them and how to teach and practice them. We need to rediscover, as participants in a pluralistic democracy, the civic virtues necessary for personal liberty in a global community.

The social contract Locke envisioned and the rights he affirmed for all men—free and equal—to life, liberty, and the pursuit of happiness now have serious caveats in community responsibilities and in complex situations. Now the importance of tolerance, civility, compassion, empathy, self-discipline, and justice come with particular implications for an increasingly diverse society. Now the definition of "all men created equal" includes men and women; men and women of color, as well as white men and women; those who are physically able and those who are physically challenged; property owners and the homeless; and those who come from any part of the globe.

If education implies preparing the individual and group for a better future, one function of...education should be to teach civic virtues so students can become responsible citizens of the world. We need to study different cultures in order to discover modern civic virtues for a globally interdependent world.

The task begins with exploring, identifying, and then practicing and teaching these virtues in the context of citizenship in the global community. Different cultures have a great deal to teach each other. A curriculum that reflects multicultural perspectives can teach the virtues commonly practiced and prized across many different cultures—as well as the distinctive virtues of specific cultures. A pluralistic curriculum should emphasize a country's traditional civic virtues, but it also can shape the basis for a commonly held set of global civic virtues.

From an article of the same title in Liberal Education *Vol. 77, No. 3, 1991, page 14 by permission of the author.*

CLAIRE L. GAUDIANI *is the former president of Connecticut College.*

Challenges

6
Resolving Racial, Ethnic, and Religious Conflicts

"Toleration makes difference possible; difference makes toleration necessary."
—Michael Walzer

Introduction by Trudy Rubin

As a journalist who has watched the spread of democracy since communism's fall, I've learned a disappointing lesson. Holding democratic elections in new democracies that are torn by bitter ethnic and religious differences will probably make those divisions worse.

The classic case of democracy as prelude to ethnic slaughter is Bosnia. And the Bosnian story tells us much about where and when democracy can be dangerous to the public's health.

In communist Yugoslavia, dictator Josef Broz Tito had suppressed ethnic hatreds, in part by force (separatists went to jail), in part by a combination of balanced patronage and education of a new generation. Those born after World War II were taught to think of themselves as Yugoslavs first.

When Yugoslav communism began to crumble, and free elections were held in the various republics, the population had no experience with democracy as a system of give and take. Compromise was an alien concept to people raised in a dictatorship. In Croatia and Serbia, the leaders who emerged were communists making a political comeback as nationalists.

In Bosnia, a republic where Muslims, Croats, and Serbs had lived together, and no ethnic group had a majority, political parties immediately formed along ethnic lines. Those who thought of themselves as Yugoslavs formed multiethnic parties, but were outnumbered by ethnic separatists, or by those who simply feared what would happen if they didn't stick with their own kind.

The results of the first free Bosnian election in 1990 separated the republic firmly into three irreconcilable political parties. This helped speed the descent of Bosnia into bloodshed. And even now that the war is over, the three separatist parties still have a vested interest in keeping power divided along ethnic lines.

True, the Bosnian experience is a worst-case scenario. Blatant outside support by Serbia and Croatia for virulently nationalist Bosnian parties who wanted to link up with their "homelands" killed the chances of liberals who wanted to establish a multiethnic state.

But Bosnia also tells us it is foolish to hope for democracy to develop instantaneously, like Athena springing full grown from the head of Zeus. The very concept of law has little meaning in countries where, for decades, constitutions were nothing more than window dressing for dictators. Joseph Stalin's constitution was terrific—on paper. Today, Russia's duma (parliament) passes many laws that remain useless pieces of paper, scoffed at by voters and unenforced by a judiciary still not used to freedom.

Absent independent institutions—a free press, independent courts, non-exclusive political parties—that command a loyalty greater than blood, elections can't smooth over ethnic hatreds. Instilling respect for such institutions takes time—lots of time. It worked in Japan and Germany, but those countries' racist regimes were defeated in battle, and both were occupied and reconstructed by a democratic superpower.

The more interesting case is India, where the British Raj introduced legal codes to keep the Indians down, but India took to the rule-of-law concept and adapted it to suit its own needs after independence. In India, the legal tradition has sunk deep roots (despite the rampant corruption that undermines it), and the Supreme Court is the most respected institution in the country.

And, in India, the election system has managed to contain enormous religious and regional differences. Even the recent election, which brought a Hindu-nationalist-led coalition to power, constrained the nationalists, who had to tone down the Hindu-first part of their platform in order to win a plurality.

However flawed the system, however poor its delivery of economic goods, Indian democracy has probably kept the country from splitting apart. But Indians had centuries to observe British institutions and learn what they wanted to copy and adapt.

In Bosnia, it is NATO's presence, not elections, that prevents the war from restarting. But NATO lacks the powers of a formal occupier which can remake institutions by fiat. And no one knows whether its troops will stay for very long. U.S., European, and nongovernmental efforts to develop a free press, and other democratic institutions, move at a snail's pace. Only time and outside pressure and help can nurture the liberal institutions that could win Bosnian allegiance away from blood ties.

TRUDY RUBIN *is foreign affairs columnist for the* Philadelphia Inquirer *and a member of its editorial board.*

Discussion Questions

1. What are some of the dangers cited by Fareed Zakaria that arise when building a democracy in a multiethnic nation with a history of authoritarian rule? What might be done to mitigate some of these dangers?

2. To Shashi Tharoor, the key to success for a nation with a population as diverse as India's is to give people the confidence that they can pursue their own interests fairly and openly. What tools, insights, and current trends does he identify that might further this goal? How do these strategies and trends apply to your country?

3. According to arguments made in Tharoor's piece, some African countries might be justified in outlawing political parties altogether. What is the basis of this position? Are there similar conditions in your country? What, if anything, might be done to change these conditions?

4. What does Michael Walzer mean when he says, "A defense of toleration does not have to be a defense of difference?"

Readings

FROM
"Ethnic Conflict and War"
BY FAREED ZAKARIA

On December 8, 1996, Jack Lang made a dramatic dash to Belgrade. The French celebrity politician, formerly minister of culture, had been inspired by the student demonstrations involving tens of thousands against Slobodan Milosevic, a man Lang and many Western intellectuals held responsible for the war in the Balkans. Lang wanted to lend his moral support to the Yugoslav opposition. The leaders of the movement received him in their offices—the philosophy department—only to boot him out, declare him "an enemy of the Serbs," and order him to leave the country. It turned out that the students opposed Milosevic not for starting the war, but for failing to win it.

Lang's embarrassment highlights two common, and often mistaken, assumptions—that the forces of democracy are the forces of ethnic harmony and of peace. Neither is necessarily true. Mature liberal democracies can usually accommodate ethnic divisions without violence or terror and can live in peace with other liberal democracies. But without a background in constitutional liberalism, the introduction of democracy in divided societies has actually fomented nationalism, ethnic conflict, and even war. The spate of elections held immediately after the collapse of communism were won in the Soviet Union and Yugoslavia by nationalist separatists and resulted in the breakup of those countries. This was not in and of itself bad, since those countries had been bound together by force. But the rapid secessions, without guarantees, institutions, or political power for the many minorities living within the new countries, have caused spirals of rebellion, repression, and, in places like Bosnia, Azerbaijan, and Georgia, war.

Elections require that politicians compete for people's votes. In societies without strong traditions of multiethnic groups or assimilation, it is easiest to organize support along racial, ethnic, or religious lines. Once an ethnic group is in power, it tends to exclude other ethnic groups. Compromise seems impossible; one can bargain on material issues like housing, hospitals, and handouts, but how does one split the difference on a national religion? Political competition that is so divisive can rapidly degenerate into violence. Opposition movements, armed rebellions, and coups in Africa have often been directed against ethnically based regimes, many of which came to power through elections. Surveying the breakdown of African and Asian democracies in the 1960s, two scholars concluded that democracy "is simply not viable in an environment of intense ethnic preferences." Recent studies, particularly of Africa and Central Asia, have confirmed this pessimism. A distinguished expert on ethnic conflict, Donald Horowitz, concluded, "In the face of this rather dismal account…of the concrete failures of democracy in divided societies…one is tempted to throw up one's hands. What is the point of holding elections if all they do in the end is to substitute a Bemba-dominated regime for a Nyanja regime in Zambia, the two equally narrow, or a southern regime for a northern one in Benin, neither incorporating the other half of the state?"[1]

Jack Snyder and Edward Mansfield contend, using an impressive data set, that over the last 200 years democratizing states went to war significantly more often than either stable autocracies or liberal democracies. In countries not grounded in constitutional liberalism, the rise of democracy brings with it hyper-nationalism and war-mongering. When the political system is opened up, diverse groups with incompatible interests gain access to power and press their demands. Political and military leaders, who are often embattled remnants of the old authoritarian order, realize that to succeed they must rally the masses behind a national cause. The result is invariably aggressive rhetoric and policies, which often drag countries into confrontation and war. Noteworthy examples range from Napoleon III's France, Wilhelmine Germany, and Taisho Japan to those in today's newspapers, like Armenia and Azerbaijan and Milosevic's Serbia. The democratic peace, it turns out, has little to do with democracy.

From the section of the same title in"The Rise of Illiberal Democracy," Foreign Affairs, *November/December 1997, pages 35–38. Reprinted by permission of* Foreign Affairs, *November/December 1997. Copyright 1997 by the Council on Foreign Relations, Inc.*

Fareed Zakaria *is editor of*Newsweek International. *Former managing editor of*Foreign Affairs, *he has written numerous articles and books, including* From Wealth to Power: The Unusual Origins of America's World Role.

---

[1]Alvin Rabushka and Kenneth Shepsle, *Politics in Plural Societies: A Theory of Democratic Instability* (Columbus: Charles E. Merrill), pp. 62–92; Donald Horowitz, "Democracy in Divided Societies," in Larry Diamond and Mark F. Plattner, eds., Nationalism, Ethnic Conflict and Democracy (Baltimore: The Johns Hopkins University Press, 1994), pp. 35–55.

India: From Midnight to the Millennium

BY SHASHI THAROOR

The vexed question of identity is one from which there is no escape in today's developing societies, and India is no exception. The plethora of sectarian agitations, religious clashes, and movements for secession or autonomy reflect periodic breakdowns in the ability of the state to convince sections of its people that their economic and political aspirations are being (or even can be) met within the state structure. Sometimes conflict arises from the competition for resources, at other times from contention for power (though power is not merely an end in itself, but a means to control the distribution of resources); but it is always predicated on the assertion of identity, a particularist identity distinct from that of the rest of the nation. Problems arise when the identity that is sought to be asserted is rigid and nonnegotiable, rather than one that is divisible (into alternative political loyalties) or fungible (through accommodation into the regional or national mainstream). The demand for a distinct territory—whether for an autonomous region, as with the Gurkhas of northern Bengal; for a separate state within the Indian Union, as with the Jharkhandis; or for complete secession and independence, as with Kashmir and some of the northeastern insurgencies—is symptomatic of this desire for self-realization, rather than an ultimate objective in itself. Each group is saying, "Give us our own space, in which we can feel we belong, we call the shots, we determine our own fate." For India to survive as an effective democracy, it has to be able to acknowledge and accommodate the various identities of its multifaceted population. Yet to give in to each demand is to generate new victims and new minorities.

There is no easy answer, but democracy is the only technique that can work to find one. In a pluralist state it is essential that each citizen feels secure in his or her identities (and, as I have explained, there will always be more than one identity for each citizen). Indians have to come to understand that while they may be proud of being Muslims or Marwaris or Mallahs, they will be secure as Muslims or Marwaris or Mallahs only because they are also Indians—in other words, that it is their Indian identity that gives them the framework within which to satisfy their material needs, to compete and coexist with other members of the broader society, to work and trade in a larger marketplace, to contend for political office, and to feel physically secure behind defensible borders. The institutions of political and economic democracy are the only ones that can provide each Indian with the sense that his interests can be pursued fairly and openly alongside those of others. Strengthening those institutions is the vital task of the next fifty years.

Recent trends may in fact give heart to those who believe that economic liberalization and political democracy will inevitably make sectarianism and bigotry impossible. Market forces militate against fundamentalisms; the *rupee*, though not quite yet as almighty as the dollar, does not recognize the faith of the man making or spending it. Many a Hindu businessman depends for his profits on a Muslim worker or tailor or weaver, who in turn depends on the Hindu for his employment; they thus develop a vested interest in keeping each other safe. A riot against the Muslim artisans of the Hindu sacred city of Benares (Varanasi) would deprive Hindus of the traditional masks and paraphernalia required for their annual Ramlila; without those industrious and experienced Muslim hands, Benares Hindus could not celebrate their own religious epic, the Ramayana. A compelling study led by Harvard's Ashutosh Varshney of six pairs of Indian cities—each city comparable demographically to the other in the pair, but one prone to communal riots and the other not—has recently established that the prior existence of social networks of civic engagement across communal lines is the key to preventing violence. Where Hindus and Muslims work together, interact together, and need each other, they tend not to attack or harm each other. This insight suggests that a governmental policy of actively encouraging the establishment of intercommunal associations (clubs, unions, committees, trade arrangements) could help promote communal peace even in the most riot-torn environments. Civic action is the key, more so than political conciliation.

Africa has responded to the dangers of political divisiveness by resorting to the non-Indian solutions of the one-party state and, more recently, the no-party state. The one-party state worked more or less successfully in Tanzania, where, under Julius Nyerere's enlightened and statesmanlike (if economically unsuccessful) leadership, it became a force for uniting a disparate congeries of tribes and clans into a viable nation-state. The no-party state is being tried in Uganda, where President Yoweri Museveni has argued that political parties are dangerously divisive because they function differently in Africa than in Western democracies. In the West, he suggests, parties draw from all sections of society, since they are organized around issues of principle or to defend class interests; in Africa, parties are organized on a tribal, ethnic, or regional basis, therefore do not draw from all sections of society, and as a result, threaten societal cohesion. Museveni's answer was to ban all political parties in Uganda, permitting opposition by individuals rather than groupings. But while aspects of his analysis are relevant to India—for there are communal and regional parties that represent impermeable and therefore divisive identities—India also has parties that are organized ideologically on Western lines and transcend such divisions.

Yet there is no denying the disillusionment that does exist in India with aspects of Indian democracy. All too often, democratic politics appears to be practiced in India as an end in itself, unconnected to the welfare of Indians. As a result, one disturbingly encounters, in conversations across middle-class India, a frequent wistful longing for benign authoritarianism. It is startling to me, for instance, how the Emergency—Mrs. Gandhi's 22-month experiment in autocratic rule—is remembered in many middle-class homes as a time of order and relative honesty in government, when officials came to work and didn't ask for bribes, when the streets were free of agitations and demonstrations, and when black-marketeers and hoarders were locked up along with troublesome politicians. Political contention breeds inefficiencies, and the subcontinental penchant for taking our differences to the streets in the form of strikes and agitations undoubtedly costs the country a great deal in lost production. Slogans do not fill stomachs, and when shouted too loudly and too often…could well scare off foreign investors. Democratic politics also distorts the complexity of governance, predicating political judgment to the short-term logic of the next election, making difficult visionary decisions (especially those that involve short-term individual pain for long-term societal gain) impossible. This is why authoritarianism holds some attraction for those who genuinely claim only to have the national good at heart. Democracy, they say, doesn't deliver the goods, it merely impedes their delivery.

Politicians of all faiths across India seek to mobilize voters by appealing to narrow identities; by seeking votes in the name of religion, caste, and region, they have urged voters to define themselves on these lines. Indians have been made more conscious than ever before of what divides us. As religion, caste, and region have come to dominate public policy, we are more and more defined by our narrow particulars, and to some it has become more important to be a Muslim, a Bodo, or a Yadav than to be an Indian.

Fortunately, the Indian idea celebrates diversity; if America is a melting-pot, then to me India is a *thali*, a selection of sumptuous dishes in different bowls.

Each tastes different, and does not necessarily mix with the next, but they belong together on the same plate, and they complement each other in making the meal a satisfying repast.

No one identity can ever triumph in India; both the country's chronic pluralism and the logic of the electoral marketplace make this impossible. In leading a coalition government, the Hindu-inclined Bharatiya Janata Party has learned that any party with aspirations to rule India will have to reach out to other groups, other interests, other minorities. After all, there are too many diversities in our land for any one version of reality to be imposed on all of us.

India is unusual in that democracy is not an elite preoccupation, but matters most strongly to ordinary people. Whereas in the United States a majority of the poor do not bother to vote, in India the poor turn out in great numbers because they know their votes make a difference.

That conviction has helped overcome some major threats to the country. Separatism in places as far afield as Tamil Nadu in the south and Mizoram in the northeast has been defused in one of the great unsung achievements of Indian democracy: yesterday's secessionists have, in many cases, become today's chief ministers. The explosive potential of caste division has also been channeled through the ballot box. Corruption is being tackled by an activist judiciary and by energetic investigative agencies that have not hesitated to indict the most powerful Indian politicians. The rule of law remains a vital Indian strength. Nongovernmental organizations actively defend human rights, promoting environmentalism and fighting injustice. The press is free, lively, and irreverent, disdainful of sacred cows.

The experiment begun fifty years ago has worked. Though there have been major threats to the nation from separatist movements, caste conflicts, and regional rivalries, political democracy has helped defuse them. Most strikingly, the power of electoral numbers has given high office to the lowest of India's low. It was unimaginable for 3000 years that an "untouchable" woman would rule as chief minister of India's most populous state. Yet Mayawati has done that twice in Uttar Pradesh. Last summer, K. R. Narayanan, a Dalit, an "untouchable," was elected president of India. He leads an India whose injustices and inequalities he has keenly felt as a member of an underprivileged community; yet it is an India that offers—through its brave if flawed experiment in constitutional democracy, secularism, affirmative governmental action, and change through the ballot-box—the prospect of overcoming these injustices.

It is true that democracy works in some ways against the larger, long-term national interest in economic policy. It privileges short-term considerations, like the populism that infected the Andhra polls of November 1994; the attitude is to seek licenses or benefits now, not to sacrifice for long-term development. It makes hard choices difficult, because of the political consequences of such necessary decisions as public-sector layoffs or the elimination of subsidies. Equally, however, it involves all shades of opinion in the problem by obliging them to exercise power in the states or the Center and to confront the same choices in the process. No wonder all three governments that have held national office in 1996 remained committed to the same basic consensus around economic liberalization. And democracy sometimes serves as a force for responsible governance by placing restraints on how far politicians can go in their profligacy; if they are so spendthrift as to provoke high inflation, voters will turn them out. As Manmohan Singh, the architect of reform under Prime Minister Rao, put it:

In the short term, democracy may be an impediment to growth, but it is not a disadvantage in the long run. Political pluralism is the wave of the future....Political societies that are rigid and monolithic are like command economies. They can produce very rapid growth in the short term, but in the long run it's not sustainable.

Adapted from the author's book of the same title, Arcade Publishing, New York, 1997, by permission of the publisher.

Shashi Tharoor *is interim head, department of public information, at the United Nations. He is author of numerous books, including* India: From Midnight to the Millennium *and the novel* Riot.

∞

FROM
On Toleration
by Michael Walzer

As an American Jew, I grew up thinking of myself as an object of toleration. It was only much later that I recognized myself as a subject too, an agent called upon to tolerate others, including fellow Jews whose idea of what Jewishness meant differed radically from my own. My dawning sense of the United States as a country where everyone had to tolerate everyone else...was the starting point of this essay. It led me to reflect on the ways in which other countries were different, and only sometimes intolerably different. All the world is not America!

Tolerating and being tolerated is a little like Aristotle's ruling and being ruled: it is the work of democratic citizens. I don't think that it is easy or insignificant work. Toleration itself is often underestimated, as if it is the least we can do for our fellows, the most minimal of their entitlements. In fact, tolerance (the attitude) takes many different forms, and toleration (the practice) can be arranged in different ways. Even the most grudging forms and precarious arrangements are very good things, sufficiently rare in human history that they require not only practical but also theoretical appreciation. As with other things that we value, we have to ask what it is that sustains toleration, how it works....Here I want only to suggest what it is that toleration sustains. It sustains life itself, because persecution is often to the death, and it also sustains common lives, the different communities in which we live. Toleration makes difference possible; difference makes toleration necessary.

A defense of toleration doesn't have to be a defense of difference. It can be, and often is, nothing more than an argument from necessity. But I write here with a high regard for difference, though not for every instance of it. In social, political, and cultural life, I prefer the many to the one. At the same time, I recognize that each regime of toleration must be singular and unified to some degree, capable of engaging the loyalty of its members. Coexistence requires a politically stable and morally legitimate arrangement, and this too is an object of value.

MICHAEL WALZER *is UPS Foundation Professor of Social Science at the Institute for Advanced Study in Princeton, N.J. A co-editor of* Dissent *and a contributing editor at* The New Republic, *he is the author of numerous books and articles.*

7
Shaping the Political Structures for Democracy

"There are no longer respectable alternatives to democracy; it is part of the fashionable attire of modernity."
—Fareed Zakaria

Introduction by Stanley N. Katz

Many of the lessons political scientists and historians thought they had learned from studying the settled democracies of Europe and North America are now being reexamined. The post-World War II movement for post-colonial democracy in Africa and Asia was the first indication that countries react to the introduction of democracy in distinctive ways. The post-Cold War movements for democracy in the Iron Curtain countries have reinforced our appreciation that political democracy takes many forms, since similar political institutions function differently in diverse political cultures. The point is also underscored by those countries in Asia and Latin America currently making the transition from authoritarianism to democracy.

Proponents of democracy in newly-democratizing countries have a difficult task in deciding what institutional models they should advocate. Should they opt for parliamentary or presidential regimes? Should they adopt bicameral legislatures, and, if so, what should the function of the upper body be? Should they write new constitutions or adopt existing constitutions? Should they put systems of judicial review in place? How seriously should they consider the United States model of a system of checks and balances? Should they permit public referenda to trump decisions of the legislature? The questions of this sort go on and on.

The larger question is how much democracy, and what type of democracy, a transitional regime can support. At a minimum, there must be free elections open to most of the citizens, but elections alone do not make democracy, as we should have learned from the socialist period. Even reasonably free elections, by themselves, amount to "votocracy" rather than democracy, if they do not enable popular participation in genuinely representative institutions. But there are perils to political stability in permitting either too much popular participation or too many checks on executive decision-making. The challenge for each country is to determine how much democracy (and what sort of democratic political and legal institutions) it can sustain without inviting weakness in response to internal and external challenges and threats.

For the student of politics and law in the older democratic countries, the current world scene provides a fascinating tableau of experiments in democratization. We now have the opportunity to apply comparative methodologies to help us understand both the nature of emerging democracies and the fundamental dynamics of our own systems, which we have for too long taken for granted.

STANLEY N. KATZ *is a professor for the Woodrow Wilson School of Public and International Affairs at Princeton University and former president of the American Council of Learned Societies.*

Discussion Questions

1   What does Stanley Katz mean by the term *votocracy*? Is your country an example of it? Why or why not?

2. Besides free and fair elections, what does Fareed Zakaria say constitutes liberal democracy? Which components of a liberal democracy exist in your country? Which are missing?

3. What is the relationship between politics and economics in Zakaria's view? Do you agree? Give examples from your own country to support your answer.

4. According to Zakaria, what is wrong with giving government strong powers to quickly accomplish reasonable goals such as breaking down feudalism or bringing order to a chaotic society?

5. According to Zakaria, whose conception of democracy displays more faith in human nature, the French or the American? What are the political consequences of this faith?

6. Martin Palouš says that with the collapse of communism, Eastern Europeans cannot simply adopt the liberal traditions established in the West, because these traditions are being challenged by a new world order. What are the challenges Palouš identifies? What does he suggest for solutions? What evidence is there in your country of Palouš's thesis?

Readings

FROM
"The Rise of Illiberal Democracy"
BY FAREED ZAKARIA

THE NEXT WAVE

The American diplomat Richard Holbrooke pondered a problem on the eve of the September 1996 elections in Bosnia, which were meant to restore civic life to that ravaged country. "Suppose the election was declared free and fair," he said, and those elected are "racists, fascists, separatists, who are publicly opposed to [peace and reintegration]. That is the dilemma." Indeed it is, not just in the former Yugoslavia, but increasingly around the world. Democratically elected regimes, often ones that have been reelected or reaffirmed through referenda, are routinely ignoring constitutional limits on their power and depriving their citizens of basic rights and freedoms. From Peru to the Palestinian Authority, from Sierra Leone to Slovakia, from Pakistan to the Philippines, we see the rise of a disturbing phenomenon in international life—illiberal democracy.

It has been difficult to recognize this problem because for almost a century in the West, democracy has meant liberal democracy—a political system marked not only by free and fair elections, but also by the rule of law, a separation of powers, and the protection of basic liberties of speech, assembly, religion, and property. In fact, this latter bundle of freedoms—what might be termed constitutional liberalism—is theoretically different and historically distinct from democracy.... Today the two strands of liberal democracy, interwoven in the Western political fabric, are coming apart in the rest of the world. Democracy is flourishing; constitutional liberalism is not.

THE ROAD TO LIBERAL DEMOCRACY

Constitutional liberalism has led to democracy, but democracy does not seem to bring constitutional liberalism. In contrast to the Western and East Asian paths, during the last two decades in Latin America, Africa, and parts of Asia, dictatorships with little background in constitutional liberalism have given way to democracy. The results are not encouraging. In the western hemisphere, with elections having been held in every country except Cuba, a 1993 study by the scholar Larry Diamond determined that 10 of the 22 principal Latin American countries "have levels of human rights abuse that are incompatible with the consolidation of [liberal] democracy."[1] In Africa, democratization has been extraordinarily rapid. Within six months in 1990, much of Francophone Africa lifted its ban on multiparty politics. Yet although elections have been held in most of the 45 sub-Saharan states since 1991 (18 in 1996 alone), there have been setbacks for freedom in many countries. One of Africa's most careful observers, Michael Chege, surveyed the wave of democratization and drew the lesson that the continent had "overemphasized multiparty elections…and corresponding-ly neglected the basic tenets of liberal governance." In Central Asia, elections, even when reasonably free, as in Kyrgyzstan and Kazakhstan, have resulted in strong executives, weak legislatures and judiciaries, and few civil and economic liberties. In the Islamic world, from the Palestinian Authority to Iran to Pakistan, democratization has led to an increasing role for theocratic politics, eroding long-standing traditions of secularism and tolerance. In many parts of that world, such as Tunisia, Morocco, Egypt, and some of the Gulf States, were elections to be held tomorrow, the resulting regimes would almost certainly be more illiberal than the ones now in place.

Many of the countries of Central Europe, on the other hand, have moved successfully from communism to liberal democracy.…Indeed, the Austro-Hungarian empire, to which most belonged, was a classic liberal autocracy. Even outside Europe, the political scientist Myron Weiner detected a striking con-nection between a constitutional past and a liberal democratic present. He pointed out that, as of 1983, "every single country in the Third World that emerged from colonial rule since the Second World War with a population of at least one million (and almost all the smaller colonies as well) and with a con-tinuous democratic experience is a former British colony."[2] British rule meant not democracy—colonialism is by definition undemocratic—but constitution-al liberalism. Britain's legacy of law and administration has proved more bene-ficial than France's policy of enfranchising some of its colonial populations.

While liberal autocracies may have existed in the past, can one imagine them today? Until recently, a small but powerful example flourished off the Asian mainland—Hong Kong. For 156 years, until July 1, 1997, Hong Kong was ruled

---

[1]Larry Diamond, "Democracy in Latin America," in Tom Farer, ed., *Beyond Sovereignty: Collectively Defending Democracy in a World of Sovereign States* (Baltimore: Johns Hopkins University Press, 1996), p. 73.

[2]Myron Weiner, "Empirical Democratic Theory," in Myron Weiner and Ergun Ozbudun, eds., *Competitive Elections in Developing Countries* (Durham: Duke University Press, 1987).

by the British Crown through an appointed governor general. Until 1991 it had never held a meaningful election, but its government epitomized constitutional liberalism, protecting its citizens' basic rights and administering a fair court system and bureaucracy. A September 8,1997, editorial on the island's future in *The Washington Post* was titled ominously, "Undoing Hong Kong's Democracy." Actually, Hong Kong has precious little democracy to undo; what it has is a framework of rights and laws. Small islands may not hold much practical significance in today's world, but they do help one weigh the relative value of democracy and constitutional liberalism....

ABSOLUTE SOVEREIGNTY

Many Western governments and scholars have encouraged the creation of strong and centralized states in the Third World. Leaders in these countries have argued that they need the authority to break down feudalism, split entrenched coalitions, override vested interests, and bring order to chaotic societies. But this confuses the need for a legitimate government with that for a powerful one. Governments that are seen as legitimate can usually maintain order and pursue tough policies, albeit slowly, by building coalitions. After all, few claim that governments in developing countries should not have adequate police powers; the trouble comes from all the other political, social, and economic powers that they accumulate. In crises like civil wars, constitutional governments might not be able to rule effectively, but the alternative—states with vast security apparatuses that suspend constitutional rights—has usually produced neither order nor good government. More often, such states have become predatory, maintaining some order but also arresting opponents, muzzling dissent, nationalizing industries, and confiscating property. While anarchy has its dangers, the greatest threats to human liberty and happiness in this century have been caused not by disorder but by brutally strong, centralized states, like Nazi Germany, Soviet Russia, and Maoist China. The Third World is littered with the bloody handiwork of strong states.

Historically, unchecked centralization has been the enemy of liberal democracy. As political participation increased in Europe over the nineteenth century, it was accommodated smoothly in countries such as England and Sweden, where medieval assemblies, local governments, and regional councils had remained strong. Countries like France and Prussia, on the other hand, where the monarchy had effectively centralized power (both horizontally and vertically), often ended up illiberal and undemocratic. It is not a coincidence that in twentieth-century Spain, the beachhead of liberalism lay in Catalonia, for centuries a doggedly independent and autonomous region. In America, the presence of a rich variety of institutions—state, local, and private—made it much easier to accommodate the rapid and large extensions in suffrage that took place in the early nineteenth century....More recently, India's semi-liberal democracy has survived because of, not despite, its strong regions and varied languages, cultures, and even castes. The point is logical, even tautological: pluralism in the past helps ensure political pluralism in the present.

Fifty years ago, politicians in the developing world wanted extraordinary powers to implement then fashionable economic doctrines, like nationalization of industries. Today their successors want similar powers to privatize those very industries. [Argentine President Carlos] Menem's justification for his methods is that they are desperately needed to enact tough economic reforms. Similar arguments are made by Abdala Bucarem of Ecuador and by [Peruvian President Alberto] Fujimori. Lending institutions, such as the International Monetary Fund and the World Bank, have been sympathetic to these pleas, and the bond market has been positively exuberant. But except in emergencies like war, illiberal means are in the long run incompatible with liberal ends. Constitutional government is in fact the key to a successful economic reform policy. The experience of East Asia and Central Europe suggests that when regimes—whether authoritarian, as in East Asia, or liberal democratic, as in Poland, Hungary, and the Czech Republic—protect individual rights, including those of property and contract, and create a framework of law and administration, capitalism and growth will follow....

Finally, and perhaps more important, power accumulated to do good can be used subsequently to do ill. When Fujimori disbanded parliament, his approval ratings shot up to their highest ever. But recent opinion polls suggest that most of those who once approved of his actions now wish he were more constrained. In 1993 Boris Yeltsin famously (and literally) attacked the Russian parliament, prompted by the parliament's own unconstitutional acts. He then suspended the constitutional court, dismantled the system of local governments, and fired several provincial governors. From the war in Chechnya to his economic programs, Yeltsin has displayed a routine lack of concern for constitutional procedures and limits. He may well be a liberal democrat at heart, but Yeltsin's actions have created a Russian super-presidency. We can only hope his successor will not abuse it.

For centuries Western intellectuals have had a tendency to view constitutional liberalism as a quaint exercise in rule-making, mere formalism that should take a back seat to battling larger evils in society. The most eloquent counterpoint to this view remains an exchange in Robert Bolt's play *A Man for*

All Seasons. The fiery young William Roper, who yearns to battle evil, is exasperated by Sir Thomas More's devotion to the law. More gently defends himself.

> MORE: What would you do? Cut a great road through the law to get after the Devil?
>
> ROPER: I'd cut every law in England to do that!
>
> MORE: And when the last law was down, and the Devil turned on you—where would you hide, Roper, the laws all being flat?

THE AMERICAN PATH

An American scholar recently traveled to Kazakhstan on a U.S. government-sponsored mission to help the new parliament draft its electoral laws. His counterpart, a senior member of the Kazak parliament, brushed aside the many options the American expert was outlining, saying emphatically, "We want our parliament to be just like your Congress." The American was horrified, recalling, "I tried to say something other than the three words that had immediately come screaming into my mind: 'No you don't!'" This view is not unusual. Americans in the democracy business tend to see their own system as an unwieldy contraption that no other country should put up with. In fact, the adoption of some aspects of the American constitutional framework could ameliorate many of the problems associated with illiberal democracy. The philosophy behind the U.S. Constitution, a fear of accumulated power, is as relevant today as it was in 1789. Kazakhstan, as it happens, would be particularly well-served by a strong parliament—like the American Congress—to check the insatiable appetite of its president.

It is odd that the United States is so often the advocate of elections and plebiscitary democracy abroad. What is distinctive about the American system is not how democratic it is but rather how undemocratic it is, placing as it does multiple constraints on electoral majorities. Of its three branches of government, one—arguably paramount—is headed by nine unelected men and women with life tenure. Its Senate is the most unrepresentative upper house in the world, with the lone exception of the House of Lords, which is powerless. (Every state sends two senators to Washington regardless of its population—California's 30 million people have as many votes in the Senate as Arizona's 3.7 million—which means that senators representing about 16 percent of the country can block any proposed law.) Similarly, in legislatures all over the United States, what is striking is not the power of majorities but that of minorities. To further check national power, state and local governments are strong and fiercely battle every federal intrusion onto their turf. Private businesses and other nongovernmental groups, what Tocqueville called intermediate associations, make up another stratum within society.

The American system is based on an avowedly pessimistic conception of human nature, assuming that people cannot be trusted with power. "If men were angels," Madison famously wrote, "no government would be necessary." The other model for democratic governance in Western history is based on the French Revolution. The French model places its faith in the goodness of human beings. Once the people are the source of power, it should be unlimited so that they can create a just society....Most non-Western countries have embraced the French model—not least because political elites like the prospect of empowering the state, since that means empowering themselves—and most have descended into bouts of chaos, tyranny, or both. This should have come as no surprise. After all, since its revolution, France itself has run through two monarchies, two empires, one proto-fascist dictatorship, and five republics.[3]

Of course cultures vary, and different societies will require different frameworks of government. This is not a plea for the wholesale adoption of the American way but rather for a more variegated conception of liberal democracy, one that emphasizes both parts of that phrase. Before new policies can be adopted, there lies an intellectual task of recovering the constitutional liberal tradition, central to the Western experience and to the development of good government throughout the world. Political progress in Western history has been the result of a growing recognition over the centuries that, as the Declaration of Independence puts it, "human beings have certain inalienable rights" and that "it is to secure these rights that governments are instituted." If a democracy does not preserve liberty and law, that it is a democracy is a small consolation.

Finally, we need to revive constitutionalism. One effect of the overemphasis on pure democracy is that little effort is given to creating imaginative constitutions for transitional countries. Constitutionalism, as it was understood by its greatest eighteenth-century exponents, such as Montesquieu and Madison, is a complicated system of checks and balances designed to prevent the accumulation of power and the abuse of office. This is done not by simply writing up a list of rights but by constructing a system in which government will not violate those rights. Various groups must be included and empowered because, as Madison explained, "ambition must be made to counteract ambition." Constitutions were also meant to tame the passions of the public, creating not simply democratic but also deliberative government.

---

[3]Bernard Lewis, "Why Turkey Is the Only Muslim Democracy," *Middle East Quarterly*, March 1994, pp. 47-48.

DEMOCRACY'S DISCONTENTS

We live in a democratic age. Through much of human history the danger to an individual's life, liberty, and happiness came from the absolutism of monarchies, the dogma of churches, the terror of dictatorships, and the iron grip of totalitarianism. Dictators and a few straggling totalitarian regimes still persist, but increasingly they are anachronisms in a world of global markets, information, and media. There are no longer respectable alternatives to democracy; it is part of the fashionable attire of modernity. Thus the problems of governance in the twenty-first century will likely be problems *within* democracy. This makes them more difficult to handle, wrapped as they are in the mantle of legitimacy.

Illiberal democracies gain legitimacy, and thus strength, from the fact that they are reasonably democratic. Conversely, the greatest danger that illiberal democracy poses—other than to its own people—is that it will discredit liberal democracy itself, casting a shadow on democratic governance.…Today, in the face of a spreading virus of illiberalism, the most useful role that the international community…can play is—instead of searching for new lands to democratize and new places to hold elections—to consolidate democracy where it has taken root and to encourage the gradual development of constitutional liberalism across the globe. Democracy without constitutional liberalism is not simply inadequate, but dangerous, bringing with it the erosion of liberty, the abuse of power, ethnic divisions, and even war. Eighty years ago, Woodrow Wilson took America into the twentieth century with a challenge, to make the world safe for democracy. As we approach the next century, our task is to make democracy safe for the world.

From an article of the same title in Foreign Affairs, *November/December 1997, excerpted from pages 22-43. Reprinted by permission of* Foreign Affairs, *November/December 1997. Copyright 1997 by the Council on Foreign Relations, Inc.*

For information about FAREED ZAKARIA, *see page 164.*

FROM
"Beyond the Liberal Paradigm"
BY MARTIN PALOUŠ

Is the process witnessed in Europe after the collapse of communism a mere homecoming of "post-totalitarians" from their Babylonian captivity to the nice, prosperous, and safe haven of the West? Or is the current rapprochement of East and West in Europe taking place at a moment of profound crisis in European civilization, when Europeans cannot go, as they might like, "back to the future," but find themselves in an unprecedented, and thus unknown situation? Is it old, familiar ideas whose time has come? Or is it not the lack of new ideas which is at the heart of our post-totalitarian problem?

What I am saying is simple: the collapse of communism could not lead to the restoration and/or expansion of the good old liberal European order, because this event has not only liberated East Central Europeans, but also has irreversibly changed Europe's political identity. With all respect to the venerable traditions of modern European liberalism, it is essential for our discussion to see the limitations of the liberal paradigm and to understand not only the similarities but also the differences in Europe before and after the ruinous attack on its identity by totalitarian ideologies.

The international system emerging after the disintegration of the bipolar Cold War architecture is more open, more interdependent, and definitely less "Eurocentric." Multiculturalism, multiple identities, and anti-foundationalism are not only fashionable themes in academic discourse today, they create the context for current international politics. The "grand opening" of the postmodern market of ideas does not necessarily generate more political freedom and improved communication between nations. On the contrary, it may lead to the emergence of new, culturally motivated conflicts and the possibility that we may be heading into an era of the "clash of civilizations."[1]

What is at stake is the present existence of and future prospects for the nation-state. The very concept of nation-state—understood as a defined state territory ruled by a sovereign power and recognized as an equal member of the international community—has been weakened in the course of the twentieth century. The experience of two horrible world wars and the growing global interdependence in practically all spheres of social, political, economic, and cultural life have dramatically changed the basic characteristics of the international system. Trends indicate clearly that globalization is unavoidable and that it will persist regardless of how strongly isolationist feelings and attitudes may influence the politics of some states.

The victory of the old, well-tested liberal ideas in the ideological conflict fueling the Cold War can change neither the endemic deficiency of the modern

---

[1]Samuel P. Huntington, "The Clash of Civilizations," *Foreign Affairs*, Summer 1993.

nation-state nor the modern liberalism that finds itself in deep crisis at the end of the twentieth century. The ever more complex network of communications connecting non-state actors across national boundaries has made it increasingly difficult for national governments to exert decisive control over important political issues, thus curtailing the possibilities of traditional liberal politics. The process by which vital decisions are made often remains opaque to most ordinary citizens—not discussed, not understood, not present in the public domain. An increasing sense of insecurity and powerlessness pervades European societies. What can be observed practically everywhere in the West is the growing "democratic deficit." The whole game of politics is more and more distant from the lives of ordinary citizens and has begun, as some commentators observe, to acquire a bogus air and a sense of a kind of "virtual reality."

Globalization and complex interdependence, the most important characteristics of mankind's existence at the end of the twentieth century, have not only changed the nature of world politics but have also introduced its negative, hidden agendas. International crime generating enormous amounts of money to infiltrate and corrupt political elites, a growing vulnerability in the population to extremist views, articulating nationalist and anti-foreigner rhetoric of the most disreputable kind, the disintegration of basic social patterns and structures in some countries or whole regions (i.e., "coming anarchy"[2])—these and other phenomena represent the dark side of our post-modern and increasingly globalized situation.

In his...seminal work on the recent wave of European revolutions [Ralf] Dahrendorf advised the post-communist politicians "to go back to the 1780s, to the lessons of the great transformations of that time" and to use The Federalist Papers, as an "unsurpassed manual of liberal democracy."[3] The biggest threat to democracy in times of transition and disordered society, warned James Madison, is weak government. The key question is what "republican remedies" can be used to make governments stronger. How can emerging open societies be stabilized and protected not only against the forces of the "*ancien régime*," but also against those new politicians who pretend to be the speakers of the people but in reality seek to "aggrandize themselves by the confusion of their country," in the words of another Federalist, Alexander Hamilton.[4]

How can we transform a closed political regime and build a republican form of government and at the same time cope with the problem of a newly emerging

---

[2]Robert D. Kaplan, "Was Democracy Just a Moment?" *Atlantic Monthly*, Dec. 1997, p. 55–80.
[3]*Ibid.*, p. 30.

international system—a New World Order? Two aspects of the dramatically changing realm of international relations were underestimated in the "realpolitik" of the past and now should be taken much more seriously into consideration. First is the internationalization of human rights. The emergence of international mechanisms for their protection, as a reaction to the unprecedented crimes committed by totalitarian criminal regimes during World War II, represents the most important change in world politics in the second half of the twentieth century....

The second aspect, largely underestimated and under-represented in international politics, is the phenomenon of trans-national civil society. All efforts to cope with the tasks that transcend the limited, closed space of territorial nation-states, whether they be problems which require "global governance" or questions of regional arrangements and "integrative" frameworks, cannot be successful without active participation of the civic element. The conflicts emerging in the post-communist world clearly demonstrate that a profound democratization of international relations is essential. The political structures needed to replace the stable bipolar system of the Cold War era cannot be imposed from above. The New World Order can be formed only when all strategies from above are complemented by actions from below....

If Europeans still believe that their civilizations are worthy of preservation in the age of multiculturalism and globalization, they must have the courage to overcome the shadows of the past and enhance and promote politics based on trans-national communication.

An ongoing international dialogue is the best, and perhaps the only, possible "republican remedy," in the Federalists' sense, to strengthen global governance and maintain in emerging world politics the element of freedom which is still the very essence of our humanity.

Adapted from an article of the same title in hCa *quarterly, Summer 1996, pages 11–13, by permission of* hCa *quarterly.*

Martin Palouš *is the Czech ambassador to the United States. He was one of the first signatories of Charter 77 and author of* Between Past & Future: The Revolutions of 1989 and Their Aftermath.

---

[4] *The Federalist Papers*, first letter of Alexander Hamilton.

8
Democracy and the Free Market

*"Markets reduce everything, including human beings (labor) and nature
(land), to commodities. We can have a market economy but we cannot
have a market society."*
—George Soros

Introduction by William M. Sullivan

Democratic societies are not perpetual motion machines. They require a con-
tinual investment of care and responsibility on the part of their citizens. The
experience of both emerging democracies and long-established democracies
confirms this. The most fundamental goods of democracy, such as the security
of individual rights, can exist only as long as most citizens share a sense of solidarity and common destiny.

Contemporary life, however, is marked by increasing volatility in all areas of
social relationship. In particular, the dynamism of technology and the market
economy poses a mounting challenge. While democracies must find ways to
cultivate a sense of moral equality and shared destiny among citizens, the rapid
spread of market values to all aspects of life is teaching, and even enforcing, very
different lessons.

Increasingly, national societies are split into a minority class of economic
winners who inhabit a cosmopolitan world of affluence, and a growing under-
class with little hope of economic ascent. Moreover, as economic competition
grows more intense, the ties of social solidarity are placed under increasing
strain. Systems of social provision are likewise threatened, further undermining
the sense of common destiny among citizens.

However, the chief threat posed by the spread of market behavior into every
sphere of life is that social relationships become stripped of their moral meaning. Thus, business ceases to acknowledge any responsibility to either its
employees, the communities where it operates, or to the nation which protects
it through law. In the same way, the individual is encouraged to think first of

self-interest, not only in business affairs but in the civic sphere, with respect to the natural environment, and finally in community and family life.

The danger to democracy of the spread of market behavior is that society will become increasingly atomized. With this, public responsibility, like social solidarity, will wither away, leaving society incapable of dealing with large-scale and long-term threats to its well-being. The chief question in the face of these threats is: How can modern nations develop their economic and technological capacities without damaging the moral and social underpinnings needed to fulfill the promise of democracy?

For information about WILLIAM M. SULLIVAN, *see page 110.*

Discussion Questions

1. William M. Sullivan believes that what he calls market behavior has begun to influence our personal relationships. Do you find evidence of this in your own life? If so, what are the effects?

2. Jacques Attali makes the case that democracy and capitalism are incompatible in terms of their underlying principles. Do you agree? Support your position.

3. Attali claims that today, the market economy is more dynamic than democracy. What evidence of this, if any, is there in your country? What are the consequences? What remedial action does Attali recommend? Is it applicable to your local and national situation?

4. Do corporations in your region or country render services to the public good? If not, what change is recommended in the excerpt from *Habits of the Heart*? Might this work under your circumstances?

Readings

FROM
"The Crash of Western Civilization: The Limits of the Market and Democracy"
BY JACQUES ATTALI

With the end of the Cold War and the collapse of the Soviet empire, the market economy and democracy appear to have triumphed. Universally praised, these two central values of Western society have become the prerequisite of any nation seeking acceptance by the international community or assistance from international financial institutions....Moreover, history would seem to suggest that the market economy and democracy together form the equivalent of a virtuous circle. Not only is it seemingly impossible to have one without the other, but in the long run the two appear to be mutually reinforcing. The market economy needs private property, entrepreneurship, and innovation, which cannot flourish without freedom of thought, speech, and movement. Democracy means that people can choose where to live, what to buy and sell, and how to work, save, and accumulate wealth, none of which is compatible with the collective ownership of industry. In sum, the market economy and democracy appear to be deeply intertwined, with both tied to the fundamental concept of private property.

Yet even the most enthusiastic proponents of both the market economy and democracy would admit that "market democracies"—a shorthand term adopted in recent years by exuberant American policymakers—are not easy to create. The development of a robust market economy in a formerly communist country such as Russia requires more than privatizing industry and allowing the market to determine prices. And the establishment of real democracy in a war-torn nation such as Cambodia calls for more than its much-celebrated free elections. A market economy and democracy can endure only in nations that maintain certain indispensable features: the rule of law, a legal system, a free media, and a social consensus on efficient tax collection.

Despite the prevalent belief that the market economy and democracy combine to form a perpetual-motion machine that propels human progress, these two values on their own are in fact incapable of sustaining any civilization. Both are riddled with weaknesses and are increasingly likely to break down....

WHERE THE MARKET AND DEMOCRACY FAIL

While the cracks in the facade of Western civilization are only just beginning to show, an x-ray of its foundation might reveal deep weaknesses that could lead to its total collapse.

Inapplicable Principles

Consider two core institutions of the West: the private corporation and the civil service. For all our talk of free markets and equality among individuals, our companies and bureaucracies are organized on the basis of fixed plans and strict hierarchies. Can we imagine a real market relationship between divisions of the same company or between a boss and her assistant? Can we imagine an internal referendum on each decision made by a minister or cabinet secretary?...

Likewise, few Western nations...would appreciate an international community where true democracy prevailed....If international financial institutions had followed such a democratic system during the so-called Global Negotiations of the 1980s, there would likely have been a drastic shift in the global distribution of wealth that would have jeopardized the interests of the West....

Similarly, applying the principles of the market economy both within and among nations is problematic and undesirable. I know of no Western nation that seeks a free market in justice, law enforcement, national defense, education, or even telecommunications—and with good reason. Few if any Westerners would want to live in a country where court rulings were for sale, citizenship and passports could be purchased at airline ticket counters, and air waves were auctioned off to the highest bidder without regard to content. And among nations, a free market for nuclear weapons, illegal narcotics, high technology, potable water, and pollution would promote the rapid growth of supranational political bodies and powerful nonstate entities capable of challenging national governments.

Inherent Contradictions

Contrary to popular belief, the market economy and democracy—the twin pillars of Western Civilization—are more likely to undermine than support one another. What follows is a list of just some of the ways in which they clash:

- In a democratic society, the promotion of the individual is the ultimate goal, while in a market economy the individual is treated as a commodity—one that can be excluded or cast aside for want of the right education, skills, physical characteristics, or upbringing.
- The market economy accepts and fosters strong inequalities between economic agents, whereas democracy is based on the equal rights of all citizens. By

depriving some people of the ability to meet their basic economic needs, the market economy also leaves them less able to exercise their full political rights. Witness the swelling ranks of unemployed workers in much of the West who can vote but are otherwise increasingly disenfranchised and alienated.

• The market economy resists the localization of power, discourages coalitions between participants, and encourages selfishness, while democracy depends upon a clear identification of political responsibility, the coalition of citizens in political parties, and a general appreciation of our common fate. Democracies need political parties that are capable of molding platforms based on compromises between individual points of view, while market economies rely on competing individual centers....

Inevitable Destruction

Both the market economy and democracy encourage a herd mentality that can be deeply destabilizing. Known as the self-fulfilling prophecy syndrome, this tendency can amplify problems, triggering runs on market and financial institutions and even political crises. Information technology is exacerbating this self-destabilizing and self-destructive tendency—in both economics and politics—by providing split-second market results and polling data.

The destructive consequences of this volatility are enormous: markets leave less and less room for long-term contracts or long-term investments. Older generations neglect the interests of the young, demanding benefits and pensions that their children will not be able to sustain, much less enjoy themselves upon retirement. In politics, unpopular decisions are deferred endlessly for immediate political considerations. Led by managers and politicians who are increasingly skilled at gauging public opinion and evading responsibility, society grows incapable of dealing with vital long-term challenges....

THE RISE OF THE MARKET DICTATORSHIP

When two concepts are contradictory, one of them has to come out on top. It seems obvious that, all over the world, the market economy today is more dynamic than democracy. Stronger forces are backing it. The frantic search for money to fund elections, the spread of corruption, and the scale of the criminal economy are all signs of the ascendancy of the market economy over democratic ethics.

The implications of a triumph of the market economy over democracy would be profound. Powerful minorities seeking to take full advantage of the market economy will want total control of their resources and will come to view the collective democratic decisions of poor majorities as intolerable burdens. As legislatures and courts lose power to central banks and corporations, market elites will become stronger than democratic elites, further shrinking the reach and appeal of the public sphere....

Eventually, democracy will fade away, having been replaced by market mechanisms and corruption. We will have a kind of market dictatorship, a "lumpen market" without strong democratic institutions to serve as countervailing powers. Political outcomes will be bought and sold, and the market will rule every element of public life from police protection, justice, education, and health to the very air that we breathe, paving the way for the final victory of "corporate" economic rights over individual human rights.

Under such circumstances, Western civilization itself is bound to collapse....

If we want to avert such a crash, we must seek honest answers to several fundamental questions: What is the real influence of citizens in major decisions? What is the reality of democracy among nations? Why are there always the same winners and losers? Can poverty be overcome by market mechanisms?

To find answers to these questions, Western Civilization should first become more modest about its own values. We must recognize the need to find a compromise between the market economy and planning, and between democratic and authoritarian decision-making mechanisms. We should be exploring ways to organize that compromise rather than indulging in triumphalist rhetoric about the globalization of values....

We also should declare openly that Western Civilization has something to learn from others. An efficient society should be able to organize both the expression of differences and the creation of an enduring collective view. Civilizations that draw on other philosophical and ethical beliefs—whether Confucianism or Buddhism—seem to be succeeding where we are failing in efforts to maintain human dignity, foster solidarity, and give long-term meaning to our decisions by fostering a vision of what sort of world we hope to have in the twenty-first century. The fact that the West may disagree with some aspects of Islam as applied in some countries—the status of women, for example—does not mean that there is nothing to learn from Islamic societies.

Indeed, while many people in non-Western civilizations are trying to imitate the West, a wellspring of opposition to Western values has erupted in many places as well. In Asia, for example, our way of organizing urban life is increasingly rejected, as demonstrated by the Malaysian experience, where planners are considering reorganizing society to deemphasize the automobile. Asian societies suggest possible answers to the contradictory tenets of the market and democracy; by allowing a stronger role for the state in protecting citizens against some of the risks of competition, these societies balance the contradictory forces.

On our own behalf, the West should improve and strengthen democracy in order to achieve a balance with the power of the market. To accomplish that, we must foster a new government role in enforcing the rule of law, supporting the principles of education, ensuring social justice and the participation of workers in corporate decision making, and leading the fight against corruption and the drug economy.

Small nations must unite with their neighbors to achieve a critical mass in the face of market-driven globalization—and to be able to summon the achievements of past generations while not limiting the freedom of choice of future generations (in terms of culture, language, lifestyle, and ethics, for example).

Western societies must decide when and by what means long-term foreign residents can be given the right to vote. As the number of expatriots grows with the development of the global market economy, the right to vote will become essential in any effort to increase the feeling of partnership between people living on the same soil. Ultimately, the civilizations capable of organizing their diasporas will be the winners. We must begin to understand multidimensional citizenship and to recognize cohesion between groups belonging simultaneously to many different entities (e.g., cities and companies). We also must agree on how to build a flexible, long-term framework for democracy that goes beyond national constitutions and their amendments. Some dimensions of human dignity (the right to childhood, the integrity of the genome, and the rights of other species) are not yet well protected by these constitutions.

Western civilization is no stranger to predictions of decline and fall. Some of these predictions have been based on historical theory, others on cultural, economic, or even racial assumptions. For the time being, they have fortunately been proven wrong. But no one should accept the assumption that any civilization, however triumphant, is here to stay. Our survival is in our hands.

Reproduced with permission from Foreign Policy *#107 (Summer 1997), pages 54–63. Copyright 1997 by the Carnegie Endowment for International Peace.*

JACQUES ATTALI *served as special adviser to France's President François Mitterand and as president of the European Bank for Reconstruction and Development. He is a contributing editor for* Foreign Policy.

Habits of the Heart

BY ROBERT N. BELLAH, ET AL.

As late as 1911…a leading Boston businessman, Henry Lee Higginson, could say, following earlier Protestant notions of stewardship, that corporate property "belongs to the community."

Reasserting the idea that incorporation is a concession of public authority to a private group *in return for* service to the public good, with effective public accountability, would change what is now called the "social responsibility of the corporation" from its present status, where it is often a kind of public relations whipped cream decorating the corporate pudding, to a constitutive structural element in the corporation itself. This, in turn, would involve a fundamental alteration in the role and training of the manager. Management would become a profession in the older sense of the word, involving not merely standards of technical competence but standards of public obligation that could at moments of conflict override obligations to the corporate employer. Such a conception of the professional manager would require a deep change in the ethos of schools of business administration, where "business ethics" would have to become central in the process of professional formation. If the rewards of success in business management were not so inordinate, then choice of this profession could arise from more public-spirited motives. In short, personal, cultural, and structural change all entail one another.

ROBERT N. BELLAH *is professor of sociology, emeritus, at the University of California, Berkeley. He is co-author of* Habits of the Heart: Individualism and Commitment in American Life *and* The Good Society.

∞

9
Adapting to the Culture of Democracy

> *"…[civil] society … makes room for the richest possible self-structuring and the riches possible participation in public life."*
> —Václav Havel

Introduction by Benjamin R. Barber

Democracy is a form of government but, John Dewey reminds us, it is also a way of life. "It is," he insists, "the idea of community life itself." It manifests itself in governing institutions, but it also manifests itself in culture. Walt Whitman's celebration of democracy in his extraordinary essay "Democratic Vistas" poses a rhetorical question that is the challenge implicit in these essays, particularly in this section on the "culture of democracy." Whitman asks:

> Did you suppose democracy was only for elections, for politics, and for party name? I say democracy is only for use there that it may pass on and come to its flower and fruits in manners, in the highest forms of interaction between men and their beliefs—in religion, literature, colleges, and schools—democracy in all public and private life.

There can be no democratic government without a democratic culture. The first rests on the second as surely as a barn rests on a stone foundation. When the political theorists of the eighteenth century like Montesquieu and Rousseau offered a vision of democracy, they first described democratic mores and the cultural conditions that alone fostered a democratic spirit. Government came afterward. When Tocqueville rode from town to town in the America of President Andrew Jackson, it was the spirit of municipal liberty manifested in local civic institutions he scrutinized most closely and celebrated most vociferously.

Today, we often seem to forget this simple lesson of the priority of culture to politics. We think a multiparty system or an independent judiciary will endow traditionally despotic societies with all the fruits of liberty. We FedEx Albania the Bill of Rights or we e-mail Afghanistan Australian ballots and assume democratization is underway. But culture counts. Hegemonic or patriarchal cultures may have a hard time supporting the legal infrastructure of democracy. And as a consequence, a bill severing foundations and civic associations from formal government control may be far more important to nourishing a democratic culture than a contested election. Local civic associations that are formed bottom up may do more for citizenship than a democratic constitution's naturalization formulas imposed top down. A free church may do more for liberty than a free economy.

It is not that we must choose. Democracy demands free governing institutions, a sufficient free market *and* democratic cultural institutions and attitudes. But somehow we get preoccupied with the first two and end up neglecting the third—the *sine die qua non* of the others!

It is not an accident that a poet and playwright, whose essay is printed in this section, became Central Europe's leading democratic spokesperson as well as the president of one of the most independent and successful of the emerging democracies. Václav Havel has never talked much about government and its laws in the narrow sense. He has manifested instead a bracing Whitmanesque disposition—the temperament of a poet of democratic mores who understands that in order to be free, a person must first free her spirit and then her community; only afterwards can she forge free governing institutions. This is the challenge of democratic culture: Rousseau's challenge, Tocqueville's challenge, Whitman's challenge, Dewey's challenge, Havel's challenge, and our challenge. Get the culture right, and the rest will follow.

For information about Benjamin R. Barber, *see page 101.*

Discussion Questions

1. Why does Adam Michnik use the color gray as a metaphor for democracy? If democracy is, as he says, prone to manipulation, corruption, banality, and empty promises, what reasons does he give for pursuing it?
2. According to Václav Havel, how does a healthy civil society help to create political stability? Do you agree? Explain.
3. Using Kim Dae Jung's article as a starting point, explore the issue of a culture's receptiveness to the concepts of democracy. Does your country's cultural traditions help or hinder democracy? Explain.

Readings

FROM
"Gray is Beautiful: Thoughts on Democracy in Central Europe"
BY ADAM MICHNIK

Communism was like a freezer. Within it, a diverse world of tensions and values, emotions and conflicts, was covered with a thick layer of ice. The defrosting process was a gradual one—so first we saw beautiful flowers, and only later, the rot. First came the grandeur of the peaceful fall of the Berlin Wall and of the Velvet Revolution in Czechoslovakia. First was the memorable "Autumn of the Nations" in 1989. Freedom returned to Central Europe, and Central Europe returned to history. It returned as a messenger not only of freedom and tolerance, but also of hatred and intolerance, both ethnic and religious. Conflicts—difficult to understand for Westerners who had perceived this territory simply as the Soviet Bloc—came to life once more. But these conflicts were understood all too well by the residents. This world of many nations and cultures had experienced the deep ambiguity of the national right of nations to sovereign existence: the right of one nation usually endangered the right of another nation. Franz Grillparzer, a great Austrian writer of the nineteenth century, warned prophetically against the road that leads "from humanism, through nationality to bestiality."

...We were put to a double test: the test of captivity and the test of freedom. Hence, certainly some of our statements will appear unclear, others perfectly banal. But they were born out of a common inspiration: a passionate dream, about freedom and democratic order. Democracy is not identical with freedom. Democracy is freedom written into the rule of law. Freedom in itself, without the limits imposed on it by law and tradition, is a road to anarchy and chaos—where the right of the strongest rules....

Why did we rebel against communism? Why did we prefer to become a small repressed minority, rather than to join the majority that made careers in the world of totalitarian dictatorship? Well, we rejected communism for several different reasons: it was a lie, and we were searching for truth; it required conformity, and we desired authenticity; communism was enslavement, fear, and censorship, and we desired freedom; it was an ongoing attack on the traditions and national identities that we held to be ours; it was social inequality and injustice, and we believed in equality and justice; communism was a grotesquely deficient economy, and we sought rationality, efficiency, and affluence; communism meant the suppression of religion, and we held freedom of conscience to be a fundamental human right. So, we rejected communism for reasons equally dear to a conservative, a socialist, and a liberal. In this way, a peculiar coalition of ideas emerged, which Leszek Kolakowski noted in his well-known essay, "How to be a Conservative-Liberal Socialist?" This coalition collapsed along with communism. But before it collapsed, the coalition had marked public debate with a specific tone of moral absolutism.

The moral absolutism of the anticommunist opposition required us to believe that communism is inherently evil, the devil of our times, and that resistance to communism is something naturally good, noble, and beautiful. The democratic opposition demonized communists and angelicized itself. I know because this moral absolutism was also my experience to a certain degree. I don't regret this experience, nor do I think I need to be ashamed of it. Standing up to the world of totalitarian dictatorship was to risk, or even to sacrifice, not only one's own safety but also that of one's friends and family. One had to believe that "human life is a serious game," as a church historian of the communist period wrote.

Moral absolutism is a great strength for individuals and groups struggling against dictatorship; but it is a weakness for individuals and groups active in a world where democratic procedures are being built on the rubble of totalitarian dictatorships. There is no room there for the utopias of a just, harmonious, and perfect world—or for moral absolutism. Both of these come down to anachronism or hypocrisy; both threaten the democratic order. Because a democratic world is a chronically imperfect one....

This world not only broke the coalition of antitotalitarian ideas, but also revealed their contradictory character. Egalitarianism found itself in conflict with the principles of liberal economy; conservatism challenged the spirit of liberal tolerance. Dilemmas appeared that the socialist, the conservative, and the liberal resolved in different ways. Let us mention some of them: dealing with the communist past, the shape of the market, the fundamental principles of the state, and the place of the church and religious values in the new reality.

For the socialist, the central issues will be to give a human face to a rapacious market economy; to defend the poorest sectors in society; the secular character of the state; and tolerance toward people of different faiths and nationalities.

The conservative would bring back the continuity of national symbols, would fight for a Christian reshaping of the Constitution and institutions, would warn against the dangers of liberalism and relativism, and would demand harsh treatment for people of the old regime.

The liberal will say: the economy first—economic growth, clear rules of the market, stable systems of taxation, privatization, exchangeable currency. He or she would be a careful defender of the idea of a tolerant state—with regard to the Catholic church, to national minorities, to the neighboring countries, and to the past. Each of these three will have to formulate ideas in a new context: the context of a populist and still unnamed ideology. There is a bit of fascism in it and a bit of communism; a bit of egalitarianism and a bit of clericalism; a radical critique of the Enlightenment and the harsh language of moral absolutism. At the same time, a nostalgia will appear, surprising to all—for the socialist, the liberal, and the conservative. A nostalgia for the security of the "good old communist days," when, as they said, "the state pretended to pay the people, and the people pretended to work."…

And finally, the Catholic church. After years of repression, the church has reasserted its claim to a place in the public debate. In communities where national identity frequently coincided with religious identity, there has been a natural temptation to allow a religious establishment. The church has called for a constitution and criminal code that would be in accordance with religious norms. The debate over abortion has in fact been an argument about the axiological foundation of the state. Does the legality of abortion imply approval of the murder of unborn children? Does the criminalization of abortion constitute an attack on the fundamental right of a woman to decide about her own maternity? These arguments made for extreme emotional tension: there have been constant appeals to moral arguments; the language of war has been used. Two opposing worlds of values have confronted one another. The heroism of the people who had resisted repression has shown its second face: intolerant, fanatical, and opposed to new, modernizing ideas. This is a natural turn of events in the post-communist democracies.

None of these disputes is fatal for democracy, which after all is a permanent debate. Fatal, indeed, would be such an intensification of conflict that all sides become incapable of compromise. Then it would be easy to undermine the procedures of the democratic state. Radical movements—whether under black or red banners—gladly use democracy in order to obliterate it. In the meantime, democracy is neither black nor red. Democracy is gray, is established only with difficulty, and its quality and flavor can be recognized best when it comes under the pressure of advancing red or black ideas. Democracy is not infallible, because in its debates all are equal. This is why it lends itself to manipulation, and may be helpless against corruption. This is why, frequently, it chooses banality over excellence, shrewdness over nobility, empty promise over true competence. Democracy is a continuous articulation of particular interests, a diligent search for compromise among them, a marketplace of passions, emotions, hatreds, and hopes; it is eternal imperfection, a mixture of sinfulness, saintliness, and monkey business. This is why the seekers of a moral state and of a perfectly just society do not like democracy. Yet only democracy, having the capacity to question itself, also has the capacity to correct its own mistakes. Dictatorships, whether red or black, destroy the human capacity for creation, they kill the taste for human life and, eventually, life itself. Only gray democracy, with its human rights, with institutions of civil society, can replace weapons with arguments.

The subject of democracy is people, not ideas. And this is why, in the framework of democratic institutions, citizens can meet and collaborate independently of their faith, nationality, or ideology. Today the classic ideological positions—liberalism, conservatism, socialism—do not dominate public debate about taxes, health reform, or insurance. Yet in each of those debates, there is a need for socialist concern for the poorest, a conservative defense of tradition, and a liberal reflection on efficiency and growth. Each of those values is needed in democratic politics. It is these that give color and diversity to our life; it is these that equip us with the capacity to choose; it is thanks to their mutual contradictions that we can afford inconsistency, experimentation, changes of opinion, and changes of government. In opposition to so-called "corrupt demo-liberalism," the fanaticism of ideological inquisitors offers again and again new projects for a "promised land." Fundamentalists of different varieties condemn the moral relativism of democracy, as though it were the state that should be the guardian of moral virtue. We, however, the defenders of gray democracy, do not grant the state this right. We want human virtues to be guarded by the human conscience. That is why we say, "gray is beautiful."

From the East and Central Europe Program Bulletin, *December 1996, of the Graduate Faculty of the New School for Social Research, translated from the Polish by Elzbieta Matynia, and published in* Dissent, *Spring 1997, pages 15–19, by permission of the New School for Social Research*

For information about ADAM MICHNIK, *see page 142.*

FROM
"The State of the Republic"
BY

In a speech on December 9, 1997 to the Parliament and Senate of the Czech Republic, on the occasion of the resignation of Prime Minister Václav Klaus, President Václav Havel outlined ten points on what must be done to transform what he called the gloomy face of Czech society. The following is the last of his ten points.

I have left culture to the end not because I consider it to be some superstructural "icing on the cake," but for precisely the opposite reason. I consider it the most important of all….I am not thinking of culture as a separate sphere of human activity, such as caring for heritage sites, producing films, or writing poetry. I mean culture in the broadest sense of the word—that is the culture of human relationships, or human existence, of human work, of human enterprise, of public and political life. I refer to the general level of our culture. I am afraid it is here that we have our greatest debt to pay and therefore have the most work ahead of us.

Culture cannot be measured by the number of splendid rock stars who visit our country, or by the beauty of fashions created by world-class designers and modeled for us by world-famous models, but by something else. It can be measured, for example, by what skinheads shout in the bar U Zabránsky'ch, by how many Roma [gypsies] have been lynched or murdered, by how terribly some of us behave to our fellow human beings simply because they have a different color of skin.

This lack of culture…is a typical expression of the post-communist syndrome and, at the same time, a consequence of how little attention we have paid to the state of our souls. Once again I repeat: it is not true that culture is a superstructure that somehow lives a parasitic existence on a flourishing economic base. On the contrary, economic prosperity is directly dependent on the cultural environment in which a given economy operates.

This is not the first time I have spoken to the members of parliament about the nonprofit sector, the reform of the civil service, and other such matters, but if I do it now, you must know I am talking about what is called a civil society. That means a society that makes room for the richest possible self-structuring and the richest possible participation in public life. In this sense, civil society is important for two reasons: in the first place it enables people to be themselves in all their dimensions, which includes being social creatures who desire, in thousands of ways, to participate in the life of the community in which they live.

In the second place, it functions as a genuine guarantee of political stability. The more developed all the organs, institutions, and instruments of civil society are, the more resistant that society will be to political upheavals or reversals. It was no accident that communism's most brutal attack was aimed precisely against this civil society. It knew very well that its greatest enemy was not an individual non-communist politician, but a society that was open, structured independently from the bottom up, and therefore very difficult to manipulate.

As you know, our country today is going through a political crisis. In democratic circumstances or conditions the essence of our crisis is a more or less banal event—the resignation of the government. A democratic system anticipates such events and has the means to deal with them.

And yet this very same crisis appears to many as the collapse of a regime, the collapse of democracy, or even of the world. In my opinion this can only happen because we have not yet created the foundations of a genuinely evolved civil society, which lives on a thousand different levels and thus need not feel that its existence depends on one government or another or on one political party or another.

If I criticize those who have resigned, it is not so much for any particular sin they may have committed, but far more for their indifference and outright hostility to everything that may even slightly resemble a civil society or contribute to its creation. In the final analysis, this indifference is precisely why so common a democratic event as the fall of one government appears nothing short of a Greek tragedy, and to some extent may even have become such a tragedy. Many people understandably feel that they are facing the collapse of a particular view of the state, a particular world view, a particular set of ideals.

However unpleasant and stressful, and even dangerous, what we are going through may be, it can also be instructive and a force for good, because it can call forth a catharsis, the intended outcome of ancient Greek tragedy. That means a feeling of profound purification and redemption. A feeling of newborn hope. A feeling of liberation.

If, then, the present crisis forces us to think seriously again about the nature of our state, about the idea behind it, about its identity, and if it leads us to imbue our work with the result of such thinking, then this crisis will have been anything but meaningless, and all the setbacks it has caused will be compensated for many times over.

We often talk about the identity of a state or a nation or a society, and more than one opponent of European integration has ranted on about national identity and tried to engender fear of its loss. Most who speak this way subconsciously understand identity as something predestined, something genetic, almost an identity of blood—that is, something over which we have no influence or control. This notion of identity is thoroughly discredited. Identity is, above all, an accomplishment, a particular work, a particular act. Identity is not something separate from responsibility, but on the contrary, is its very expression.

If the current crisis is to be an invitation to action, if it once more gives substance to our identity, then we have no reason to regret it. Let us therefore understand it as a lesson, a schooling, a test, a challenge which may well have come just in time to warn us of our vanity and save us from something far worse.

Translated from the Czech by Paul Wilson and published in The New York Review of Books, *March 5, 1998, pages 45-46. Reprinted with permission from* The New York Review of Books. *Copyright © 1998 NYREV, Inc.*

For information about VÁCLAV HAVEL, *see page 151.*

FROM
"Is Culture Destiny? The Myth of Asia's Anti-Democratic Values"
BY KIM DAE-JUNG

Lingering doubts remain about the applicability of and prospects for democracy in Asia. Such doubts have been raised mainly by Asia's authoritarian leaders, Lee [Kuan Yew, Singapore's former prime minister] being the most articulate among them. They have maintained that cultural differences make the "Western concept" of democracy and human rights inapplicable to East Asia. Does Asia have the philosophical and historical underpinnings suitable for democracy? Is democracy achievable there?

SELF-SERVING SELF-RELIANCE

…I too believe in the importance of culture, but I do not think it alone determines a society's fate, nor is it immutable. Moreover, Lee's view of Asian culture is not only unsupportable but self-serving. He argues that Eastern societies, unlike Western ones, "believe that the individual exists in the context of his family" and that the family is "the building brick of society." However, as an inevitable consequence of industrialization, the family-centered East Asian societies are also rapidly moving toward self-centered individualism. Nothing in human history is permanent.

Lee asserts that, in the East, "the ruler or the government does not try to provide for a person what the family best provides." He cites this ostensibly self-reliant, family-oriented culture as the main cause of East Asia's economic successes and ridicules Western governments for allegedly trying to solve all of society's problems, even as he worries about the moral breakdown of Western societies due to too much democracy and too many individual rights. Consequently, according to Lee, the Western political system, with its intrusive government, is not suited to family-oriented East Asia. He rejects Westernization while embracing modernization and its attendant changes in lifestyle—again strongly implying that democracy will not work in Asia.

FAMILY VALUES (REQUIRED HERE)

But the facts demonstrate just the opposite. It is not true, as Lee alleges, that Asian governments shy away from intervening in private matters and taking on all of society's problems. Asian governments intrude much more than Western governments into the daily affairs of individuals and families. In Korea, for example, each household is required to attend monthly neighborhood meetings to receive government directives and discuss local affairs. Japan's powerful government constantly intrudes into the business world to protect perceived national interests, to the point of causing disputes with the United States and other trading partners. In Lee's Singapore, the government stringently regulates individual actions—such as chewing bubble-gum, spitting, smoking, littering, and so on—to an Orwellian extreme of social engineering. Such facts fly in the face of his assertion that East Asia's governments are minimalist.…

Opinions like Lee's hold considerable sway not only in Asia but among some Westerners because of the moral breakdown of many advanced democratic societies. Many Americans thought, for example, that the U.S. citizen Michael Fay deserved the caning he received from Singaporean authorities for his act of vandalism. However, moral breakdown is attributable not to inherent shortcomings of Western cultures but to those of industrial societies; a similar phenomenon is now spreading through Asia's newly industrializing societies. The fact that Lee's Singapore, a small city-state, needs a near-totalitarian police state to assert control over its citizens contradicts his assertion that everything would be all right if governments would refrain from interfering in the private affairs of the family. The proper way to cure the ills of industrial societies is not to impose the terror of a police state but to emphasize ethical education, give high regard to spiritual values, and promote high standards in culture and the arts.

WE ARE THE WORLD

...Instead of making Western culture the scapegoat for the disruptions of rapid economic change, it is more appropriate to look at how the traditional strengths of Asian society can provide for a better democracy. In Asia, democracy can encourage greater self-reliance while respecting cultural values. Such a democracy is the only true expression of a people, but it requires the full participation of all elements of society. Only then will it have legitimacy and reflect a country's vision.

Asian authoritarians misunderstand the relationship between the rules of effective governance and the concept of legitimacy. Policies that try to protect people from the bad elements of economic and social change will never be effective if imposed without consent; the same policies, arrived at through public debate, will have the strength of Asia's proud and self-reliant people.

A global democracy will recognize the connection between how we treat each other and how we treat nature, and it will pursue policies that benefit future generations. Today we are threatening the survival of our environment through wholesale destruction and endangerment of all species. Our democracy must become global in the sense that it extends to the skies, the earth, and all things with brotherly affection....

The movement for democracy in Asia has been carried forward mainly by Asia's small but effective army of dedicated people in and out of political parties, encouraged by nongovernmental and quasi-governmental organizations for democratic development from around the world. These are hopeful signs for

Asia's democratic future. Such groups are gaining in their ability to force governments to listen to the concerns of their people, and they should be supported.

Asia should lose no time in firmly establishing democracy and strengthening human rights. The biggest obstacle is not its cultural heritage but the resistance of authoritarian rulers and their apologists. Asia has much to offer the rest of the world; its rich heritage of democracy-oriented philosophies and traditions can make a significant contribution to the evolution of global democracy. Culture is not necessarily our destiny. Democracy is.

From an article of the same title in Foreign Affairs, *November/December 1994, pages 189-94. Reprinted by permission of* Foreign Affairs, *November/December 1994. Copyright 1994 by the Council on Foreign Relations, Inc.*

KIM DAE-JUNG *is president of South Korea. He was a dissident and human rights activist during a political career of more than four decades in the Republic of Korea.*

Promise

10
Rapid Growth of the Civil Sector

"A society in which the piling up of special interests replaces a single voice for the common good is unlikely to fare well."
—Jessica T. Mathews

Introduction by Miklos Marschall

"**C**itizens are at the center of the global drama unfolding today. They are the lead actresses and actors in building global democratic governance....The security of our common future lies in the hands of an informed, inspired, committed, engaged citizenry."[1]

The growth of citizen initiatives today is unprecedented. From Argentina to South Africa, from the Philippines to Poland, tens of thousands of associations and other civil organizations have sprung up. CIVICUS: World Alliance for Citizen Participation, which was established in 1994 by a handful of people to promote civil society and citizen action, by 1998 was operating in eighty-two countries.

In the last two decades, according to Lester M. Salamon, "we are in the midst of a global 'associational revolution' that may prove to be as significant to the latter twentieth century as the rise of the nation-state was to the latter nineteenth."[2]

---

[1]Citizens: Strengthening Global Civil Society, (Washington, D.C.: CIVICUS, 1994), p. 16.
[2]Lester M. Salamon, "The Rise of the Nonprofit Sector," *Foreign Affairs*, July/August 1994, p. 109.

This emerging third sector provides not only help and care but millions of jobs, and represents a fast-growing share in the gross domestic product of a number of countries. Most important, it offers new career paths to many young people.

New communication technologies allow non-state actors to access, process, and share information in a way that is indeed revolutionary. For the first time in history, bonds and alliances, communities and action groups can be created quickly across distant cultures and continents, easing the transition from closed to open societies. More people participate in the decision-making process; more informed voices can be heard in democratic discussions; more civil society organizations play a role, not only in the legislative process, but in diplomatic actions as well.

What drives the emergence of civil society differs from region to region. In the developing world, after decades of failed, state-centered development strategies, the lesson was driven home that without the participation of indigenous communities, these strategies will not succeed. In post-communist countries, it has become clear that civil society is what makes democracy work. And in Western consumer societies, there is a growing recognition of the need for a renewal of civic values.

What connects these diverse movements is a global claim for a new division of power. Empowered citizens taking their place alongside government and commerce will mark the new democratic era. We don't know how to achieve and sustain people power, nor what new institutions, rules, and laws will emerge. We do know that social and political innovations created by and for people craving freedom are needed more than ever before. What we need is open discussion about governance for the new century.

For information about MIKLOS MARSCHALL, *see page 52.*

Discussion Questions

1. Jessica T. Mathews both admires and fears the burgeoning nongovernmental organizations that she claims are eroding the powers of national governments. As international players, what are some of the assets and liabilities of these organizations?

2. Explain Ulrich Beck's concept of "public work." Would it have potential in your country? Why or why not?

Readings

FROM
"Power Shift"
BY JESSICA T. MATHEWS

THE RISE OF GLOBAL CIVIL SOCIETY

The end of the Cold War has brought no mere adjustment among states but a novel redistribution of power among states, markets, and civil society. National governments are not simply losing autonomy in a globalizing economy. They are sharing powers—including political, social, and security roles at the core of sovereignty—with businesses, with international organizations, and with a multitude of citizens groups, known as nongovernmental organizations (NGOs). The steady concentration of power in the hands of states that began in 1648 with the Peace of Westphalia is over, at least for a while.[1]

DIAL LOCALLY, ACT GLOBALLY

No one knows how many NGOs there are or how fast the tally is growing. Published figures are badly misleading. One widely cited estimate claims there are 35,000 NGOs in the developing countries; another points to 12,000 irrigation cooperatives in South Asia alone. In fact, it is impossible to measure a swiftly growing universe that includes neighborhood, professional, service, and advocacy groups, both secular and church-based, promoting every conceivable cause and funded by donations, fees, foundations, governments, international organizations, or the sale of products and services. The true number is certainly in the millions, from the tiniest village association to influential but modestly funded international groups like Amnesty International to larger global activist organizations like Greenpeace and giant service providers like care, which has an annual budget of nearly $400 million.

Except in China, Japan, the Middle East, and a few other places where culture or authoritarian governments severely limit civil society, NGOs' role and influence have exploded in the last half-decade. Their financial resources and—often more important—their expertise, approximate and sometimes exceed

---

[1]The author would like to acknowledge the contributions of the authors of ten case studies for the Council on Foreign Relations study group, "Sovereignty, Nonstate Actors, and a New World Politics," on which this article is based.

those of smaller governments and of international organizations. "We have less money and fewer resources than Amnesty International, and we are the arm of the UN for human rights," noted Ibrahima Fall, head of the UN Centre for Human Rights, in 1993. "This is clearly ridiculous." Today NGOs deliver more official development assistance than the entire UN system (excluding the World Bank and the International Monetary Fund). In many countries they are delivering the services—in urban and rural community development, education, and health care—that faltering governments can no longer manage.

The range of these groups' work is almost as broad as their interests. They breed new ideas; advocate, protest, and mobilize public support; do legal, scientific, technical, and policy analysis; provide services; shape, implement, monitor, and enforce national and international commitments; and change institutions and norms.

Increasingly, NGOs are able to push around even the largest governments. When the United States and Mexico set out to reach a trade agreement, the two governments planned on the usual narrowly defined negotiations behind closed doors. But NGOs had a very different vision. Groups from Canada, the United States, and Mexico wanted to see provisions in the North American Free Trade Agreement on health and safety, transboundary pollution, consumer protection, immigration, labor mobility, child labor, sustainable agriculture, social charters, and debt relief. Coalitions of NGOs formed in each country and across both borders. The opposition they generated in early 1991 endangered congressional approval of the crucial "fast track" negotiating authority for the U.S. government. After months of resistance, the Bush administration capitulated, opening the agreement to environmental and labor concerns. Although progress in other trade venues will be slow, the tightly closed world of trade negotiations has been changed forever.

Technology is fundamental to NGOs' new clout. The nonprofit Association for Progressive Communications provides 50,000 NGOs in 133 countries access to the tens of millions of Internet users for the price of a local call. The dramatically lower costs of international communication have altered NGOs' goals and changed international outcomes. Within hours of the first gunshots of the Chiapas rebellion in southern Mexico in January 1994, for example, the Internet swarmed with messages from human rights activists. The worldwide media attention they and their groups focused on Chiapas, along with the influx of rights activists to the area, sharply limited the Mexican government's response. What in other times would have been a bloody insurgency turned out to be a largely nonviolent conflict. "The shots lasted ten days," José Angel Gurría, Mexico's foreign minister, later remarked, "and ever since, the war has been...a war on the Internet."

NGOs' easy reach behind other states' borders forces governments to consider domestic public opinion in countries with which they are dealing, even on matters that governments have traditionally handled strictly between themselves. At the same time, cross-border NGO networks offer citizens' groups unprecedented channels of influence. Women's and human rights groups in many developing countries have linked up with more experienced, better funded, and more powerful groups in Europe and the United States. The latter work the global media and lobby their own governments to pressure leaders in developing countries, creating a circle of influence that is accelerating change in many parts of the world.

OUT OF THE HALLWAY, AROUND THE TABLE

In international organizations, as with governments at home, NGOs were once largely relegated to the hallways. Even when they were able to shape governments' agendas, as the Helsinki Watch human rights groups did in the Conference on Security and Cooperation in Europe in the 1980s, their influence was largely determined by how receptive their own government's delegation happened to be. Their only option was to work through governments.

All that changed with the negotiation of the global climate treaty, culminating at the Earth Summit in Rio de Janeiro in 1992. With the broader independent base of public support that environmental groups command, NGOs set the original goal of negotiating an agreement to control greenhouse gases long before governments were ready to do so, proposed most of its structure and content, and lobbied and mobilized public pressure to force through a pact that virtually no one else thought possible when the talks began.

More members of NGOs served on government delegations than ever before, and they penetrated deeply into official decision-making. They were allowed to attend the small working group meetings where the real decisions in international negotiations are made. The tiny nation of Vanuatu turned its delegation over to an NGO with expertise in international law (a group based in London and funded by an American foundation), thereby making itself and the other sea-level island states major players in the fight to control global warming. ECO, an NGO-published daily newspaper, was negotiators' best source of information on the progress of the official talks and became the forum where governments tested ideas for breaking deadlocks.

Whether from developing or developed countries, NGOs were tightly organized in a global and half a dozen regional Climate Action Networks, which were able to bridge North-South differences among governments that many had expected would prevent an agreement. United in their passionate pursuit of a treaty, NGOs would fight out contentious issues among themselves, then take an agreed position to their respective delegations. When they could not agree, NGOs served as invaluable back channels, letting both sides know where the other's problems lay or where a compromise might be found.

As a result, delegates completed the framework of a global climate accord in the blink of a diplomat's eye—16 months—over the opposition of the three energy superpowers, the United States, Russia, and Saudi Arabia. The treaty entered into force in record time just two years later. Although only a framework accord whose binding requirements are still to be negotiated, the treaty could force sweeping changes in energy use, with potentially enormous implications for every economy.

The influence of NGOs at the climate talks has not yet been matched in any other arena, and indeed has provoked a backlash among some governments. A handful of authoritarian regimes, most notably China, led the charge, but many others share their unease about the role NGOs are assuming. Nevertheless, NGOs have worked their way into the heart of international negotiations and into the day-to-day operations of international organizations, bringing new priorities, demands for procedures that give a voice to groups outside government, and new standards of accountability....

FOR BETTER OR WORSE?

A world that is more adaptable and in which power is more diffused could mean more peace, justice, and capacity to manage the burgeoning list of humankind's interconnected problems. At a time of accelerating change, NGOs are quicker than governments to respond to new demands and opportunities. Internationally, in both the poorest and richest countries, NGOs, when adequately funded, can outperform government in the delivery of many public services. Their growth, along with that of the other elements of civil society, can strengthen the fabric of the many still-fragile democracies. And they are better than governments at dealing with problems that grow slowly and affect society through their cumulative effect on individuals—the "soft" threats of environmental degradation, denial of human rights, population growth, poverty, and lack of development that may already be causing more deaths in conflict than are traditional acts of aggression.

As the computer and telecommunications revolution continues, NGOs will become more capable of large-scale activity across national borders. Their loyalties and orientation, like those of international civil servants and citizens of non-national entities like the EU, are better matched than those of governments to problems that demand transnational solutions. International NGOs and cross-border networks of local groups have bridged North-South differences that in earlier years paralyzed cooperation among countries....

There are at least as many reasons, however, to believe that the continuing diffusion of power away from nation-states will mean more conflict and less problem-solving both within states and among them.

For all their strengths, NGOs are special interests, albeit not motivated by personal profit. The best of them, the ablest and most passionate, often suffer most from tunnel vision, judging every public act by how it affects their particular interest. Generally, they have limited capacity for large-scale endeavors, and as they grow, the need to sustain growing budgets can compromise the independence of mind and approach that is their greatest asset.

A society in which the piling up of special interests replaces a single strong voice for the common good is unlikely to fare well. Single-issue voters, as Americans know all too well, polarize and freeze public debate. In the longer run, a stronger civil society could also be more fragmented, producing a weakened sense of common identity and purpose and less willingness to invest in public goods, whether health and education or roads and ports. More and more groups promoting worthy but narrow causes could ultimately threaten democratic government....

DISSOLVING AND EVOLVING

Whether the rise of nonstate actors ultimately turns out to be good news or bad will depend on whether humanity can launch itself on a course of rapid social innovation, as it did after World War II. Needed adaptations include a business sector that can shoulder a broader policy role, NGOs that are less parochial and better able to operate on a large scale, international institutions that can efficiently serve the dual masters of states and citizenry, and, above all, new institutions and political entities that match the transnational scope of today's challenges while meeting citizens' demands for accountable democratic governance.

From an article of the same title in Foreign Affairs, *January/ February 1997, pages 50-66.*
Reprinted by permission of Foreign Affairs, *January/February 1997. Copyright 1997 by the*
Council on Foreign Relations, Inc.

JESSICA T. MATHEWS *is president of the Carnegie Endowment for International Peace. She*
is the author of numerous articles, including, "Power Shift" (Foreign Affairs, 1997), which
was chosen as one of the most influential articles in the journal's seventy-five years.

FROM
"Capitalism Without Work"
BY ULRICH BECK

In the old industrial society, two "employers" occupied the dominant position:
capital and the state. In the future, both will be chronically absent in this function. Capitalism is creating joblessness and will more and more be jobless. To
call the public coffers "empty" is more than an understatement. We have the
choice of wailing about that or creating a new focus of activity and identity that
will revitalize the democratic way of life: "public work." If public discourse is the
art of involving strangers in a continuing discussion of what affects them most
intimately, public work is the art of making deeds follow the words. So what
does this concept imply?

First, active compassion....Active resistance to indifference has many goals
and many faces: work with the elderly and the handicapped, with the homeless
and with AIDS patients, with illiterates and the excluded, with women's centers,
Greenpeace, Amnesty International, and so forth. "Public work" in this sense
means an odd blend of politics, care for others, and everyday cooperation.

Second, practical critique: many lawyers, tax consultants, physicians, busi-
nesspeople, and administrators want to use their professional skills in different
settings for a change—exerting influence over public opinion and legislation,
devising economic strategies for self-help groups, providing information on
avoiding tax liability, advising people on handling debt, calling attention to
health and safety risks, and so on. Why not establish prizes and awards for such
forms of civil resistance? (Of course, citizens should be the ones to award them.)

Third, active democracy: citizen participation and decentralization. In the
administration of many cities and communities, a small cultural revolution has
broken out. It promises to bring not only greater efficiency but also a gain in

democracy. "All these citizen initiatives just duplicate existing governmental bodies," a city councilman grumbles. But that is precisely the point: people acquire a taste for democracy by practicing it. Freedom begets, strengthens, and expands freedom.

What all this means is that we have to invest in civil society. We have to delegate power and authority to it, and in every respect: technologically (information media), economically (basic investment), educationally (certification that will be valid on the labor market as well).

How do the values and goals of an earnings-based society relate to the grassroots organization of civil society? The relationship is one not of mutual exclusion but of complementarity. In the future, what will probably win out is a blending of formal work and voluntary organization, the dismantling of legal and mobility barriers between the two sectors, the creation of opportunities for leaving or changing one's principal occupation (in an annual, monthly, or weekly rhythm). Two things would thus become possible: first, the equation of public activity with [un]remunerated employment would be broken. Second, public work would create new foci of political action and identity-formation within and opposed to a fragmented society. The material and cultural foundations for "individualism coupled with solidarity" would be established.

Four objections will serve to sharpen this apparently simple idea and show how it can be turned into a viable reality. First: won't public work come to grief the moment it encounters the selfishness that has overrun our society? Second: who is supposed to pay for this? Third: is such a thing possible under conditions of globalization? Fourth: won't "creative unemployment" (Ivan Illich's term) make people unhappy? Doesn't identity crumble when gainful employment is taken away?

Let's look first at the much maligned "selfish society." The American sociologist Robert Wuthnow has shown that without voluntary efforts dedicated to others, all modern societies would collapse immediately. Eighty million Americans, or 45 percent of those above the age of eighteen, commit five hours or more, week after week, to helping others or working for charitable purposes. The monetary value of these efforts amounts to about $150 billion per year.

This study also shows that for 75 percent of the American population solidarity, helpfulness, and concern for the general welfare are as important as self-actualization, professional success, and expansion of personal freedom. The notion of the "selfish society" assumes that two things are mutually exclusive that in fact belong together: self-actualization and being there for others.

That the situation is any different in Europe can be believed only by those who confuse commitment with membership in organizations. Although young people are staying away in droves from organized churches, parties, unions, and associations, private initiatives of all sorts are attracting participants in record numbers. According to a poll of European Community countries, these same young people who shun the tedium of collective organizations express strong support (over 80 percent) for environmental causes; 73 percent see homelessness as a major issue and want to do something about it personally; 71 percent demand more rights for the handicapped; 71 percent support feminism and see it as important for both men and women.

As for the decline in values and the growth of indifference among young people, a trend already bemoaned by Plato, these too are connected to a "blockage of institutional commitments." Young people are given rights, but citizen initiatives are more and more hemmed in by governmental restrictions. Power is not really delegated; many are reluctant to get involved because they have already found that "nothing comes of it."

WHO PAYS?

Who is supposed to finance investment in "social capital" in an active society? In Germany we have over four trillion marks in private household accounts, very unequally distributed. Ten percent of all households account for a good 49 percent of the wealth; 40 percent of households for the next 49 percent; 50 percent of households have only 2.4 percent of all private wealth.

The entrepreneurs have discovered the mother lode. Their new magic formula goes this way: capitalism without work plus capitalism without taxes. Revenue from the corporation tax, the tax on company profits, fell between 1989 and 1993 by 18.6 percent; its share in the total tax revenue was cut almost in half (from 6.4 to 3.7 percent), while at the same time profits rose by more than 10 percent. These data reveal, among other things, the new power relationships created by globalization. Many companies are becoming taxpayers only in principle, not in fact.

Capital is globally mobile; nation-states, on the other hand, have to stay put. When the manufacture of a product is spread over several countries and continents, it becomes increasingly difficult to assign the profit to a specific locale; at the same time, strategies whereby companies can undermine the tax system become easier to implement.

The internationalization of production gives companies two strategic advantages: global competition springs up between expensive and inexpensive labor, and the tax structures and monitoring systems of various countries can be played off against each other and subverted. In the newfound power of the multinational corporations we can observe the successful application of the laws of the free market to the political realm. In reality, however, the situation is much more dicey. Since utilization of numerous social resources (expensive universities, hospitals, transportation systems, the courts, research funds) is not restricted to the place where taxes are assessed, many corporations are in a position to minimize their tax burden while establishing their headquarters in the countries that maintain the best infrastructures.

The sites of investment, production, taxation, and residence can now be completely uncoupled from one another. Once again, business leaders take advantage of the low tax rates of the poor countries while enjoying the high standard of living found in the rich countries. They pay taxes where it is cheapest and live where conditions are most appealing. This situation carries considerable potential for social conflict. First of all, tension arises between virtual and real taxpayers—that is, those individuals who still have work and the smaller companies that are not in a position to move and thereby escape regular taxation. These are the losers in the globalization game.

Then, too, it is precisely the champions of economic growth, assiduously wooed by the politicians, who are undermining the authority of the state by taking advantage of its offerings while snatching away its revenues. These new virtuosi of virtual taxation are subverting the general welfare in a legal but illegitimate fashion, and along with it political life and the democratic state. Neoliberal policies, which uncritically embrace the free market, have much in common with those proponents of efficiency in business who make themselves superfluous.

There is only one conclusion to be drawn: we must break the taboo on speaking of this new social injustice. Those who profit from globalization must be made accountable for the general welfare. Our system of social welfare needs reforming in many respects, but paradoxically the answer is not less but more money, properly invested and distributed! For investments in public work the watchword is: a little goes a long way. Society flourishes, public wealth grows.

Here it becomes clear that we need a new definition of "wealth." Among other things, this definition must include such indicators as social participation and political freedom. For a society whose economy is flourishing while putting people out of work is not a "rich" society but only a rump society for the rich....

As for the alleged monopoly that gainful employment has on identity formation, empirical studies have already shown that a far-reaching change of attitude is underway: more and more people are looking for both meaningful work and opportunities for commitment outside of work. If society can upgrade and reward such commitment and put it on a level with gainful employment, it can create both individual identity and social cohesion.

The scenario I have sketched here can be summed up in a plea to take the invisible practice of social self-help and grassroots political organization and make it visible. Give it economic, organizational, and political weight. This becomes possible only if we invest in civil society, thereby democratizing democracy, so to speak. What we need is a citizen-state alliance for civil society, if need be in opposition to work and capital. But this alliance should attract all those who hold democracy dear.

From an article of the same title in Dissent, Winter 1997, pages 53-56, *by permission of the author. The article first appeared in* Der Spiegel, no. 20, 1996. *It was translated from the German by Krishna Winston.*

ULRICH BECK *is a professor at the Institute for Sociology at the Hudwig-Maximians University, Munich. He is the author of* The Brave New World of Work.

11
A New Vision for Education

"An education in the humanities is only a frill if human freedom is a frill."
—Sondra Myers

Introduction by Sondra Myers

In a Speech entitled "An Education for Freedom," the late A. Bartlett Giamatti, President of Yale University from 1978 to 1986, observed, "the best way…to combat indoctrination by any system that would exclude or master others as slaves is to promote a view of education that is not intended to indoctrinate. Such an education would constantly test, rather than impose, the values it cherishes and would posit seeking the truth—not simply propounding the truth—as its goal. Such an education is a process, not a closed and static system of beliefs, and its goal is to free the mind rather than enclose it."

The essence of an education to free the mind, according to Giamatti, is the humanities. To understand the humanities, he claimed, we must go back to the Renaissance. It was then that scholars, first in Italy and later across Europe, revived Greek and Latin writings and used them as living models. For these scholars, the five core studies of the humanities were grammar, rhetoric, history, poetry, and moral philosophy. Following their ancient precursors, they believed that an education in the humanities joined wisdom and eloquence for the purpose of improving human beings in civil or political terms; it was an education with an active, civic goal. Humanistic learning is, of course, much more. It is a source of pleasure, recollection, and vision. It adds depth and breadth to our understanding of human life, expanding our capacities for analysis, criticism, empathy, and creativity. It is, however, the purpose of this essay to discuss the connection between the humanities and freedom. For if the study of the humanities had no other virtue, that connection would suffice to preserve its sanctity.

Giamatti believed that "at the heart of the humanities lives the conviction that freedom of thought is the necessary precondition to political freedom." He understood that only those whose minds were free and who had a keen awareness of their own freedom and a strong immunity to indoctrination could build a free society.

The study of the humanities is inextricably linked to the quest for freedom and justice; it is necessary, though not sufficient, to the work of citizens in democratic societies. An education in the humanities, in history and ethics and in the art of expression, is fundamental to our functioning effectively as citizens in a democracy.

Tyranny, the archenemy of democracy, comes in many forms. Whether the tyrant is a self-appointed dictator who possesses the rights and leaves citizens with no responsibilities, or the demagogue who is elected because he promises simple solutions to complex problems, we must have the wisdom to understand him and the vigor to reject him. We must have the skills, the patience, and the will to discuss, negotiate, and compromise—that is, to employ the tools of democracy.

In the last years of a century as remarkable for reaching new heights of knowledge and freedom as it has been for descending to new depths of brutality and cynicism, we must arm ourselves for the ordinary yet heroic task of accepting the glorious burden of civic responsibility.

We must learn to live with revolutionary change and perpetual uncertainty, resolved to maintain our freedom as individuals and as societies. Giamatti cites legal philosopher Alexander Bickel, who admonishes us to "fix our eyes on the middle distance where values are provisionally held, are tested, and evolve within the legal order—derived from the morality of process, which is the morality of consent...."

No argument for an education in the humanities is more powerful, none more essential, than that it is an education of, by, and for a free people—an education for freedom.

Democratic societies are works in progress. To sustain them and make sure they remain dynamic and responsive, yet solidly grounded in the principles of "liberty and justice for all," we require the intellectual rigor, the expressive eloquence, and the civic commitment of the humanities.

An education in the humanities is a frill only if human freedom is a frill. It is both daunting and exhilarating to realize that a "future of freedom" rests not in the power of charismatic leaders, but in the hands of responsible citizens.

Adapted from a speech delivered at the conference "Developing Values: The Role of Education, the Media, and the Arts," Bellagio, Italy, April 3–7, 1995, by permission of the author.

Sondra Myers *is the editor of the* Democracy Is a Discussion *handbooks, an independent consultant on international, civic, and cultural projects, and senior associate to the Democracy Collaborative at the University of Maryland.*

Discussion Questions

1. According to Sondra Myers, what do the study of grammar, poetry, and history have to do with maintaining a free society? Do you agree? Why or why not? What is central to A. Bartlett Giamatti's concept of "education to free the mind"?
2. According to Claire L. Gaudiani, what are some of the challenges students will face in the new era? What recommendations does she have for teachers as they guide students to meet these new challenges?

Readings

FROM

"Tossed into a New Frame: Learning Before Teaching"

BY CLAIRE L. GAUDIANI

Since the dissolution of the USSR and the fall of the Berlin Wall, we are in a completely different ball game with new rules, and colleges must rethink the framework for education. In the 50 years before the end of the Cold War, there existed, in the words of one of our presidents, "an evil empire." So life was simple. We knew who the enemy was, who our allies were, and that courses would be taught essentially within a certain frame of reference. Compared to the post-Cold War world we face today, that world appears almost one dimensional.

Juan Somavía, Chilean representative to the United Nations, and a number of people working on the United Nations–sponsored global summits taking place since 1990 were, in a sense, prescient in seeing the transformation that was occurring around the world as we moved away from a bipolar and bimodal structure to something much more complicated. These summits—focusing on children, the environment, human rights, population, global social development, women, and most recently, on habitat—are guided by the notion that there is an emerging global consensus around some locally-appropriate form of democracy that balances individual rights and opportunities with responsibility for the common good. The summits also acknowledged the growing consensus that some form of market economy is, for the moment, the optimal economic system. But what we have not developed anywhere is a consensus on an optimal social system.

As teachers and administrators, we guide students into a world where most of the big questions remain problematic. For instance, why are some of the Asian countries doing so well economically in light of a substantial absence of democracy? We need to figure out what this means in terms of our curriculum and how to teach students not to be simply followers of systems, but transformers—creators of democracies, economies, and societies that are more just and prosperous for all citizens.

But before we think about politics and economics, we must think about human beings. As faculty teaching in the context of the liberal arts, we are connecting with a tradition that is as old as recorded human thought. The tradition of the liberal arts connects us across cultures, around the world, and throughout time to a continuing conversation regarding who we are as human beings. This conversation adds an important element to the pursuit of education in this post-Cold War environment. The ethical framework in which one thinks about political, economic, and social systems has to be considered first and then persistently through the rest of the decisions we make, both in society and education. We must talk with colleagues not only about who we are, but what kind of people we must be in order to be teachers in this new time, and what we need to do to become these people.

The faculty at Connecticut College decided it was willing to put itself in Third World environments—now we say "pursuing roads less traveled"—because it realized that many had not spent time in these areas, unless they had been in the Peace Corps or a similar program. The faculty realized that we live in one frame of reference and were preparing students for another—a world we do not know ourselves. And what makes the two frameworks so vitally different is the ethos in which the action and the thinking take place. We need to experience these new worlds to legitimize our teaching.

Our faculty has gone to Mysore, India, Ghana, Capetown, South Africa, and Puebla, Mexico. Usually, two faculty and between 20 and 30 students go to live in these countries for a semester. They participate in a kind of learning characterized by statements such as, "I don't know what to do about this either," or "I've never done my work in this environment before, but I am going to try to do it." The everyday life is dramatically different from home—the food, the thinking, the coming-to-terms, after all is said and done, with brothers and sisters, with people who teach in their simplicity or in their complexity, or as much as they are willing to share their lives. These are "places I will never forget once I have left there," some faculty members have said.

Our faculty has found in certain settings that students must be allowed to lead, because their flexibility and openness makes them better able to be with people who are different from them. We, who are so well- educated and trained in our thinking and expectations, may miss the very kernel we need to grasp in order to be who we need to be in this unfamiliar setting. We must be willing to change ourselves as midcareer people. We must be willing to take ourselves back to the beginning, and say to ourselves, "I will start all over again. I will go to a new place, and I will be like a graduate student again."

We all wish we could go back and start over again, knowing what we know now. In fact, this is the chance; we can start again and examine all the premises and assumptions on which we built our world view. It helps to get tossed into a frame where everything is different. Maybe as women who think we understand feminism, we ought to spend some time with women who understand feminism and come from places with names we cannot pronounce. We need to do this for ourselves, and then provide such opportunities for our colleagues, but we must begin with ourselves. We need to reexamine our own thinking and be willing to put ourselves in vulnerable positions—vulnerable in the sense that our assumptions are thrown into the air and come down in unfamiliar ways, making us truly rethink, truly throw out whole aspects of the syllabus and let new things into our curriculum. But it is not just changing the curriculum or developing the programs, it is starting with ourselves.

It may well be that the world for students entering the twenty-first century will be focused on developing a social system in which everyone can experience some democratic rights and the benefits of a productive market economy. This will be tremendously difficult work. It will create different kinds of allegiances. It will call on people to function in ways unknown in the past; that is, to talk and listen to each other, actually demonstrate deep listening—not just waiting to speak—and demonstrate it by asking follow-up questions. We need to understand fundamentally that democracy is a discussion.

Our habits as academics are to analyze, criticize, and break things down into component parts. In the coming century, we will need to synthesize. We have to rethink our training, not only in terms of its content and how things have changed since we were educated, but how we were taught to speak and reason in an academic context. Is it enough to leave students with the ability to analyze and criticize, and not to create, in the end, synthesis? Is it enough to help them create a hypothesis and prove a position, and not help them find a way to mediate a best solution under the circumstances? It is not enough. It might have been enough in a very neat, bipolar, bimodal, Cold War world frame, but it is not enough now.

A liberal arts education gives students and faculty a renewed chance to reexamine the wisdom of humankind throughout the ages. As we study it in the present, go to places we have never been before, and try to let ourselves be transformed there, we will be able to transform education, so that the future will not simply be an extrapolation from what has happened, but the result of what we have chosen—not just with each other and our students, but also with people around the world. We all know that Americans still have a disproportionate influence on what happens in the global frame. It is more important than ever in this post-Cold War, complex environment that we be learners and listeners in the global frame before we decide to be educators and transformers.

Adapted from an address delivered at a conference of the Toor Cummings Center for International Studies and the Liberal Arts entitled "The Future of International Studies in the Liberal Arts Context," Connecticut College, New London, Conn., June 1996, by permission of the author.

For information about CLAIRE L. GAUDIANI, *see page 159.*

❧

FROM
"Textbook Citizens: Education for Democracy and Political Culture in El Salvador"
BY LUCY TAYLOR

One of the central ways in which El Salvador's legacy of exclusion, violence and failed institutionalization is being tackled is through education for democracy. A diverse range of actors has embarked on the education crusade, including the state (which is busy inculcating ideas through the Ministry of Education's new curriculum in human rights), the NGOs (which have launched projects working particularly with the poor communities) and the human rights social movements (which build on their denunciation work by emphasizing the defense of human rights)....

Broadly speaking, education for democracy is thought to have four potential ways of impacting on Salvadoran politics. First, educating people in their human rights is understood to be crucial because it is empowering. It allows ordinary people to know and understand what the 'authorities' can and cannot do, dignifying and justifying their cause should they have need to defend their human rights. Moreover, it sends two key messages to ordinary people; 'you are just as important as anyone else' and 'you are not alone in your struggle'. These simple ideas mirror those of democracy—equality and universality—and contrast dramatically with the unequal and authoritarian relationships of the lower classes with the landowners, the employers, the local government officials and agents of the security forces. One NGO works particularly with rural people for precisely this reason 'so that they are awakened, so that they understand more and participate but in an active manner, so that they can really become the subjects of their own development'.[1]

Secondly, education in democracy explains to citizens how the political system should work, for example by examination of the constitution. Such knowledge allows citizens to identify if and when democratic procedures are distorted or ill-used and to become active agents in maintaining transparency and accountability. The argument proposed is that if political leaders are aware that they can no longer pull the wool over the peoples eyes, they will be less inclined towards subterfuge, corruption and deceit and will adopt more straightforward dealings rather than risk exposure and the consequent loss of legitimacy....

Thirdly, armed with self-confidence and understanding, citizens might go on to become active participants in politics themselves. The arena favoured is that of the community and local government, not only because the councillors and officers of the municipality are easily accessible and well known, but also because participation in the local arena allows people to contribute directly to the quality of their lives and to the improvement of their immediate environment. Most typically such participation is not linked to party activism but to organizations within civil society, the idea being that these act as counterweights to municipal power and contribute towards more effective policy-making and implementation....

Fourthly, each of these (knowledge, appropriation, participation) contributes towards the creation of a culture of democracy....[An] activist states that his NGO is involved in moulding new Salvadoran citizens: 'We are generating a culture with new values, democracy, liberty, solidarity, equality, justice...How do we go about this? We inculcate the values, trying to get people to appropriate the values for themselves, so that then they practice them and so we generate a new type of culture'.[2] Most activists believe that in learning of their own rights, people will come to understand and respect the rights of others too.

---

[1] NGO Coordinator, *ISD* (*Iniciativa Social por la Democracia*), San Salvador, 13 May 1998.
[2] Interview, *ISD*, 13, May 1998.

Although this might be rather naïve, the widespread dissemination of a discourse of rights, and the assumptions that accompany it concerning duties and conduct, all contribute to creating a climate of democratic interaction. The action of participation also contributes to a democratic culture through the development of negotiation skills and encouragement of co-operative efforts based on consensus, rather than zero-sum games based on conflict.

Constructing faith in democracy and in one's politicians requires a demonstration that democracy 'works'. It also, though, takes a leap of the imagination, a leap which translates dreams of peace, equality, rights and democracy into a practicable set of norms and relationships which can create the foundation of a 'democratic way of life'. Such an enterprise is not easy, though, as it requires that people purposefully forget sections of the past, override their natural caution or fear and defy the logic of confrontation which made sense of their former lives. In other words, it requires people to start not from the beginning of the process but from right in the middle, to 'act as if' everyone, all at once, had adopted these democratic norms and ideas in a conscious manner. This requires not a little courage….Democracy may be 'adopted' overnight, but overcoming prejudices will require the ascendance of a new political generation in order for a deep democratic culture to become a tangible reality.…

Clearly, a new political culture cannot be created and inculcated overnight, just as the past cannot be completely forgotten, and overall El Salvador's problems far outweigh the palpable levels of optimism. Yet it is such optimism which, in many ways, sustains the process of transformation and democratization and is in turn the product of a 'miracle'; the end of civil war and the beginning of inclusive political system based on the concept of equal rights. El Salvador has shown that it *is* possible to create a new political order through will power alone and that a people does not have to be a hostage to its past forever.

From Democratization, *Frank Cass Publishers, London. Volume 6.3, Autumn, 1999.*

LUCY TAYLOR *is a lecturer of comparative politics at the University of Wales. Her most recent book is* Citizenship, Participation and Democracy: Changing Dynamics in Chile and Argentina.

12
The Moral Factor in the Democratic Equation

"In individual change and personal action lies the origin of the true transformation of a society."
—Juan Somavía

Introduction by Juan Somavía

I should like to focus my statement on the question that is in the minds of many people: what is going to happen in Bosnia and Herzegovina on the day when the troops of North Atlantic Treaty Organization (NATO) withdraw?...To what extent is the peace process self-sustaining?

How deeply has the Peace Agreement penetrated into the hearts of the men and women of Bosnia and Herzegovina? How deeply rooted is the ideal of reconciliation, which is mentioned in the preamble of the Constitution of Bosnia and Herzegovina itself? In short, can there truly be reconciliation if peace depends on an international military presence?...

It is extremely difficult to hope to see love and mutual understanding in a society that has gone through the fratricidal struggle that Bosnia and Herzegovina has experienced. But such change can happen, and it must come from the power of the heart, from men and women who see the fulfillment of the peace process as a search for a higher goal for them as human beings.

Throughout our time in the Security Council, Chile has sought to untangle the ethical dimension present in each conflict as a way of contributing to the conflict's solution. Despite the obstacles, and we realize how great they are, we must have faith that ethical values can bring about important changes. Individuals have the capacity to raise themselves above their society's conditioning factors and to transform the lives of their communities. In individual change and personal action lies the origin of the true transformation of a society.

However, just as genuine forgiveness is necessary to reconciliation, the latter cannot be achieved in a society where justice is not practiced. Reconciliation is not and cannot be a synonym for forgetting. I come from a country which, in other circumstances, had to meet the difficult challenge of reconciliation. Today we are beginning in my society to enjoy the fruits of that effort, having travelled a road fraught with difficulties and many tragedies.

The United Nations and the Security Council can do more to encourage those people in Bosnian civil society, in community affairs, in the schools, and in the workplaces who have the inner strength to break the bonds of the present and are prepared to assume the costs involved in the search for reconciliation.

We all know that those who dare to forsake the "official culture" always run risks in any society. That is even more difficult, however, in a society in conflict, like that of Bosnia and Herzegovina. Intimidating demagogy is unleashed against them, because those who believe in violence as a source of power deeply fear those who dare to act as sane and sensible human beings, rejecting violence and hatred in their own lives. An example of this are the media—radio, television, and newspapers—in which we still see the desire to shape public opinion by discounting one's opponents and perpetuating the spirit of conflict.

I have focused on only one aspect of the conflict in Bosnia and Herzegovina because many of us are convinced that that region is symbolic in the context of this issue and that, if the challenge of national reconciliation is met with success, it will impart very important lessons to other peoples in other situations brought to this Council's attention. We trust that this will prove possible.

I wish to conclude my statement by referring to the ideal of change embodied by one of the greatest figures ever produced by the United Nations: Dag Hammarskjold, who gave his life for the sake of an ideal of change. It is incumbent on us today to follow his legacy: his faith in political, economic, and social change through conviction and the transforming power of the spirit, and not only as an ethical dimension of the way he lived life. As he told us in his extraordinary book Markings, in our times the road to sainthood necessarily leads through the world of action.

From the minutes of the 3,842nd meeting of the UN Security Council, December 18, 1997.

JUAN SOMAVÍA *is director general at the International Labor Organization in Geneva and former ambassador to the Permanent Mission of Chile to the United Nations.*

Discussion Questions

1. What does Juan Somavía believe can be accomplished through the power of the heart? Do you agree? Why or why not? Do you think there is a relationship between reconciliation and justice? Explain. Is there a conflict in your region that might benefit from the approach Somavía suggests?

2. What analogy does Mamphela Ramphele use to explain why reconciliation is important? How does she use that same analogy to establish the importance of defining the scope of a reconciliation effort. How good is her analogy? Explain.

3. What important condition does Ronald Dworkin apply to the idea that in governing a country, the majority should have its way?

4. Dworkin maintains that if you are what he calls a moral member of a community, you are responsible for what it does, even if you oppose its actions. What is a moral member? Do you agree with Dworkin's point? Why or why not?

5. What does Dworkin say about the role of moral values in the rule of law? Should an "impartial" judge use his personal convictions to decide legal cases? What constraints to this practice does Dworkin recommend? Do you agree with Dworkin's position? Support your position.

6. Padraig O'Malley says richer countries must help poorer ones before, not after, conditions deteriorate into civil war. Do you agree? Why or why not? What is the difference between current conflicts and the conditions under which the Marshall Plan was implemented? What kinds of help might richer countries provide in today's "hot spots"?

7. After reading Oscar Arias's piece, would you say that Costa Rica has followed a moral path? Support your position. Is peace the only moral option? Is fighting ever morally justified? Explain.

Readings

The Challenge Facing South Africa

BY MAMPHELA RAMPHELE

Novelists have an advantage over ordinary mortals like us. They can let their thoughts free-wheel and this allows them to ask uncomfortable questions. I have taken the liberty of drawing on the words of author J.M. Coetzee, which he utters through the character Michael K, a man with a harelip, in *The Life and Times of Michael K.*

> At least I have not been clever and come back to Sea Point full of stories of how they beat me in the camps till I was thin as a rake and simple in the head. I was mute and stupid in the beginning; I will be mute and stupid in the end. There is nothing to be ashamed of in being simple. They were locking up simpletons before they locked up anyone else. Now they have camps for children whose parents run away, camps for people who kick and foam at the mouth, camps for people with big heads and people with little heads, camps for people with no visible means of support, camps for people chased off the land, camps for people they find living in storm-water drains, camps for street girls, camps for people who can't add two and two, camps for people who forget their papers at home, camps for people who live in the mountains and blow up bridges in the night. Perhaps the truth is that it is enough be out of the camps, out of all the camps at the same time. Perhaps that is enough of an achievement for the time being.

Chinua Achebe's *Anthills of the Savannah*, in looking at post-colonial African woes of corruption, coups, and more coups, poses a question that is relevant to this debate: "What must a people do to appease an embittered history?" In our exploration of the theme of dealing with the past, we must pause and ask ourselves hard questions. Why do we feel compelled to deal with the past? What do we hope to achieve at the end of the day? An appeasement of our embittered history? What would constitute such an appeasement? The truth? Whose truth? Truth about what? About the camps referred to by Michael K where simple people were locked up; or only the camps in which important people were locked up?

A medical metaphor best captures what I perceive to be the issue facing us in relation to "appeasing the past." An abscess cannot heal properly unless it is thoroughly incised and cleaned out. But the process of incision and cleansing is not without pain, even with modern anaesthesia. Pain is thus an integral component of the cleansing process which precedes healing. But there is a danger posed by incisions of this nature: vital organs can be damaged in the process and the patient's life thereby threatened. There is also the risk that too much pain may cause such a shock to the system—vasovagal shock, in medical parlance—that the heart stops and the patient dies.

The options we face as a society are not whether we incise the abscess; the question is how to do so without endangering the life of our brand new democracy. To simply put a plaster over the infection will not do, but too much enthusiasm may lead to serious difficulties and prolong, if not completely derail, the healing process that we so desperately yearn for.

A precondition to healing is an acknowledgment of one's suffering. I believe that to be behind many of the pleas from victims to know the truth. Acknowledgment is an affirmation that one's pain is real and worthy of attention.

A definition of the scope of the exercise of dealing with the past is essential to ensure its efficacy. It is in this regard that I have some misgivings about how much thought has gone into the proposed commission. First, the use of the phrase the "truth commission" raises some fundamental philosophical and practical questions. Whose truth is to be pursued by this commission? Is there any scope for more than one truth to be explored? How is the process to be managed to ensure that the voices of even "simple people" are heard?

Secondly, what offenses are to be examined by this commission? The definitions of "political offenses," "crimes against humanity," and "human rights violations" are not unproblematic. Are we to include only acts perpetrated to achieve political repression and subjugation of disenfranchised South Africans, or is the scope to be widened to include acts which violate the human rights of workers, children, and women in both the private and public spheres? Is the personal political? Is there any bigger crime against humanity than the destruction of family life? We should pause and ask what we mean by human rights violations in light of the extreme position in which many poor South African families find themselves as a result of the destruction of the fabric of the family.

Will "camps for children whose parents run away" and "camps for street girls" be reviewed alongside "political detention camps"? What about crimes perpetrated by the oppressed themselves as part of a survival culture under apartheid or as part of struggles for political liberation? Are we to include or exclude these and what are the implications?

Thirdly, what would constitute appeasement of our embittered history? Would it be enough to simply know who did what to whom or is there an intention to institute some redress? What form of redress could compensate for the losses people have suffered? What mechanism would be appropriate to achieve such redress and who would fund it? Should the entire society pay and if so how will this be determined given the competing needs on the public purse? If the individual perpetrators are to pay, on what basis should those who were carrying out instructions, often couched in national service terms, be expected to take personal responsibility for their actions? Who are the real criminals, the policeman who physically committed the acts of torture, the general who sent him, or the politician who presided over policies which created the environment for torture? What about the silent voters who did not stand up and say "no!" loudly enough? Are they innocent? It is interesting how few people one can now find in this country who supported apartheid—they must have emigrated in droves.

In addition to all this, it is important to recognize that human rights abuses did not start in South Africa in 1948; they have been with us for 300 years. Afrikaners may have many monopolies but a monopoly on human rights abuses is not one of them.

We have to be careful how we incise this huge abscess. If the desired goal is reconciliation then the incision must be wide enough yet it must spare the vital organs. But who is to define what constitutes the vital organs of society? Who has the moral integrity to make such a judgement? There are countless ordinary South Africans whose human rights have been violated as a direct consequence of apartheid or conquest—abused youth and children, abused wives who abuse children, abused workers who abuse their wives, their children, and their fellow workers. There are also abused activists who in turn abuse members of their community. How will society facilitate their healing?

We should heed Achebe's concluding words in his novel: "Truth is beauty, isn't it? It must be, you know, to make someone dying in that pain, to make him...smile. He sees it and it is—how can I say it?—it is unbearably, yes, unbearably, beautiful."

From The Healing of a Nation? *edited by Alex Boraine and Janet Levy, pages 33–36, published by Justice in Transition, Cape Town, South Africa 1995. Reprinted by permission of the author.*

MAMPHELA RAMPHELE *was trained as a medical doctor and an anthropologist and served as vice-chancellor of the University of Cape Town, South Africa. Since 2000, she has been a managing director of the World Bank.*

FROM

"Freedom's Law, The Moral Reading of the American Constitution"

BY RONALD DWORKIN

THE MAJORITARIAN PREMISE

Democracy means government by the people. But what does that mean? No explicit definition of democracy is settled among political theorists or in the dictionary. On the contrary, it is a matter of deep controversy what democracy really is. People disagree about which techniques of representation, which allocation of power among local, state, and national governments, which schedule and pattern of elections, and which other institutional arrangements provide the best available version of democracy. But beneath these familiar arguments over the structures of democracy there lies, I believe, a profound philosophical dispute about democracy's fundamental *value* or *point*, and one abstract issue is crucial to that dispute, though this is not always recognized. Should we accept or reject what I shall call the majoritarian premise?

This is a thesis about the fair *outcomes* of a political process: it insists that political procedures should be designed so that, at least on important matters, the decision that is reached is the decision that a majority or plurality of citizens favors, or would favor if it had adequate information and enough time for reflection. That goal sounds very reasonable, and many people, perhaps without much reflection, have taken it to provide the very essence of democracy....

In the United States, however, most people who assume that the majoritarian premise states the ultimate definition of and justification for democracy nevertheless accept that on some occasions the will of the majority should *not* govern. They agree that the majority should not always be the final judge of when its own power should be limited to protect individual rights, and they accept that at least some of the Supreme Court's decisions that overturned popular legislation...were right. The majoritarian premise does not rule out exceptions of that kind, but it does insist that in such cases, even if some derogation from majoritarian government is overall justified, something morally regrettable has happened, a moral cost has been paid. The premise supposes, in other words, that it is always unfair when a political majority is not allowed to have its way, so that even when there are strong enough countervailing reasons to justify this, the unfairness remains....

The constitutional conception of democracy...takes the following attitude to majoritarian government. Democracy means government subject to conditions—we might call these the "democratic" conditions—of equal status for all citizens. When majoritarian institutions provide and respect the democratic conditions, then the verdicts of these institutions should be accepted by everyone....But when they do not....there can be no objection, in the name of democracy, to other procedures that protect and respect them better. The democratic conditions plainly include, for example, a requirement that public offices must in principle be open to members of all races and groups on equal terms. If some law provided that only members of one race were eligible for public office, then there would be no moral cost—no matter for moral regret at all—if a court that enjoyed the power to do so under a valid constitution struck down that law as unconstitutional. That would presumably be an occasion on which the majoritarian premise was flouted, but though this is a matter of regret according to the majoritarian conception of democracy, it is not according to the constitutional conception....

WE THE PEOPLE

Powerful as the idea of democratic self-governance is, it is also deeply mysterious. Why am I *free*—how could I be thought to be governing *myself*—when I must obey what other people decide even if I think it wrong or unwise or unfair to me and my family? What difference can it make how many people must think the decision right and wise and fair if it is not necessary that I do? What kind of freedom is that? The answer to these enormously difficult questions begins in the communal conception of collective action. If I am a genuine member of a political community, its act is in some pertinent sense my act, even when I argued and voted against it, just as the victory or defeat of a team of which I am a member is my victory or defeat even if my own individual contribution made no difference either way. On no other assumption can we intelligibly think that as members of a flourishing democracy we are governing ourselves.

That explanation may seem only to deepen the mystery of collective self-government, however, because it appeals to two further ideas that seem dark themselves. What could *genuine* membership in a political community mean? And in what sense *can* a collective act of a group also be the act of each member? These are moral rather than metaphysical or psychological questions: they are not to be answered by counting the ultimate constituents of reality or discovering when people feel responsible for what some group that they belong to does. We must describe some connection between an individual and a group that makes it *fair* to treat him—and *sensible* that he treat himself—as responsible for what it does. Let us bring those ideas together in the concept of moral membership, by which we mean the kind of membership in a political community that engages self-government. If true democracy is government by the people, in the communal sense that provides self-government, then true democracy is based on moral membership....

What are the conditions of moral membership, and hence of positive freedom, and hence of democracy on the constitutional conception? I have tried to describe them elsewhere, and will only summarize my conclusions here.[1] There are two kinds of conditions. The first set is *structural*: these conditions describe the character the community as a whole must have if it is to count as a genuine political community. Some of these structural conditions are essentially historical. The political community must be more than nominal: it must have been established by a historical process that has produced generally recognized and stable territorial boundaries....Our interest lies in the second set of conditions.

These are *relational* conditions: they describe how an individual must be treated by a genuine political community in order that he or she be a moral member of that community. A political community cannot count anyone as a moral member unless it gives that person a *part* in any collective decision, a stake in it, and *independence* from it. First, each person must have an opportunity to make a difference in the collective decisions, and the force of his role— the magnitude of the difference he can make—must not be structurally fixed or limited in ways that reflect assumptions about his worth or talent or ability, or the soundness of his convictions or tastes. It is that condition that insists on universal suffrage and effective elections and representation, even though it does not demand that these be the only avenues of collective decision....

Second, the political process of a genuine community must express some bonafide conception of equal concern for the interests of all members, which means that political decisions that affect the distribution of wealth, benefits, and burdens must be consistent with equal concern for all. Moral membership involves reciprocity: a person is not a member unless he is treated as a member by others....So the communal conception of democracy explains an intuition

---

[1]See *Law's Empire*, Harvard University Press, 1986, and "Equality, Democracy, and Constitution: We the People in Court," *Alberta Law Review*, vol. 28 (1990), p. 324.

many of us share: that a society in which the majority shows contempt for the needs and prospects of some minority is illegitimate as well as unjust....

WHAT FOLLOWS?

In a decent working democracy, like the United States, the democratic conditions set out in the Constitution are sufficiently met in practice so that there is no unfairness in allowing national and local legislatures the powers they have under standing arrangements. On the contrary, democracy would be extinguished by any general constitutional change that gave an oligarchy of unelected experts power to overrule and replace any legislative decision they thought unwise or unjust. Even if the experts always improved the legislation they rejected—always stipulated fairer income taxes than the legislature had enacted, for example—there would be a loss in self-government which the merits of their decisions could not extinguish. It is different, however, when the question is plausibly raised whether some rule or regulation or policy itself undercuts or weakens the democratic character of the community, and the constitutional arrangement assigns that question to a court....

Certainly it impairs democracy when an authoritative court makes the wrong decision about what the democratic conditions require—but no more than it does when a majoritarian legislature makes a wrong constitutional decision that is allowed to stand. The possibility of error is symmetrical....

How should a political community that aims at democracy decide whether the conditions of democracy requires are met? Should it have a written constitution as its most fundamental law? Should that constitution describe a conception of the democratic conditions in as great detail as possible, trying to anticipate, in a constitutional code, all issues that might arise? Or should it set out very abstract statements of the democratic conditions, as the American Constitution and many other contemporary constitutions do, and leave it to contemporary institutions to interpret these generation by generation? If the latter, which institutions should these be? Should they be the ordinary, majoritarian parliamentary institutions, as the British constitution has for so long insisted? Or should they be special constitutional chambers, whose members are elected, but perhaps for much longer terms or in different ways than the ordinary parliamentarians are? Or should they consist in a hierarchy of courts?...

A community might combine these different answers in different ways. The United States Constitution...combines very specific clauses, about quartering soldiers in peacetime, for example, with...majestically abstract clauses....It is settled in the United States that the Supreme Court does have authority to hold legislation invalid if it deems it unconstitutional....

The moral reading [of a constitution] is consistent with all these institutional solutions to the problem of democratic conditions. It is a theory about how certain clauses of some constitutions should be read—about what questions must be asked and answered in deciding what those clauses mean and require. It is not a theory about who must ask these questions, or about whose answer must be taken to be authoritative. So the moral reading is only part, though it is an important part, of a general theory of constitutional practice....

COMMENTS AND CAUTIONS

So of course the moral reading encourages lawyers and judges to read an abstract constitution in the light of what they take to be justice. How else could they answer the moral questions that [an] abstract constitution asks them? It is no surprise, or occasion for ridicule or suspicion, that a constitutional theory reflects a moral stance. It would be an occasion for surprise—and ridicule—if it did not. Only an unbelievably crude form of legal positivism—a form disowned by the foremost positivist of the century, Herbert Hart—could produce that kind of insulation.[2] Text and integrity do act as important constraints....But though these constraints shape and limit the impact of convictions of justice, they cannot eliminate that impact. The moral reading insists, however, that this influence is not disreputable, so long as it is openly recognized, and so long as the convictions are identified and defended honestly, by which I mean through proper arguments of principle, not just thin slogans or tired metaphors....

It is in the nature of legal interpretation—not just but particularly constitutional interpretation—to aim at happy endings.[3] There is no alternative, except aiming at unhappy ones, because once the pure form of originalism is rejected there is no such thing as neutral accuracy. Telling it how it is means, up to a point, telling it how it should be. What is that point? The American constitutional novel includes, after all, the Supreme Court's Dred Scott decision, which treated slaves as a kind of property, and the Court's twentieth-century "rights of property" decisions, which nearly swamped Roosevelt's New Deal. How happy an overall view of that story is actually on offer? Many chapters raise that question, and it cannot be answered except through detailed interpretive arguments

---

[2] H. L. A. Hart, *The Concept of Law*, "Postscript" to the 1994 edition, Oxford University Press, 1994.
[3] See *Law's Empire*.

like those they provide. But political and intellectual responsibility, as well as cheerfulness, argue for optimism. The Constitution is America's moral sail, and we must hold to the courage of the conviction that fills it, the conviction that we can all be equal citizens of a moral republic. That is a noble faith, and only optimism can redeem it.

RONALD DWORKIN *is university professor of jurisprudence at Oxford University and a professor of law at New York University.*

∞

FROM
"Beyond the Marshall Plan: Wanted: Somebody to Take Responsibility for the Civil before the War"
BY PADRAIG O'MALLEY

Almost fifty years have elapsed since the Marshall Plan was conceived to rescue Western Europe, especially West Germany, from the ravages of World War II. The brainchild of then U.S. Secretary of State George C. Marshall, it was, in terms of its scale, ambition, and sheer generosity, one of the most visionary and humane foreign policy initiatives of our time. In the aftermath of the twentieth century's most bloody conflict, the victors offered the vanquished a program of financial resources they needed to rebuild their infrastructure, reopen factories, and take advantage of the most sophisticated technology. The outcome? A "vanquished" West Germany transformed itself into an economic superpower by the 1960s.

Like most great initiatives, the Marshall Plan was a response to economic and political considerations we still hold dear, and also to humane considerations—the immense deprivations suffered by the populations of the defeated countries—that we continue to pay lip-service to.

On the pragmatic side were the economic and political imperatives: the U.S. was concerned with the containment of communism, and needed to make allies out of its former enemies lest their continuing destitution made them ripe for plucking by an expansionist Soviet Union. The U.S., having been lifted out of its own depression by World War II, also needed new industrial markets to sustain its own prosperity. This placed it in the ironic position of rebuilding countries it had so efficiently destroyed in the waning days of the war.

Given the undeniable success of the Marshall Plan in rebuilding Europe, it is not unreasonable to ask why similar initiatives cannot be formulated to deal with the aftermath of civil conflicts that have become endemic in the twilight years of the twentieth century.

Since the fall of the Berlin Wall alone, more than four million people have been killed in violent conflicts. According to the Carnegie Commission on Preventing Deadly Conflict, at the start of 1997 there were 35 million refugees and internally displaced people around the world. The world has borne witness to protracted violence in Bosnia, in Chechnya, and in Rwanda.

And our response? We make legalistic distinctions between "ethnic cleansing" and genocide. Meanwhile, the hope that the post-Cold War era would give birth to a New World Order has largely evaporated.

Gone too is the nexus of stability created by the political rigidities, fixed-in-stone orthodoxies, and almost naively simplistic interpretations of global behavior that characterized the Cold War. At the very least, the super powers had to provide their client states with pocket money, if only to keep them firmly aligned on the "right" side.

Without this Cold War framework, absurd as it was, and any kind of replacement, the resolution of today's civil wars hinges on a grim cost/benefit calculation that deeply discounts those without marketable resources. Conveniently for the rich countries, this formula nearly always produces the answer that non-intervention is cheaper than getting involved—even when this is palpably untrue.

For instance, it is well documented that there were innumerable warnings that mass violence was germinating in Rwanda. Equally well documented is the fact that genocide occurs in the absence of external constraints, especially external preventative action. Yet the world community chose to ignore the painfully accumulated evidence on both counts, doing nothing to put the brakes on the momentum that built until genocide was inevitable.

Rwanda, considered miserable, backward, and with nearly hopeless prospects for sustainable development, could be ignored. It had no significance as an emerging market, and—barring its murderous intentions towards itself—posed no ideological threat to anyone. Why bother "rebuilding" what did not exist in the first place? Where were the markets to whet the voracious appetites of the global economy?

There was a cost, however, to turning a blind eye: relief and reconstruction efforts in the wake of the slaughter cost the international community U.S. $2 billion. Preventative intervention would have cost a third as much, and saved countless thousands of lives. But there is an absence of the moral will and authority needed for the international community to take these steps.

This lack of moral will stands not only in the way of preventative intervention; it undermines any chance of implementing the kind of program that will do for countries threatened by civil war what the Marshall Plan did for nations devastated by conventional war. And what is that program? It is economic and social development, funded in large degree by the richer nations without regard to the market potential of the recipients.

At the moment, just the opposite is happening. The U.S. is busily cutting back on foreign aid, its international development agency is shuttering missions around the world, and the country is turning inward, content to "levitate" in its status as the world's only superpower this side of Mars.

Within the U.S. and other advanced industrial countries there is a growing—and well-chronicled—gulf between rich and poor. It is a gulf that the mass of the adequately comfortable have gotten used to, and this moral indifference is even more pronounced when its subjects are the world's poorest nations. Home to a fifth of the world's population, the 50 poorest countries account for less than 2 percent of global income—and their share is dropping.

The drop is tied to the increasing willingness of the more affluent nations to marginalize the poorer ones, assigning them a utility that accounts for all of their shortcomings but none of their potential. It is a point of view that leads inevitably to the rich getting richer while the poor are consigned to a vast pool of disposable humanity whose claim on resources gets easier and easier to ignore.

My point is this: until this amoral calculus changes, any twenty-first-century Marshall Plan will likely be useless, an expensive, after-the-fact sop to the consciences of those living in rich countries. Only when these people and their leaders accept that they have a moral obligation to the truly disadvantaged will effective plans emerge, plans which give poorer nations a chance to develop in ways that alleviate the tensions and hatred that so often degenerate into civil war. We have forgotten how much we depend on affluence to rob social and ethnic grievances of their sting.

If we can embrace a new global ethic that weighs more than market share, then perhaps we can talk again of Marshall Plans. After all, it was a moral vision that gave great weight to ordinary humanity which made the Marshall Plan possible in the first place.

From an article of the same name in the WorldPaper, *March 1998, by permission of the* WorldPaper.

PADRAIG O'MALLEY *is a senior fellow at the University of Massachusetts' John W. McCormack Institute and author of* The Uncivil Wars: Ireland Today.

FROM
"Reconciliation and Community: The Future of Peace in Northern Ireland"
BY OSCAR ARIAS

I come from Costa Rica, a small land at peace. But it was not always so. After many years of fragile governance, strife and, finally, a brief civil war that left thousands dead, we Costa Ricans in 1948 decided to take a radical step. We abolished our army and created a civilian police force.

Instead of investing in weapons and barracks, we began to invest purposely and massively, in education, health care, housing, and welfare. Instead of emphasizing our differences, we began to celebrate compromise, community, democracy, and freedom. We have not been at war, internally or externally, since that time.

But none of us lives in isolation in this modern world. Our region, Central America, is small. And our neighbors, Panama, Nicaragua, Honduras, El Salvador, and Guatemala have a long history of violence. Over the decades, these long-simmering distempers exploded in a series of bloody wars that killed more than 200,000 of our peoples in Central America. Hundreds of thousands of others were wounded or tortured. Three million others fled or were driven into exile.

In its final deadly death throes, the Cold War swept over our isthmus with sectarian certainties of Left and Right, tons of weapons, and the rhythmic sound of boots, helicopters, gunships, and clanking armor. Instead of learning how to read, ply a trade, and share with their fellow citizens, our young people began to learn the easy arts of hating and killing. We lost more than a generation. As Ezra

Pound once wrote in the wake of another terrible conflict: "there died a myriad, and of the best among them"—slain, tortured, embittered, afraid, exiled.

When I became president of Costa Rica in 1986, I was determined that, somehow, the killing must end. I did not know how. I only knew that it must—and that it was up to us, Central Americans, to end it.

All around me I heard a steady chorus of voices telling me it would be impossible. There had been too much killing. There was too much hatred. People's minds and spirits had hardened. It was impossible to negotiate with murderous terrorists; it was impossible to negotiate with homicidal army officers. The Russians and the Americans and the Cubans would not permit peace. Killing, it seemed, was too popular. Peace, it seemed, was just too difficult to risk.

Perhaps it was one of those moments when it was good to be a Latin American. We are, after all, children of Cervantes, of Unamuno and Neruda, of Borges, García Márquez, Bunuel, Miro, Picasso and Dali. Yes, we are often led to passion and fantasy. But, like Don Quixote, we are also led to dream and to act on our dreams. In 1986, surrounded by the corpses of our young and the cries of our mothers, we dreamt of peace—even as everyone told us we were fantasists; that we were naive; that we were irresponsible; that we were risking democracy by seeking to negotiate, rather than continue to arm ourselves and lacerate one another.

Perhaps we were just lucky. But we lowered our lances, charged every windmill in sight—and after a long, hard struggle, the guns were silent.

It was not easy. At times as we negotiated for reconciliation in Nicaragua and El Salvador and Panama, I would be filled with doubt and anguish. As we sought to strengthen reason, another act of violence would devastate a neighborhood or erase another handful of innocent lives. Army generals and hardened guerrilla commanders had to face what were, to them, unthinkable steps of disarming, of re-entering civilian life, of admitting responsibility for their acts of terror before the process of forgiveness, if not forgetting, could begin. Hundreds of thousands of mines, rockets, bombs, bullets, and rifles had to be collected and destroyed. And in every home and village people had to learn to hope once again—and to act on that hope.

The past several years have seen a plethora of miracles, from the streets of Pretoria, to the deserts of the Middle East, to the meadows of Northern Ireland. These are miracles that have riveted the world—inspired and encouraged us—

indeed, proven to us, that no conflict is impossible to end and, most importantly, that peace is infinitely more important and valuable than war.

In the past eight years, Central Americans have learned a very important lesson about peace. We have learned that peace is not the signing of a treaty or the shaking of hands. We cannot define peace as the cessation of war—we cannot define peace in terms of war at all. Peace possesses and offers beauty and goodness that is inherently valuable, and stands no comparison. To live in peace, my friends, is to live without fear.

We have learned that peace demands a strong, lasting commitment. We have come to understand that true peace may not be achieved for many years to come. But we persist in our quest, because we know—as you do—that peace is our only option.

From a keynote address delivered at a conference of the Foundation for a Civil Society entitled "Reconciliation and Community: The Future of Peace in Northern Ireland," Belfast, June 6, 1995.

OSCAR ARIAS *was president of Costa Rica from 1986 to 1990. He was awarded the Nobel Peace Prize in 1987.*

Globalization: Its Dimensions and Dynamic

Introduction by Sondra Myers

While globalization is not new to the world, having reared its head repeatedly in human history, it is important to examine its contemporary manifestations. We cannot halt globalization, nor should we want to. But we can identify and even limit its detrimental impact and find ways to use its advantages for democratic and humane purposes. That will require a robust political will as well as a set of creative civic skills, and, above all, a commitment to international cooperation and collaboration.

How can we contain the rampant commercialism of the global economy within the structures of democratic politics? How can we reduce the impact of religious fundamentalism on those reluctant to face the uncertainties of modernity? How can we give religion and the spiritual aspects of life more "public space" and respect in the democratic context? How can we relieve the sufferings of poverty and disease, which are the seedbeds of hopelessness and anger? How can we reduce the prospects of terrorism? These and other questions will be addressed in the readings that follow.

13
The Globalization of the Market is Not Enough

"The democratic project is to globalize democracy as we have globalized the economy; to democratize the globalism that has been so efficiently marketed."
—Benjamin R. Barber

Discussion Questions

1. According to Benjamin R. Barber, democracy reduces or "contains" the negative impacts of "sterile cultural monism" ("McWorld") and "raging cultural fundamentalism" ("Jihad"). How does that work? Does your community feel the impact of McWorld and/or Jihad?
2. Why did efforts at modernizing the social structure and economic and political order in countries such as Iran and Egypt fail while Turkey made substantial progress in these areas? Compare and contrast their respective approaches to modernization.
3. What approach does Franklin Sonn suggest for small nations in their dealings with large and powerful nations? Is the approach useful in your country?

Readings

On Globalization
BY BENJAMIN R. BARBER

Only the globalization of civic and democratic institutions is likely to offer a way out of the global war between modernity and its aggrieved critics. For democracy responds both to Jihad and to McWorld. It responds directly to the resentments and spiritual unease of those for whom the trivialization and homogenization of values is an affront to cultural diversity and spiritual and moral seriousness. But it also answers the complaints of those mired in poverty and despair as a consequence of unregulated global markets and of a capitalism run wild because it has been uprooted from the humanizing constraints of the democratic nation state. By extending the compass of democracy to the global market sector, it can promise to those wishing to join the modern world and take advantage of its economic blessings opportunities for accountability, participation and governance; by securing cultural diversity and a place for worship and faith insulated from the shallow orthodoxies of McWorld's cultural monism, it can address the anxieties of those who fear secularist materialism and are fiercely committed to preserving their cultural and religious distinctiveness. On the capacity of moderns to make the world safe for women and men in search of both justice and faith will depend the outcome of the cruel battle between Jihad and McWorld, which will be won only if democracy is the victor.

If democracy is to be the instrument by which the world avoids the stark choice between a sterile cultural monism (McWorld) and a raging cultural fundamentalism (Jihad), neither of which service diversity or civic liberty, then America, Britain and their allies will have to open a crucial second civic and democratic front aimed not against terrorism per se but against the anarchism and social chaos—the economic reductionism and its commercializing homogeneity—that have created the climate of despair and hopelessness which terrorism has so effectively exploited. A second democratic front will be advanced not only in the name of retributive justice and secularist interests, but in the name of distributive justice and religious pluralism.

The democratic front in the war on terrorism is not a battle to dissuade terrorists from their campaigns of annihilation. Their deeds are unspeakable, and their purposes can neither be rationalized nor negotiated. When they hijacked innocents and turned civilian aircraft into lethal weapons, these self-proclaimed "martyrs" of faith in truth subjected others to a compulsory martyrdom indistinguishable from mass murder. The terrorists offer no terms and can be given none in exchange. When Jihad turns nihilistic, bringing it to justice can only take the form of extirpation—root, trunk, and branch. Eliminating terrorists will depend on professional military, intelligence and diplomatic resources whose deployment will leave the greater number of citizens in America and throughout the world sitting on the sidelines, anxious spectators to a battle in which they cannot participate, a battle in which the nausea that accompanies fear will dull the appetite for revenge. The second front, however, engages every citizen with a stake in democracy and social justice whether within nation states or in the relations between them. It transforms anxious and passive spectators into resolute and engaged participants—the perfect antidote to fear....

[A]n environment of despairing rage exists in too many places in the third world as well as too many third world neighborhoods of first world cities, enabling terrorism by endowing it with a kind of a quasi-legitimacy it does not deserve. It is not terrorism itself but this facilitating environment against which the second front battle is directed. Its constituents are not terrorists for they are themselves terrified by modernity and its costs, and as a consequence vulnerable to ameliorative actions if those who embrace democracy can find the will to take such actions. What they seek is justice not vengeance....

The democratic project is to globalize democracy as we have globalized the economy; to democratize the globalism that has been so efficiently marketized. The issue is no longer utopian longing for global democracy against the siren call of consumerism or the passionate war cries of Jihad; it is the securing of safety. Following September 11, global governance has become a sober mandate of political realism.

From Jihad vs. McWorld *(New York: Ballentine Books, 2001), pages xi-xxiii.*

For information about Benjamin R. Barber, *see page 101.*

❦

On the Compatibility of Political and Economic Rights
by Morton Halperin

We must resist the temptation to argue about whether political rights are more important than economic rights; there is no incompatibility between the two. On the one hand, we cannot eliminate poverty except in democratic societies; on the other, democratic societies cannot survive unless they eliminate poverty. So the political and economic agendas must be consistent with each other.

We must, therefore, find a way to take control of existing international institutions like the World Trade Organization, the United Nations, and regional and multilateral institutions in the name of democracy. They were created in very different periods and for very different purposes. During the

Cold War they were frozen because otherwise they became instruments of either one side or the other of the arenas in which the battles of the Cold War were being fought. We now have an opportunity to transform them into institutions that exist for the promotion, preservation, and enhancement of democracy. That means democratizing the process in each country by which we deal with these institutions....

Edited remarks made at the Democracy Collaborative's International Roundtable, "The Theory and Practice of Civic Globalism," held in Washington, D.C., January 2001.

Morton Halperin *is senior fellow at the Council on Foreign Relations and former director of policy planning, U.S. Department of State.*

∞

FROM
"Why Do They Hate Us?: The Politics of Rage"
BY FAREED ZAKARIA

I. THE RULERS

If poverty produced failure in most of Arabia, wealth produced failure in the rest of it. The rise of oil power in the 1970s gave a second wind to Arab hopes. Where Nasserism failed, petroleum would succeed. But it didn't. All that the rise of oil prices has done over three decades is to produce a new class of rich, superficially Western gulf Arabs, who travel the globe in luxury and are despised by the rest of the Arab world....

By the late 1980s, while the rest of the world was watching old regimes from Moscow to Prague to Seoul to Johannesburg crack, the Arabs were stuck with their aging dictators and corrupt kings. Regimes that might have seemed promising in the 1960s were now exposed as tired, corrupt kleptocracies, deeply unpopular and thoroughly illegitimate....

II. FAILED IDEAS

America thinks of modernity as all good—and it as been almost all good for America. But for the Arab world, modernity has been one failure after another. Each path followed—socialism, secularism, nationalism—has turned into a dead end. While other countries adjusted to their failures, Arab regimes got stuck in their ways. And those that reformed economically could not bring themselves to ease up politically. The Shah of Iran, the Middle Eastern ruler who tried to move his country into the modern era fastest, reaped the most violent reaction in the Iranian revolution of 1979. But even the shah's modernization—compared, for example, with the East Asian approach of hard work, investment and thrift—was an attempt to buy modernization with oil wealth.

It turns out that modernization takes more than strongmen and oil money. Importing foreign stuff—Cadillacs, Gulfstreams and McDonald's—is easy. Importing the inner stuffings of modern society—a free market, political parties, accountability and the rule of law—is difficult and dangerous. The gulf states, for example, have gotten modernization "lite," with the goods and even the workers imported from abroad. Nothing was homegrown; nothing is even now. As for politics, the gulf governments offered their people a bargain: we will bribe you with wealth, but in return let us stay in power. It was the inverse slogan of the American revolution—no taxation, but no representation either.

The new age of globalization has hit the Arab world in a very strange way. Its societies are open enough to be disrupted by modernity, but not so open that they can ride the wave. They see the television shows, the fast foods and the fizzy drinks. But they don't see genuine liberalization in the society, with increased opportunities and greater openness. Globalization in the Arab world is the critic's caricature of globalization—a slew of Western products and billboards with little else. For some in their societies it means more things to buy. For the regimes it is an unsettling, dangerous phenomenon. As a result, the people they rule can look at globalization but for the most part not touch it....

The Arab world has a problem with its Attas[1] in more than one sense. Globalization has caught it at a bad demographic moment. Arab societies are going through a massive youth bulge, with more than half of most countries' populations under the age of 25. Young men, often better educated than their parents, leave their traditional villages to find work. They arrive in noisy, crowded cities like Cairo, Beirut and Damascus or go to work in the oil states....In their new world they see great disparities of wealth and the disorienting effects of modernity; most unsettlingly, they see women, unveiled and in public places, taking buses, eating in cafes and working alongside them....

---

[1]Mohammed Atta is one of the alleged suicide bombers on September 11, 2001.

III. ENTER RELIGION

In his seminal work, "The Arab Predicament," Fouad Ajami explains, "The fundamentalist call has resonance because it invited men to participate…[in] contrast to a political culture that reduces citizens to spectators and asks them to leave things to their rulers. At a time when the future is uncertain, it connects them to a tradition that reduces bewilderment." Fundamentalism gave Arabs who were dissatisfied with their lot a powerful language of opposition.

On that score, Islam has little competition. The Arab world is a political desert with no real political parties, no free press, few pathways for dissent. As a result, the mosque turned into the place to discuss politics. And fundamentalist organizations have done more than talk. From the Muslim Brotherhood to Hamas to Hizbullah, they actively provide social services, medical assistance, counseling and temporary housing. For those who treasure civil society, it is disturbing to see that in the Middle East these illiberal groups *are* civil society.…

IV. WHAT TO DO

America must now devise a strategy to deal with this form of religious terrorism. As is now widely understood, this will be a long war, with many fronts and battles small and large. Our strategy must be divided along three lines: military, political and cultural. On the military front—by which I mean war, covert operations and other forms of coercion—the goal is simple: the total destruction of Al Qaeda. Even if we never understand all the causes of apocalyptic terror, we must do battle against it.…

The political strategy is more complex and more ambitious. At the broadest level, we now have a chance to reorder the international system around this pressing new danger. The degree of cooperation from around the world has been unprecedented. We should not look on this trend suspiciously. Most governments feel threatened by the rise of subnational forces like Al Qaeda. Even some that have clearly supported terrorism in the past, like Iran, seem interested in re-entering the world community and reforming their ways.

We can define a strategy for the post-cold-war era that addresses America's principal national-security need and yet is sustained by broad international consensus. To do this we will have to give up some cold-war reflexes, such as an allergy to multilateralism.…

The purpose of an international coalition is practical and strategic. Given the nature of this war, we will need the constant cooperation of other governments—to make arrests, shut down safe houses, close bank accounts and share intelligence. Alliance politics has become a matter of high national security. But there is a broader imperative. The United States dominates the world in a way that inevitably arouses envy or anger or opposition. That comes with the power, but we still need to get things done. If we can...work with institutions like the United Nations Security Council, U.S. might will be easier for much of the world to bear....

The third, vital component to this battle is a cultural strategy. The United States must help Islam enter the modern world. It sounds like an impossible challenge, and it certainly is not one we would have chosen. But America— indeed the whole world—faces a dire security threat that will not be resolved unless we can stop the political, economic and cultural collapse that lies at the roots of Arab rage. During the cold war the West employed myriad ideological strategies to discredit the appeal of communism, make democracy seem attractive and promote open societies. We will have to do something on that scale to win this cultural struggle.

First, we have to help moderate Arab states, but on the condition that they embrace moderation....[W]e must persuade Arab moderates to make the case to their people that Islam is compatible with modern society, that it does allow women to work, that it encourages education and that it has welcomed people of other faiths and creeds. Some of this they will do—Sept. 11 has been a wake-up call for many. The Saudi regime denounced and broke its ties to the Taliban (a regime that it used to glorify as representing pure Islam). The Egyptian press is now making the case for military action. The United States and the West should do their own work as well. We can fund moderate Muslim groups and scholars and broadcast fresh thinking across the Arab world, all aimed at breaking the power of the fundamentalists.

Obviously we will have to help construct a new political order in Afghanistan after we have deposed the Taliban regime. But beyond that we have to press the nations of the Arab world—and others, like Pakistan, where the virus of fundamentalism has spread—to reform, open up and gain legitimacy....

Perhaps most important, Islamic fundamentalism still does not speak to the majority of the Muslim people. In Pakistan, fundamentalist parties have yet to get more than 10 percent of the vote. In Iran, having experienced the brutal puritanism of the mullahs, people are yearning for normalcy. In Egypt, for all the repression, the fundamentalists are a potent force but so far not dominant.

If the West can help Islam enter modernity in dignity and peace, it will have done more than achieved security. It will have changed the world.

From an article of the same title printed in Newsweek, *October 15, 2001, pages 27–40. Copyright © 2001 Newsweek, Inc. All rights reserved. Reprinted with permission.*

For information about FAREED ZAKARIA, *see page 164.*

∽

"Strategies for Emerging Democracies"
BY FRANKLIN SONN

We are trying to create the parameters of society. The post-Cold War regime which determines civilization is perceived by emerging democracies as a *pax americana*....We [poorer nations] must take on the transnationals, but we must take them on in a productive way. We must say we are part of globalization because that's a reality, not because we like it. And at the same time, we must say what's acceptable to us and what's not. We say we are not going to pay your drug prices because we are not a G-8 country. And we are going to question what you present to us as intellectual property rights. We want to sell generic drugs in order to meet the health demands of our poor, which is almost 50% of the South African population. The drug companies mustered an enormous fight against us. We conducted this fight respectful of the rules and won. Today, we sell generic drugs and our relationship with the U.S. is still perfectly good. So my suggestion is that we do *not* allow the big monoliths to dictate terms all together; that we do not look upon the U.S. and all the G-8 countries as an insurmountable problem. And we do that like we "eat the elephant"—piece by piece.

Where we have the advantage is that the superpower is a democracy, and it is less sure of itself than emerging economies and markets often think it is....

I hope that emerging democracies will develop a sense of coherence; that we will come at this issue collectively and cleverly, and that we will participate in the writing of the rules of *pax americana* globalization, and thereby play a constructive role....[W]e are dealing with power relations in the global community and those power relations are skewed. How do we move forward, given that reality of skewed power relations? We need to accept the inevitability of the political and economic strength and power of concentrated capital, and we need to analyze the monolith and find entry points where we can promote the interest of the G-8 and at the same time promote our own interests and move the global community forward.

How was it possible in South Africa for Mandela to step forward and say to de Klerk, "Let's talk capitulation"? First was the destruction of the Berlin Wall, which created a special environment in which he could talk. Second, he found out exactly what the interests of de Klerk and his people were and played to those interests rather than threatening them....We need to find ways and means of promoting this strategy...because if we find and identify those entry points, we can build strength.

Edited remarks made at the Democracy Collaborative's International Roundtable, "The Theory and Practice of Civic Globalism," held in Washington, D.C., January 2001.

FRANKLIN SONN *served as the first ambassador of the Democratic South Africa to the United States from 1995 to 1998. He is former rector and president of Peninsula Technikon and currently serves as executive chairman of Africa Group Corporation.*

14
Creating the Political Context for Civic Globalism

"…[the] act if debating in a global forum about who is there legitimately and who is not, in the same room, talking about global problems, will itself be a process that helps build global norms and gives more voice to those who will bear the consequences of globalization."
—Michael W. Doyle

Discussion Questions

1. Are civic groups in your community addressing such issues as the environment, education, human rights, and health? How might you work to initiate or strengthen this kind of civic action?
2. What are the challenges that face global democratization, according to Michael W. Doyle? How can they best be addressed?
3. George Soros speaks of a "global open society" and its challenges. What are the major obstacles to a global civil society?
4. Thomas Friedman notes that the Muslim communities in India and Bangladesh prosper both economically and socially. Patrice Brodeur notes that Indonesia, the largest Muslim country in the world, has had similar successes. What are the characteristics in these nations that have allowed Muslims to prosper in them?

Readings

FROM
"An Emerging Global Civil Society"
BY MIGUEL DARCY DE OLIVEIRA AND RAJESH TANDON

"Our world cannot survive one-fourth rich and three-fourths poor, half democratic and half authoritarian with oases of human development surrounded by deserts of human deprivation."
—Human Development Report 1994

People coming together and helping each other solve problems is by no means a novelty. Since time immemorial, human beings have banded together for caring and mutual protection. Compassion for one another is a distinctive attribute of humanity. Solidarity and cooperation have always characterized relationships and social ties within families, communities, and friendship networks. The concerns and obligations that we feel toward our relatives, friends, and neighbors are not determined by self-interest nor imposed by an external coercive authority. We help those close to us on a spontaneous, sympathetic, and reciprocal basis.

What is distinctive about today is the extension of these virtues of solidarity and responsibility to the public sphere on a global scale. True enough, faith and revolution also had a global outreach. Missions of different religions inspired many to leave their homes to bring conversion and, therefore, salvation to strangers. The socialist internationals tried to link all the oppressed in their quest for a "promised land" in the here and now. In both cases, the global drive was promoted by a centrally organized institution, be it a church or a political organization, spreading its compass to the periphery.

Today's massive, almost universal movement toward greater citizen participation and influence is a new phenomenon. It is not being promoted by one all-encompassing structure. It has no fixed address. It seeks neither converts nor political militants. Its target is not state power. At its center is the figure of the citizen. And there are many citizens, with their myriad faces, concerns and sources of inspiration in today's world.

Citizen action is as multidimensional as the diversity of human endeavors. It may be local or global, small or massive, permanent or ephemeral, highly dramatic or almost invisible, confrontational or collaborative, spontaneous or organized, promoted by associations of like-minded individuals or by large civic movements. Or any combination of these, depending on the needs of the moment.

Its breadth and diversity range from women in India hugging trees to save them from being felled to global environmental organizations lobbying governments to come to terms with ecological imbalance. From students in Scandinavia donating the proceeds of their voluntary work for educational projects in the Third World to the mothers of political prisoners in Argentina barehandedly confronting a ferocious military dictatorship. From Polish workers challenging a totalitarian regime to entire villages in Asia mobilizing for self-governance and self-development. From medical doctors disregarding national frontiers to rescue the victims of civil strife to millions of Americans reading for the blind, collecting money for a health charity, or doing volunteer work in the local library, art gallery, or soup kitchen. From courageous Arab women standing up for their rights to citizens worldwide demanding the safeguard of the physical integrity of persecuted people whose names they can hardly pronounce and whose political beliefs they often do not share.

The sources of inspiration may be spiritual, religious, moral, or political. The common thread, however, in this ever-changing quilt is to be found in the realm of values: solidarity and compassion for the fate and well-being of others, including unknown, distant others; a sense of personal responsibility and reliance on one's own initiative to do the right thing; the impulse toward altruistic giving and sharing; the refusal of inequality, violence, and oppression.

These are the compelling moral values that generate people's social energy and enhance the texture of civil society. The themes and concerns vary from place to place and from time to time, but citizen movements are now a constant, global phenomenon.

In counterpoint both to the power and the impersonal rules of governments and to the quest for profit and personal gain intrinsic to the market, third sector—nonprofit and nongovernmental—now coexists in practically every society. All over the world, civil society now interacts with and exercises a countervailing power to markets and government.

Yet the richness and diversity of citizen initiatives still far outweigh their public visibility and recognition. "Private action for the public good" is a new concept in many parts of the world. Despite the recent multiplication at the local and national levels of innovative experiences that cut across the boundaries of class and culture, cross-sectoral partnerships and interactions among the different components of the nonprofit sector are still the exception rather than the rule.

In the countries of the South, NGOs [non-government organizations] possess a rich history of solidarity and collaboration with popular movements, but have so far had little contact with the emerging initiatives of corporate philanthropy. Private foundations and development agencies have been actively supporting civil society associations, but donors and donees hardly ever share equal responsibility for joint programs on issues of common concern. Only now are the government and business sectors, the academic world, and the media beginning to acknowledge the role and potential of the third sector. Many countries lack the appropriate legislation to encourage citizen action, private giving, and volunteering....

Expressing this new global spirit in deeds is one of the foremost challenges to citizens and civil society institutions. Private action for the public good has been lost in the shrill of public for public good or private for private good. Citizens' actions for public good are conceptually and qualitatively different from private, profit-oriented initiatives. Likewise, the government is not the sole repository of all wisdom, concern, and capacity to act for the common good.

Citizen initiatives aimed at addressing public issues and problems are no longer to be considered residual actions. They are now in the center, not the periphery. The actors of civil society are not following the prescriptions of the state or of the market, but creating their own initiatives. In this sense, the nonprofit sector can be said to be not the third, but the primary sector of society....

The reassertion of the primacy of civil society calls for the articulation of a set of universal human values. The current crisis of morality is being countered by inspired and value-based citizens' actions worldwide. The source of inspiration for human response to the needs and suffering of individuals and groups is essentially spiritual throughout the world. Spontaneous and committed citizen initiatives are premised on love, compassion, concern for others. These values and inspirations provide meaning and substance to people.

In a world where material acquisitions and consumption are becoming the dominant ethos, there is an urgent need to bring spirituality to the core of human endeavor. This will constitute the fountainhead of a universal moral code based on our common humanity. The values of diversity, of tolerance and pluralism, of peace and justice, of solidarity and responsibility to unknown others and to future generations need to be proposed and practiced as the anchor for universal humanity and global citizen action.

From an article of the same name in Citizens Strengthening Global Civil Society *(Washington, D.C. 1994), 1-11, by permission of CIVICUS: World Alliance for Citizen Participation.*

MIGUEL DARCY DE OLIVEIRA *is co-founder and executive secretary of Instituto de Ação Cultural and consultant to the International Labor Organization and UNESCO. He is a graduate instructor at The Catholic University of America and co-author of* Citizens: Strengthening Global Civil Society.

RAJESH TANDON *is executive director of the Society for Participatory Research in Asia (PRIA). He is a founding board member of CIVICUS and currently serves as chairman of the board of directors of the Montreal International Forum.*

"On Global Democratization"
BY MICHAEL W. DOYLE

...International governance and global democracy are two big, controversial, confusing, and important themes. Just in the past year, what is promiscuously known as "the international community" has engaged in forceful instances of international governance. In the summer of 1999, NATO's campaign of bombing and threats of invasion coerced Serbia (the former Yugoslavia) into accepting international governance of Kosovo by the United Nations, all in the interest of protecting Kosovan Albanians, who are a majority in that territory, from forced expulsion. In effect, the international community declared Serbian sovereignty temporarily null and void. In Indonesia, again pressure (economic, not military) produced consent by Indonesia to accepting the self-determination of the people of East Timor. The East Timorese, like the Kosovars, are under the temporary benign governance of the United Nations for two or more years. Significant international governance is taking place today.

Participatory democratization also rose to the international agenda in the past year. In Seattle, the new World Trade Organization, at a meeting designed to be a celebration of the new Millennium Round of further reductions of barriers to global trade, was derailed by an informal coalition of outraged states from the world's majority of developing countries, combined with a group of nongovernmental organizations claiming to represent civil society in the industrialized world. Their aims were different, but together they derailed the entire proceeding and exposed important differences in priority among the developed states, and particularly the United States and Europe. Charlene Barshefsky, the U.S. Trade Representative and the meeting's chair, later conceded, "We needed a process which had a greater degree of internal transparency and inclusion to accommodate a larger and more diverse membership."…

Responding to the concerns noted above, some have begun to wonder, "Don't we need some increased accountability, increased legitimacy, to contain and govern the practical negotiations among the experts? Don't we need to have norms that are more broadly shared, or even decisions that are legitimate because people across borders have participated in outlining their direction?" We want expert pilots to fly the planes we ride in, but do we want them to choose our destinations?[1]

Realistically, however, no strong version of global democracy is viable at the present time. We will not soon see global decisions, global legislation, deciding new regulatory standards for the global economy. Why not? Because global democracy is not about being willing to win democratically, it is about being willing to lose democratically. None of the popular advocates of increased democratization, whether in Seattle or Strasbourg or New Delhi, are willing to lose an issue and accept it because it went through a democratic process. The world is simply too unequal and too diverse. To give an example, the top one-fifth of the countries have 74 times the income of the bottom one-fifth of the countries, and it is getting worse. That is more than double the greatest degree of inequality within the most unequal domestic economy, the Brazilian economy, where the ratio between the top fifth and the bottom fifth is 32 to 1. More than double the Brazilian ratio, and yet Brazil does not qualify as a particularly stable democracy.

With respect to culture as well, the globe falls far short of the preconditions of ordinary democracy. India, the largest and one of the most linguistically diverse democracies, has 81 percent of its population describing itself as Hindu and an elite all of whom are fluent in English. That is a huge core of common identity that helps sustain the Indian democracy despite all of its diversity and internal dissention. There is no such core identity in the globe today. There is no single such identity, other than the thin commitment to human rights, to which 81 percent of the world will subscribe.

Therefore, I suggest that we must be more moderate in our democratizing ambitions. The role of global democratization should be limited to helping to

---

[1]Robert A. Dahl, *On Democracy* (New Haven: Yale University Press, 1998).

develop norms. Not legislation, but norms that will make the process of cooperation among the bureaucrats easier, more readily achievable, more legitimate, less contested. We must be very modest because norms usually do not do that much work. What they do, however, is make it easier for national politicians and international bureaucrats to cut pragmatic deals. Therefore, global democratization should be limited to endorsing measures such as those advocated in Ingvar Carlsson and Shridath Ramphal's *Our Global Neighborhood: The Report of the Commission on Global Governance*. In addition to sending diplomats to the annual meetings of the United Nations General Assembly, we should also send legislators. Every country can put five members in the General Assembly. At least two of them should be elected from the legislatures of their home countries. Bringing in the other branches of government, those somewhat more tied to the people, may help to begin to create a transmission belt between globe and home, fostering a more legitimate articulation of global standards at the international level.

The second way to enhance global normative articulation is to bring in civil society. Establish an annual global forum that brings together representatives of global civil society, meeting the week before the General Assembly meets each year. Nongovernmental organizations (NGOs) will be invited from all over the world to discuss and issue recommendations about global standards for the environment, humanitarian intervention, international economic assistance, and reforms of international institutions such as the International Monetary Fund, the World Bank, or the United Nations itself.

These recommendations constitute far from a cure-all. Electing legislators from nondemocratic legislatures to the U.N. does not enhance global democracy strikingly. Others will ask who elected the NGOs, for whom there is no internal process of democratic accountability to their members or to those whom their policies affect. But, merely that act of debating in a global forum about who is there legitimately and who is not, in the same room, talking about global problems, will itself be a process that helps build global norms and gives more voice to those who will bear the consequences of globalization. This is far short of democratic legitimation. In terms of democratic evolution, this represents little more than a Runnymede—cautious consultation far short of effective accountability....But like the meeting at Runnymede that produced the Magna Carta of English liberties, it can be the preliminary to increasingly responsible deliberation. And that may well be, I would like to suggest in conclusion, as well as we can do in the world as it is today.

From the 2000 Welling Lecture, "A More Perfect Union?" delivered March 9, 2000, Elliott School of International Affairs, The George Washington University, Washington, D.C..

Michael W. Doyle *is special adviser to United Nations Secretary-General Kofi Annan. He is author of* New Thinking in International Relations Theory *and* Ways of War and Peace.

൲

"Toward a Global Open Society"
BY George Soros

I have argued that we cannot have a global economy without a global society. But how can the idea of a global society be reconciled with the sovereignty of states? States have interests but no principles. How can the global common interest be left in their care? Only if the citizens of democratic states exert influence on governments and make them responsive to the needs of a global society.

I propose that the democratic states of the world should form an alliance with the purpose of creating a global open society. This would involve two distinct but related tasks: fostering the development of open societies throughout the world, and establishing certain rules and institutions that would govern the behavior of states toward their citizens and one another. This is a rather grandiose project, and it could be dismissed as an utopian idea; but open society recognizes the limitations imposed by reality. Perfect solutions are not attainable. We must therefore content ourselves with the second-best: imperfect arrangements that can be improved by a process of trial and error. The arrangements must vary according to time and place. Above all we must remember that well-intentioned actions often have adverse unintended consequences. This is particularly true of external interventions. When people try to impose their version of the ultimate truth on others it is liable to lead to religious, ideological, or communal warfare and there will be no end to the fighting. That is what happened in the Thirty Years' War. By basing the international political architecture on the principles of open society, this danger could be avoided. Open society rests on the recognition that the ultimate truth is beyond our reach. We must accept that people have different views and interests and we must find ways to allow them to live together in peace.

The creation of a global open society would inevitably involve some external meddling in internal affairs. It follows both from the principle of fallibility and the principle of sovereignty (which is today's reality) that to the greatest extent possible the intervention should be consensual and constructive rather than coercive. The emphasis should be on crisis prevention rather than punitive intervention. Prevention cannot start early enough, but at an early stage it is impossible to identify potential trouble spots. The best way to prevent crises is to foster the development of open societies throughout the world. The development has to be economic as well as political. The point is well made by Amartya Sen when he defines development as political freedom.[1]

I believe the concept of open society could provide some guiding principles to govern international relations, but to serve in that capacity the abstract concept must be transformed into an operational one. To prepare a blueprint for global open society would run counter to the principles of open society; it would also be an exercise in futility. Open society cannot be designed from first principles: It must be created by the people who live in it.

Open society as an operational concept needs to be developed by every society and every age for itself. A global open society has to be created by the open societies of the world working together. That is exactly what I propose.

The process that Karl Popper recommends is piecemeal social engineering. I am not entirely happy with the term, because in times of revolutionary regime change, the tempo is too fast to allow us the luxury of piecemeal action; that is why events spin out of control. The collapse of the Soviet system was such a moment in history. But that moment has passed, and we missed a historic opportunity. The international political scene is now much calmer, with specific problems slowly coming to the boil. Therefore a piecemeal approach is appropriate.

From Open Society: Reforming Global Capitalism *(New York, 2000), by permission of PublicAffairs.*

GEORGE SOROS *is an investor and philanthropist and the chairman of the Open Society Institute, an international charitable foundation based in New York.*

---

[1]Amartya Sen, *Development as Freedom* (New York: Alfred A. Knopf, 1999).

"Today's News Quiz"

BY Thomas L. Friedman

NEW DELHI

So, class, time for a news quiz: name the second largest Muslim community in the world. Iran? Wrong. Pakistan? Wrong. Saudi Arabia? Wrong....

Answer: India....India, with nearly 150 million Muslims, is believed to have more Muslim citizens than Pakistan or Bangladesh, and is second only to Indonesia. Which brings up another question that I've been asking here in New Delhi: Why is it you don't hear about Indian Muslims—who are a minority in this vast Hindu-dominated land—blaming America for all their problems or wanting to fly suicide planes into the Indian Parliament?

Answer: Multi-ethnic, pluralistic, free-market democracy. To be sure, Indian Muslims have their frustrations, and have squared off over the years in violent clashes with Hindus, as has every other minority in India. But they live in a noisy, messy democracy, where opportunities and a political voice are open to them, and that makes a huge difference.

"I'll give you a quiz question: Which is the only large Muslim community to enjoy sustained democracy for the last 50 years? The Muslims of India," remarked M.J. Akbar, the Muslim editor of *Asian Age*, a national Indian English-language daily funded by non-Muslim Indians. "I am not going to exaggerate Muslim good fortune in India. There are tensions, economic discrimination and provocations, like the destruction of the mosque at Ayodhya. But the fact is, the Indian Constitution is secular and provides a real opportunity for the economic advancement of any community that can offer talent. That's why a growing Muslim middle class here is moving up and, generally, doesn't manifest the strands of deep anger you find in many non-democratic Muslim states."

In other words, for all the talk about Islam and Islamic rage, the real issue is: Islam in what context? Where Islam is imbedded in authoritarian societies it tends to become the vehicle of angry protest, because religion and the mosque are the only places people can organize against autocratic leaders. And when those leaders are seen as being propped up by America, America also becomes the target of Muslim rage.

But where Islam is imbedded in a pluralistic, democratic society, it thrives like any other religion. Two of India's presidents have been Muslims; a Muslim woman sits on India's supreme court. The architect of India's missile program,

A.P.J. Abdul Kalam, is a Muslim. Indian Muslims, including women, have been governors of many Indian states, and the wealthiest man in India, the info-tech whiz Azim Premji, is a Muslim. The other day the Indian Muslim film star and parliamentarian Shabana Azmi lashed out at the imam of New Delhi's biggest mosque. She criticized him for putting Islam in a bad light and suggested he go join the Taliban in Kandahar. In a democracy, liberal Muslims, particularly women, are not afraid to take on rigid mullahs....

[Bangladesh]...has almost as many Muslims as Pakistan. Over the last 10 years, though, without the world noticing, Bangladesh has had three democratic transfers of power, in two of which...Muslim women were elected prime ministers. Result: All the economic and social indicators in Bangladesh have been pointing upward lately, and Bangladeshis are not preoccupied hating America. Meanwhile in Pakistan, trapped in the circle of bin Ladenism—military dictatorship, poverty and anti-modernist Islamic schools, all reinforcing each other—the social indicators are all pointing down and hostility to America is rife....

Those who argue that we needn't press for democracy in Arab-Muslim states, and can rely on repressive regimes, have it all wrong. If we cut off every other avenue for non-revolutionary social change, pressure for change will burst out anyway—as Muslim rage and anti-Americanism.

If America wants to break the bin Laden circles across the Arab-Muslim world, then, "it needs to find role models that are succeeding as pluralistic, democratic, modernizing, societies, like India—which is constantly being challenged by religious extremists of all hues—and support them," argues Raja Mohan, strategic affairs editor of *The Hindu* newspaper.

So true. For Muslim societies to achieve their full potential today, democracy may not be sufficient, but it sure is necessary. And we, and they, fool ourselves to think otherwise.

The New York Times, *November 20, 2001.*

THOMAS L. FRIEDMAN *has served as the* New York Times *foreign-affairs columnist on the Op-Ed page since 1995. A two-time Pulitzer Prize winner for* The New York Times, *he is the author of* The Lexus and the Olive Tree *and* From Beirut to Jerusalem.

Islam and Democracy: The Hopeful Sign of Indonesia

BY PATRICE BRODEUR

Indonesia is the fourth largest country in the world with 215 million people. It is also the largest Muslim country in the world with about ninety percent of its inhabitants identifying as Muslims. Extremely rich in ethnic and linguistic diversity, the inhabitants of this vast archipelago reflect religious diversity too: Christianity (7%), Hinduism (2%), and Buddhism (1%), with various forms of local animistic practices integrated into the religious practices of different religious identities. While these religious statistics are highly debated, it is clear that the predominance of Islam makes of Indonesia a vital piece of the Islamic mosaic worldwide, comprising close to twenty percent of the total Muslim world population of over one billion.

Since its independence from the Dutch in 1945, Indonesia has had two dictators: Sukarno from 1945 to 1966 and Suharto from 1966 to 1998. It was not until 1998 that pro-democracy forces were able to take power. The reason why Indonesia is a hopeful sign in the potential for a constructive relationship between Islam and democracy is that its population was able to put in place as its first President resulting from democratic elections in 1999, Abdurrahman Wahid, a Muslim cleric with a clear preference for new forms of Islamic pluralism and tolerance. The tense but peaceful takeover by the current president, Megawati Sukarnoputri, in July 2001 also indicates that there is no going back on the democratic advances achieved in Indonesia, even though the process of stabilizing this new democracy still faces major challenges.

This new reality did not happen overnight. In *Civil Islam: Muslims and Democratization in Indonesia,* published in 2000, Robert Hefner presents the spectrum of Muslim participation in and rejection of democratization in post-colonial Indonesia between 1945 and 1999. His book is cast in the context of the late 1990s' famous debate around Samuel Huntington's thesis of civilizational clashes and it offers a powerful counter-argument, both theoretical and factual. From Sukarno to Suharto, Hefner recounts the use and misuse of various Islamic discourses and alliances for gaining, asserting, and perpetuating political power at the highest nation-state level. He demonstrates how between the two extreme Islamic goals of either state conquest or separatist isolation, a large majority of Indonesia's two hundred million Muslims has developed a culture of civil Islam that promotes the values of tolerance and pluralism. Hefner carefully describes the relationship between Islam and democratization with his analysis of both the democratic successes and the many setbacks. He does not "suggest that the outcomes of today's democratic struggles, whether Indonesian or others, are guaranteed. There is no end of history, no definitive triumph of democratic ideals....But of this the Indonesian experience should make us certain: that the desire for democracy and civil decency is not civilizationally circumscribed."

Hefner argues that "[c]ivil Islam is an emergent tradition and comes in a variety of forms. Most versions begin, however, by denying the wisdom of a monolithic Islamic state and instead affirming democracy, voluntarism, and a balance of countervailing powers within a state and society. In embracing the ideals of civil society, this democratic Islam insists that formal democracy cannot prevail unless government power is checked by strong civic associations. At the same time, it is said, civic associations and democratic culture cannot thrive unless they are protected by a state that respects society by upholding its commitment to the rule of law. Recovering and amplifying elements of Islamic tradition, civil Islam is not merely a facsimile of a Western original." This definition of "civil Islam" is the result of a historical process unique to Indonesia, as described in a brief historical overview of the "civic seedlings" that emerged out of a form of nationalism based on multi-ethnicity similar to that of European nations, rather than mono-ethnicity.

Within the complex mix of ethno-religious polities that co-existed within the growing Dutch colony of Indonesia, the inroads of Islamic conversions which had, in pre-colonial times, taken a dynastic top-down approach, began to take a more grassroots approach. They did so in response to the Dutch colonial centralization of power, which resulted in the strengthening of the *pesantren*[1] Islamic schooling system apart from the State. This "translocal network of native authority" provided a necessary element for a democratic public culture: extra-state associations, a native "model of political culture that affirms principles of autonomy, mutual respect, and voluntarism," an application of this ideal model into the public sphere, and a supportive network of state and social institutions to buttress this ideal model.

[Hefner maintains that] "our democratic confidence should be based on the conviction that the message of freedom, equality, and plurality is not narrowly circumscribed, as some prophets of the new civilizational relativism argue. Democratic ideals are broadly appealing because they respond to circumstances

---

[1] *Pesantren*: traditional school for children and early teenagers to study the Qur'an and Islamic studies.

and needs common across modern cultures." If the idea of nation-state, with its equally Western genealogy, could become so fully integrated in a myriad of ways into the reality of Muslim politics today…it is only a matter of time for the idea of democracy to become equally integrated, with a unique set of Islamic family traits, into Muslim politics worldwide.

Revised by the author from a book review to be published spring 2002 in The Muslim World Journal.

PATRICE BRODEUR *is assistant professor of Islamic and religious studies at Connecticut College, New London, Connecticut.*

15
"Signs of an Emerging Global Consciousness"

"An international public is beginning to emerge, but it is not yet fully effective because it has no institutional articulation."
—Bhikhu Parekh

Discussion Questions

1. Discuss the political, cultural and moral aspects of globalization that are noted by Bhikhu Parekh. How can they be encouraged in your community?

2. How might a modern democratic Islamic society differ from western democracy? What do they have in common?

3. Martin Palouš sees the expanding acceptance of human rights and the emergence of international mechanisms for the protection of human rights as a positive aspect of globalization. Do you see these positive signs in your country? Where else?

4. Discuss the challenges democracy faces as the powers of the globalized market compete for control. Why, according to Benjamin Barber, is it important to sustain a strong public sector, particularly a duly elected democratic government, as well as a civic sector and an economic sector?

5. In building a global civil community, how critical is it for nations to develop a strong sense of interdependence and responsibility for each other? What can we do as individuals to foster an engaged and informed interdependence?

6. Kofi Annan believes the United Nations' mission in the 21st century should be to develop a global awareness of the human rights of every individual on the planet. What can you do in your community to make people aware of their global as well as their local responsibility?

Readings

"Globalization Recognizes a Common Humanity"

BY BHIKU PAREKH

Are we simply concerned with free speech and basic rights—the political infrastructure of democracy—or do we also have something much deeper in mind, the promotion of human well-being and the elimination of poverty? Democracy is not just concerned with liberal freedoms but also with two central ideas which have been at the heart of it since the time of Aristotle, namely the idea of equality and the idea of community. Take away those two ideas and there is nothing left of democracy but liberalism.

During the Cold War we said *we* were a free society and they were a totalitarian society. What's the difference between them and us? We have voluntary associations and they don't; they don't allow religious liberty and a host of other things. In other words, in our discussions the notion of a free society came to be equated almost entirely with voluntary associations. This understanding of civil society, in my view, constricts us and prevents us from asking important questions. I propose that we take a critical look at the concept of civil society and decide whether it's going to perform the functions we want it to perform.

Third, I question the romanticism of civil society. When I reflect on the experience of India and many of the developing societies including China, it is clear that the state has been a progressive, emancipating institution in a way that very often civil society has not been. Take the status of the Untouchables in India. Voluntary associations attempted but failed to make an impact on it. It took the state enacting the Constitution and declaring that all have certain rights to make the difference. Before a civil society can function you need at least two basic conditions. You need a "space of freedom" where voluntary associations can function, and you need people with civic virtues who are concerned about each other. In addition, you need a fairly stable political structure, or civil society simply doesn't get off the ground.

On globalization, I want to advance three theses. First, we have tended to discuss globalization as if it is an abstract, autonomous phenomenon confined merely to the economic realm. In fact, globalization is simply a consequence of a larger moral and cultural process that has been going on for a very long time. Globalization recognizes a common humanity, so that if something happens to the Buddha statues in Afghanistan, we all feel concerned. There is a development of a common sense of humanity, a concern for rights, and a recognition that the earth belongs to us all. It is within the context of an emerging global consciousness that we need to locate globalization. Otherwise we will get it completely wrong; we will see globalization only as something to be frightened about. Globalization is a complex process with a very complex dialectic. It has a moral dimension and a cultural dimension. Films travel, cultural ideas travel, novels travel; and, of course, goods travel, companies travel, capital travels, people travel, immigrants travel. Let's locate globalization within a larger context and see it not just as an economic phenomenon, but also as a political, cultural, and moral phenomenon.

Second, we need to recognize that globalization has advantages and disadvantages. In India, where globalization has come in a very big way, the reactions have been of the following kind. It's a good thing in that it brings in foreign capital, encourages competition, and breaks up domestic industries including television. It also brings benefits to consumers because goods are cheaper. But it also has profound disadvantages. It increases inequality; it creates a footloose class of technocrats whose interest are linked to international corporations outside and not with locals. Therefore, it destroys what we would call a political community. When you feel that your way of life is increasingly being destabilized, it creates cultural panic—and fundamentalism.

[Economic] globalization has a tendency to weaken democracy, not just in the receiving countries but more important or equally important, in the United States and other metropolitan countries. Once corporations take the lead in globalization, they insist that their government force other governments to create certain conditions for globalization, and democracy at home begins to suffer. This is the experience one learned during the imperial expansion. Not only were liberties destroyed in the countries that were the object of the expansion, but they were destroyed at home as well.

And here is my final thesis, which I think is absolutely crucial. We need to ask: What kinds of institutional structures are needed to get the maximum advantage of globalization while at the same time regulating it; without some kind of regulation of currency transactions and currency speculation, no international justice is possible. We need political structures of global governance. The United Nations must be radically reformed so that it doesn't merely represent nation-states, but also NGOs.

We need to think in imaginative terms. I propose, as an example, that if you want to create a global civil society, why not create a global income tax? Several economists have been considering the following two strategies, and I have done some work in this area. If, for example, income tax in all of the advanced countries were to be increased by one-tenth of one percent it would generate something like $28 billion available for international distribution. Suppose, too, that progressive-minded people were to say: We would like to help, but we don't want to give to charities; we want our money to be properly channeled. Suppose that every month one percent or one-half of one percent of our salaries were taken away—through voluntary transactions by the tax department—to be distributed for certain services such as countering AIDS, or malaria, or other things in other parts of the world. Economists who did the work for me tell me that even if between five percent and ten percent of the people were to volunteer to do this kind of thing all over the world, not just in advanced countries, it would generate something like £36 billion. Imagine the capacity that gives us to tackle great international problems, including epidemics of all kinds!

I believe that in the context of a global public the tax concept is critically important. Because all ideas, if they are going to be implemented, need a social battle. You need a global public to mount and pilot ideas through. Is there a global public? I think one is beginning to emerge. We have seen it in the case of South Africa and the pharmaceutical companies; and we have seen it in the case of the Taliban and the Buddha statues.

An international public is beginning to emerge, but it is not yet fully effective because it has no institutional articulation. In order to checkmate corporations you need international trade unions. Likewise, we need international academic associations, meetings of universities the world over, meetings of journalists, meetings of young people, meetings of indigenous peoples, consumers, etc. If we think in terms of setting up international forums at multiple levels, then we will gradually begin to see a crisscrossing international global public that would be there to carry some of these ideas through.

International Roundtable, edited remarks made at the Democracy Collaboratives Report on "The Theory and Practice of Civic Globalism," held in Washington, D.C., January 2001

BHIKHU PAREKH *is a professor of politics and Asian studies at Hull University and member of the British House of Lords.*

Faith-Based Initiatives

BY RAY TAKEYH

The televised footage of an airliner crashing into the World Trade Center is now the prevailing image of Islam. Media pundits decry anti-Muslim bigotry and hasten to remind the public that Islam is a religion of peace and tolerance, notwithstanding the actions of an extremist minority. But in the same breath many of those pundits warn of a clash of civilizations—a war that pits the secular, modernized West against a region mired in ancient hatreds and fundamentalist rage.

This simplistic choice between "Islam" and "modernity" ignores a third option that is emerging throughout the Middle East. Lost amidst the din of cultural saber-rattling are the voices calling for an Islamic reformation: A new generation of theological thinkers, led by figures such as Iranian President Muhammad Khatami and Tunisian activist Rached Ghannouchi, is reconsidering the orthodoxies of Islamic politics. In the process, such leaders are demonstrating that the region may be capable of generating a genuinely democratic order, one based on indigenous values. For the Middle East today, moderate Islam may be democracy's last hope. For the West, it might represent one of the best long-term solutions to "winning" the war against Middle East terrorism.

Militant Islam continues to tempt those on the margins of society (and guides anachronistic forces such as Afghanistan's Taliban and Palestine's Islamic Jihad), but its moment has passed. In Iran, the Grand Ayatollah's autocratic order degenerated into corruption and economic stagnation. Elsewhere, the Islamic radicals' campaign of terror—such as Gamma al-Islamiyya in Egypt and Hezbollah in Lebanon—failed to produce any political change, as their violence could not overcome the brutality of the states they encountered. The militants' incendiary rhetoric and terrorism only triggered public revulsion, not revolutions and mass uprisings. Indeed, the Arab populace may have returned to religion over the last two decades, but they turned to a religion that called for a violent displacement of the existing order with utopias.

Political Islam as a viable reform movement might have petered out were it not for one minor detail: The rest of the world was changing. The collapse of the Soviet Union and the emergence of democratic regimes in Eastern Europe, Latin America, and East Asia electrified the Arab populace. Their demands were simple but profound. As one Egyptian university student explained in 1993, "I want what they have in Poland, and Czechoslovakia. Freedom of thought and freedom of speech." In lecture halls, street cafes, and mosques, long dormant ideas of representation, identity, authenticity, and pluralism began to arise.

The task of addressing the population's demand for a pluralistic society consistent with traditional values was left to a new generation of Islamist thinkers, who have sought to legitimize democratic concepts through the reinterpretation of Islamic texts and traditions. Tunisia's Ghannouchi captures this spirit of innovation by stressing, "Islam did not come with a specific program concerning life. It is our duty to formulate this program through interaction between Islamic precepts and modernity." Under these progressive readings, the well-delineated Islamic concept of *shura* (consultation) compels a ruler to consider popular opinion and establishes the foundation for an accountable government. In a modern context, such consultation can be implemented through the standard tools of democracy: elections, plebiscites, and referendums. The Islamic motion of *ijma* (consensus) has been similarly accommodated to serve as a theological basis for majoritarian rule. For Muslim reformers, Prophet Mohammed's injunction that "differences of opinion within my community is a sign of God's mercy" denotes prophetic approbation of diversity of thought and freedom of speech.

The new generation of Islamists has quickly embraced the benefits wrought by modernization and globalization in order to forge links between Islamist groups and thinkers in the various states of the Middle East. Through mosques, Islamists easily distribute pamphlets, tracts, and cassettes of Islamic thinkers and writers. In today's Middle East, one can easily find the Egyptian Brotherhood's magazine *Al-Dawa* in bookstores in the Persian Gulf while the Jordanian Islamist daily *Al-Sabil* enjoys wide circulation throughout the Levant. The advent of the internet has intensified such cross-pollination, as most Islamist journals, lectures, and conference proceedings are posted on the Web. The writings of Iranian philosopher Abdol Karim Soroush today appear in Islamic curricula across the region, and Egypt's Islamist liberal Hassan Hanafi commands an important audience in Iran's seminaries.

In the future, such Islamists will likely vie to succeed the region's discredited military rulers and lifetime presidents. But what will a prospective Islamic democracy look like? Undoubtedly, Islamic democracy will differ in important ways from the model in post-Reformation Europe. Western systems elevated the primacy of the individual above the community and thus changed the role of religion from that of the public conveyor of community values to a private guide for individual conscience. In contrast, an Islamic democracy's attempt to balance its emphasis on reverence with the popular desire for self-expression will impose certain limits on individual choice. An Islamic polity will support fundamental tenets of democracy—namely, regular elections, separation of powers, an independent judiciary, and institutional opposition—but it is unlikely to be a libertarian paradise.

The question of gender rights is an excellent example of the strengths—and limits—of an Islamic democracy. The Islamists who rely on women's votes, grass-roots activism, and participation in labor markets cannot remain deaf to women's demands for equality. Increasingly, Islamic reformers suggest the cause of women's failure to achieve equality is not religion but custom. The idea of black-clad women passively accepting the dictates of superior males is the province of Western caricatures. Iran's parliament, cabinet, and universities are populated with women, as are the candidate lists for Islamic opposition parties in Egypt and Turkey. But while an Islamic democracy will not impede women's integration into public affairs, it will impose restrictions on them, particularly in the realm of family law and dress codes. In such an order, women can make significant progress, yet in important ways they may still lag behind their Western counterparts.

Moderate Islamists are likely to be most liberal in the realm of economic policy. The failure of command economies in the Middle East and the centrality of global markets to the region's economic rehabilitation have made minimal government intervention appealing to Islamist theoreticians. Moreover, a privatized economy is consistent with classical Islamic economic theory and its well-established protection of market and commerce. The Islamist parties have been among the most persistent critics of state restrictions on trade and measures that obstruct opportunities for middle-class entrepreneurs.

The international implications of the emergence of Islamic democracies are also momentous. While revolutionary Islam could not easily coexist with the international system, moderate Islam can serve as a bridge between civilizations. The coming to power of moderate Islamists throughout the Middle East might lead to a lessening of tensions both within the region and between it and other parts of the world. Today, security experts talk of the need to "drain the swamps" and deprive terrorists of the state sponsorship that provides the protection and funding to carry out their war against the West. Within a more open and democratic system, dictatorial regimes would enjoy less freedom to support terrorism or engage in military buildups without any regard for economic consequences.

Ultimately, however, the integration of an Islamic democracy into global democratic society would depend on the willingness of the West to accept an Islamic variant on liberal democracy. Islamist moderates, while conceding that there are in fact certain "universal" democratic values, maintain that different civilization must be able to express these values in a context that is acceptable and appropriate to their particular region. Moderate Islamists, therefore, will continue to struggle against any form of U.S. hegemony, whether in political or cultural terms, and are much more comfortable with a multipolar, multi-"civilizational" international system. Khatami's call for a "dialogue of civilizations" presupposes that there is no single universal standard judging the effectiveness of democracy and human rights.

Certainly, the West should resist totalitarian states who use the rhetoric of democracy while rejecting its essence through false claims of cultural authenticity. But even though an Islamic democracy will resist certain elements of post-Enlightenment liberalism, it will still be a system that features regular elections, accepts dissent and opposition parties, and condones a free press and division of power between branches of states. As such, any fair reading of Islamic democracy will reveal that it is a genuine effort to conceive a system of government responsive to popular will. And this effort is worthy of Western acclaim.

Reproduced with permission from Foreign Policy #127 *(November/December 2001). Copyright 2001 by the Carnegie Endowment for International Peace.*

RAY TAKEYH *is a Soref research fellow at the Washington Institute for Near East Policy and the author of* The Receding Shadow of the Prophet: Radical Islamic Movements in the Modern Middle East *(New York: Praeger, forthcoming).*

On Globalization and Human Rights

BY MARTIN PALOUŠ

The globalization or complex interdependence which characterizes life at the end of the twentieth century has important positive implications, but it has also introduced some negative, hidden agendas: international crime generating enormous amounts of money used to infiltrate and corrupt the political elites; the growing vulnerability in the population to extremist views; an epidemic of nationalistic and anti-foreigner rhetoric of the most disreputable kind; the disintegration of basic social patterns and structures in some countries or whole regions. These and other phenomena represent the dark side of our post-modern, increasingly globalized situation.

Can we meet the enormous challenge of transforming a closed political regime into a republican form of government, and at the same time deal with the problem of a newly emerging international system—a new world order? There is one aspect in the dramatically changing realm of international relations which was quite underestimated in the "realpolitik" of the past and should be taken much more seriously. It is the internationalization of human rights— the emergence of international mechanisms for their protection—as a reaction to the unprecedented crimes committed by totalitarian criminal regimes during World War II, that represents, arguably, the most important change in world politics in the second half of the twentieth century. The demise of the bipolar system in Europe only accelerated and strengthened this development. The issue of human rights has now lost the dimension of ideological confrontation. The existence of international human rights law—which deals with the protection of individuals and groups against violations of their rights by state governments—has an increasing impact on theformation, self-perception and practices of the international community. Respect for international legal norms, active participation in their creation and observance, become essential conditions for twenty-first Century international relations—and for the creation of a truly transnational human community. It seems to me that it is this new type of communication, a kind of dialogue of humankind, which is the best, and perhaps the only possible "republican way" for our time, to preserve the freedom which is still the essence of our humanity.

For information about MARTIN PALOUŠ, *see page 182.*

On Interdependence

BY BENJAMIN R. BARBER

How can the myth of independence survive September 11? The [U.S.] Declaration of Independence that announced a new coming, a new kind of society, has achieved its task of nation-building. To build the new world that is now required calls for a new Declaration of Interdependence, a declaration recognizing the interdependence of a human race that can no longer survive in fragments—whether the pieces are called nations or tribes, peoples or markets. There are no oceans wide enough to protect a nation from a tainted atmosphere or a spreading plague, no walls high enough to defend a people against a corrupt ideology or a vengeful prophet, no security strict enough to keep a determined martyr from his sacrificial rounds. Nor is any nation ever again likely to experience untroubled prosperity and plenty unless others are given the same opportunity; suffering too has been democratized and those most likely to experience it will find a way to compel those most remote from it to share the pain. If there cannot be an equity of justice there will be an equity of injustice, if all cannot partake in plenty, impoverishment—both material and spiritual—will be the common lot. That is the hard lesson of interdependence.

To declare interdependence is then in a sense merely to acknowledge what is already a reality. It is to embrace willingly and constructively a fate terrorists would like to shove down our throats. Their message is: "your sons want to live, ours are ready to die." Our response must be: "we will create a world in which the seductions of death hold no allure because the bounties of life are accessible to everyone."

Pope John Paul said in his Apostolic Exhortation on the Mission of the Roman Catholic Church in the Americas: "If globalization is ruled merely by the laws of the market applied to suit the powerful, the consequences cannot but be negative."[1] Of course one expects the Pope to moralize in this fashion. More startling is a similar message from another more powerful [leader] of the secular world, who wrote recently: "You hear talk about a new financial order, about an international bankruptcy law, about transparency, and more…but you don't hear a word about people….Two billion people live on less than two dollars a day….We live in a world that gradually is getting worse and worse and worse. It is not hopeless, but we must do something about it now." The moralist here is the hardheaded James Wolfensohn, President of the World Bank, who has begun to replace the bank's traditional energy and industrialization projects thought to favor the interests of foreign investors with environmental and health projects aimed at the interests of the populations being directly served.[2]…

---

[1]Pope John Paul's Apostolic Exhortation, cited in *The New York Times*, January 24, 1999.
[2]James. D. Wolfensohn, President of the World Bank. Cited by Jim Hoagland, "Richer and Poorer," *Washington Post National Weekly Edition*, May 3, 1999, p. 5.

George Soros has labeled market fundamentalism (an appropriate implicit comparison to Jihadic fundamentalism) as an ideology that saps democracy by attacking government and its culture of public power. By arguing that markets can do everything government once did better than government, and with more freedom for citizens, privatization within nation states opens the way for a deregulation of markets that in turn facilitates the globalization of the economy. It softens up citizens to accept the decline of political institutions and tries to persuade them that they will be better off—more "free"—when their collective democratic voice is stilled, when they think of themselves not as public citizens but private consumers. Consumers are poor substitutes for citizens, however, as corporate CEOs are poor substitutes for statesmen. It is telling that on the morning of September 12, no American called Bill Gates or Michael Eisner to ask for assistance in dealing with terrorism. Long neglected public institutions reacquired overnight their democratic legitimacy and their role as defenders of public goods. Can this renewed legitimacy be employed on behalf of international institutions dedicated to public rather than private goods? If it can, new forms of civic interdependence can be quickly established....Consumer choice is always and necessarily private and personal choice. Private choices, autonomous or not, cannot affect public outcomes. Democratic governance is not just about choosing, it is about public choosing, about dealing with the social consequences of private choices and behavior. In the global sector this is crucial, because only public and democratic decisions can establish social justice and equity. Private markets cannot, not because they are capitalist but because they are private. In Rousseau's language, through participation in the general will, global citizens can regulate the private wills of global consumers and global corporations....

Only a struggle of democracy against not only Jihad but also McWorld can achieve a just victory for the planet. A just, diverse, democratic world will put commerce and consumerism back in its place and make space for religion; it will combat the terrors of Jihad not by making war on it but by creating a world in which the practice of religion is as secure as the practice of consumption and in which the defense of cultural values is not in tension with liberty but part of how liberty is defined. Terror feeds off of the parasitic dialectics of Jihad and McWorld. In a democratic world order, there will be no need for militant Jihad because belief will have a significant place; and there will be no advantage to McWorld because cultural variety will confront it on every television station and at every mall, the world over. When Jihad and McWorld have vanished as primary categories, terror may not wholly disappear (it is lodged in a small but impregnable crevice in the dark regions of the human soul), but it will become irrelevant to the hopes and aspirations of women and men who will have learned to love life too much to confuse religion with the courtship of death.

From Jihad vs. McWorld *(New York: Ballantine Books, 2001).*

For information about Benjamin R. Barber, *see page 101.*

⸎

FROM
"the 2001 Nobel Lecture"
by Kofi Annan

...The idea that there is one people in possession of the truth, one answer to the world's ills, or one solution to humanity's needs, has done untold harm throughout history—especially in the last century. Today, however, even amidst continuing ethnic conflict around the world, there is a growing understanding that human diversity is both the reality that makes dialogue necessary, and the very basis for that dialogue.

We understand, as never before, that each of us is fully worthy of the respect and dignity essential to our common humanity. We recognize that we are the products of many cultures, traditions and memories; that mutual respect allows us to study and learn from other cultures; and that we gain strength by combining the foreign with the familiar.

In every great faith and tradition one can find the values of tolerance and mutual understanding. The Qur'an, for example, tells us that "We created you from a single pair of male and female and made you into nations and tribes, that you may know each other." Confucius urged his followers: "When the good way prevails in the state, speak boldly and act boldly. When the state has lost the way, act boldly and speak softly." In the Jewish tradition, the injunction to "love thy neighbour as thyself," is considered to be the very essence of the Torah.

This thought is reflected in the Christian Gospel, which also teaches us to love our enemies and pray for those who wish to persecute us. Hindus are taught that "truth is one, the sages give it various names." And in the Buddhist tradition, individuals are urged to act with compassion in every facet of life.

Each of us has the right to take pride in our particular faith or heritage. But the notion that what is ours is necessarily in conflict with what is theirs is both false and dangerous. It has resulted in endless enmity and conflict, leading men to commit the greatest of crimes in the name of a higher power.

It need not be so. People of different religions and cultures live side by side in almost every part of the world, and most of us have overlapping identities which unite us with very different groups. We can love what we are, without hating what—and who—we are not. We can thrive in our own tradition, even as we learn from others, and come to respect their teachings.

This will not be possible, however, without freedom of religion, of expression, of assembly, and basic equality under the law. Indeed, the lesson of the past century has been that where the dignity of the individual has been trampled or threatened—where citizens have not enjoyed the basic right to choose their government, or the right to change it regularly—conflict has too often followed, with innocent civilians paying the price, in lives cut short and communities destroyed.

The obstacles to democracy have little to do with culture or religion, and much more to do with the desire of those in power to maintain their position at any cost. This is neither a new phenomenon nor one confined to any particular part of the world. People of all cultures value their freedom of choice, and feel the need to have a say in decisions affecting their lives.

The United Nations, whose membership comprises almost all the States in the world, is founded on the principle of the equal worth of every human being. It is the nearest thing we have to a representative institution that can address the interests of all states, and all peoples. Through this universal, indispensable instrument of human progress, States can serve the interests of their citizens by recognizing common interests and pursuing them in unity. No doubt, that is why the Nobel Committee says that it "wishes, in its centenary year, to proclaim that the only negotiable route to global peace and cooperation goes by way of the United Nations."

I believe the Committee also recognized that this era of global challenges leaves no choice but cooperation at the global level. When States undermine the rule of law and violate the rights of their individual citizens, they become a menace not only to their own people, but also to their neighbours, and indeed the world. What we need today is better governance—legitimate, democratic governance that allows each individual to flourish, and each State to thrive.

...I began my address with a reference to the girl born in Afghanistan today. Even though her mother will do all in her power to protect and sustain her, there is a one-in-four risk that she will not live to see her fifth birthday. Whether she does is just one test of our common humanity—of our belief in our individual responsibility for our fellow men and women. But it is the only test that matters.

Remember this girl and then our larger aims—to fight poverty, prevent conflict, or cure disease—will not seem distant, or impossible. Indeed, those aims will seem very near, and very achievable—as they should. Because beneath the surface of states and nations, ideas and language, lies the fate of individual human beings in need. Answering their needs will be the mission of the United Nations in the century to come.

The Nobel Lecture, given by the 2001 Nobel Peace Prize Laureate, Kofi Annan, Oslo, December 10, 2001.

Kofi Annan *is secretary-general of the United Nations. He was awarded the Nobel Peace Prize, along with the United Nations, in 2001.*

Documents

The Declaration of Independence

THE UNANIMOUS DECLARATION OF THE THIRTEEN UNITED STATES OF AMERICA

When in the Course of human events, it becomes necessary for one people to dissolve the political bands which have connected them with another, and to assume among the Powers of the earth, the separate and equal station to which the Laws of Nature and of Nature's God entitle them, a decent respect to the opinions of mankind requires that they should declare the causes which impel them to the separation.

We hold these truths to be self-evident, that all men are created equal, that they are endowed by their Creator with certain unalienable Rights, that among these are Life, Liberty and the pursuit of Happiness. That to secure these rights, Governments are instituted among Men, deriving their just powers from the consent of the governed. That whenever any Form of Government becomes destructive of these ends, it is the Right of the People to alter or to abolish it, and to institute new Government, laying its foundation on such principles and organizing its powers in such form, as to them shall seem most likely to effect their Safety and Happiness. Prudence, indeed, will dictate that Governments long established should not be changed for light and transient causes; and accordingly all experience hath shown that mankind are most disposed to suffer, while evils are sufferable, than to right themselves by abolishing the forms to which they are accustomed. But when a long train of abuses and usurpations, pursuing invariably the same Object evinces a design to reduce them under absolute Despotism, it is their right, it is their duty, to throw off such Government, and to provide new Guards for their future security.—Such has been the patient sufferance of these Colonies; and such is now the necessity which constrains them to alter their former Systems of Government. The history of the present King of Great Britain is a history of repeated injuries and usurpations, all having in direct object the establishment of an absolute Tyranny over these States. To prove this, let Facts be submitted to a candid world.

[petition of 27 specific grievances]

In every stage of these Oppressions We have Petitioned for Redress in the most humble terms: Our repeated Petitions have been answered only by repeated injury. A Prince, whose character is thus marked by every act which may define a Tyrant, is unfit to be the ruler of a free People.

Nor have We been wanting in attention to our British brethren. We have warned them from time to time of attempts by their legislature to extend an unwarrantable jurisdiction over us. We have reminded them of the circumstances of our emigration and settlement here. We have appealed to their native justice and magnanimity, and we have conjured them by the ties of our common kindred to disavow these usurpations, which would inevitably interrupt our connections and correspondence. They too have been deaf to the voice of justice and of consanguinity. We must, therefore, acquiesce in the necessity, which denounces our Separation, and hold them, as we hold the rest of mankind, Enemies in War, in Peace Friends.

We, therefore, the Representatives of the United States of America, in General Congress, Assembled, appealing to the Supreme Judge of the world for the rectitude of our intentions, do, in the Name, and by Authority of the good People of these Colonies, solemnly publish and declare, That these United Colonies are, and of Right ought to be Free and Independent States; that they are Absolved from all Allegiance to the British Crown, and that all political connection between them and the State of Great Britain, is and ought to be totally dissolved; and that as Free and Independent States, they have full Power to levy War, conclude Peace, contract Alliances, establish Commerce, and to do all other Acts and Things which Independent States may of right do. And for the support of this Declaration, with a firm reliance on the Protection of Divine Providence, we mutually pledge to each other our Lives, our Fortunes and our sacred Honor.

July 4, 1776

The Constitution of the United States

PREAMBLE

We the People of the United States, in Order to form a more perfect Union, establish Justice, insure domestic Tranquility, provide for the common defense, promote the general Welfare, and secure the Blessings of Liberty to ourselves and our Posterity, do ordain and establish this Constitution for the United States of America.

THE BILL OF RIGHTS

Amendment I
Congress shall make no law respecting an establishment of religion, or prohibiting the free exercise thereof; or abridging the freedom of speech, or of the press; or the right of the people peaceably to assemble, and to petition the government for a redress of grievances.

Amendment II
A well regulated Militia, being necessary to the security of a free State, the right of the people to keep and bear Arms, shall not be infringed.

Amendment III
No Soldier shall, in time of peace be quartered in any house, without the consent of the Owner, nor in time of war, but in a manner to be prescribed by law.

Amendment IV
The right of the people to be secure in their persons, houses, papers, and effects, against unreasonable searches and seizures, shall not be violated, and no Warrants shall issue, but upon probable cause, supported by Oath or affirmation, and particularly describing the place to be searched, and the persons or things to be seized.

Amendment V
No person shall be held to answer for a capital, or otherwise infamous crime, unless on a presentment or indictment of a Grand Jury, except in cases arising in the land or naval forces, or in the Militia, when in actual service in time of War or public danger; nor shall any person be subject for the same offense to be twice put in jeopardy of life or limb; nor shall be compelled in any criminal case to be a witness against himself, nor be deprived of life, liberty, or property, without due process of law; nor shall private property be taken for public use, without just compensation.

Amendment VI
In all criminal prosecutions, the accused shall enjoy the right to a speedy and public trial, by an impartial jury of the State and district wherein the crime shall have been committed, which district shall have been previously ascertained by law, and to be informed of the nature and cause of the accusation; to be confronted with

the witnesses against him; to have compulsory process for obtaining witnesses in his favor, and to have the Assistance of Counsel for his defense.

Amendment VII

In Suits at common law, where the value in controversy shall exceed twenty dollars, the right of trial by jury shall be preserved, and no fact tried by a jury, shall be otherwise reexamined in any Court of the United States, than according to the rules of the common law.

Amendment VIII

Excessive bail shall not be required, nor excessive fines imposed, nor cruel and unusual punishments inflicted.

Amendment IX

The enumeration in the Constitution, of certain rights, shall not be construed to deny or disparage others retained by the people.

Amendment X

The powers not delegated to the United States by the Constitution, nor prohibited by it to the States, are reserved to the States respectively, or to the people.

March 4, 1789

The Gettysburg Address

ADDRESS DELIVERED AT THE DEDICATION OF THE CEMETERY AT GETTYSBURG, PENNSYLVANIA

Four score and seven years ago our fathers brought forth on this continent, a new nation, conceived in Liberty, and dedicated to the proposition that all men are created equal.

Now we are engaged in a great civil war, testing whether that nation, or any nation so conceived and so dedicated, can long endure. We are met on a great battlefield of that war. We have come to dedicate a portion of that field, as a final resting place for those who here gave their lives that that nation might live. It is altogether fitting and proper that we should do this.

But, in a larger sense, we can not dedicate—we can not consecrate—we can not hallow—this ground. The brave men, living and dead, who struggled here, have consecrated it, far above our poor power to add or detract. The world will little note, nor long remember what we say here, but it can never forget what they did here. It is for us the living, rather, to be dedicated here to the unfinished work which they who fought here have thus far so nobly advanced. It is rather for us to be here dedicated to the great task remaining before us—that from these honored dead we take increased devotion to that cause for which they gave the last full measure of devotion—that we here highly resolve that these dead shall not have died in vain—that this nation, under God, shall have a new birth of freedom—and that government of the people, by the people, for the people, shall not perish from the earth.

November 19, 1863
Abraham Lincoln

Universal Declaration of Human Rights
ADOPTED AND PROCLAIMED BY THE GENERAL ASSEMBLY OF THE UNITED NATIONS ON DECEMBER 10, 1948.

PREAMBLE

WHEREAS recognition of the inherent dignity and of the equal and inalienable rights of all members of the human family is the foundation of freedom, justice and peace in the world,

WHEREAS disregard and contempt for human rights have resulted in barbarous acts which have outraged the conscience of mankind, and the advent of a world in which human beings shall enjoy freedom of speech and belief and freedom from fear and want has been proclaimed as the highest aspiration of the common people,

WHEREAS it is essential, if man is not to be compelled to have recourse, as a last resort, to rebellion against tyranny and oppression, that human rights should be protected by the rule of law,

WHEREAS it is essential to promote the development of friendly relations between nations,

WHEREAS the peoples of the United Nations have in the Charter reaffirmed their faith in fundamental human rights, in the dignity and worth of the human person and in the equal rights of men and women and have determined to promote social progress and better standards of life in larger freedom,

WHEREAS Member States have pledged themselves to achieve, in co-operation with the United Nations, the promotion of universal respect for and observance of human rights and fundamental freedoms,

WHEREAS a common understanding of these rights and freedoms is of the greatest importance for the full realization of this pledge,

Now, therefore,

THE GENERAL ASSEMBLY proclaims THIS UNIVERSAL DECLARATION OF HUMAN RIGHTS as a common standard of achievement for all peoples and all nations, to the end that every individual and every organ of society, keeping this Declaration constantly in mind, shall strive by teaching and education to promote respect for these rights and freedoms and by progressive measures, national and international, to secure their universal and effective recognition and observance, both among the peoples of Member States themselves and among the peoples of territories under their jurisdiction.

FROM
Charter 77

...**R**esponsibility for the maintenance of civil rights in our country naturally devolves in the first place on the political and state authorities. Yet not only on them: everyone bears his or her share of responsibility for the conditions that prevail and accordingly also for the observance of legally enshrined agreements, binding upon all individuals as well as upon governments.

It is this sense of co-responsibility, our belief in the importance of its conscious public acceptance and the general need to give it new and more effective expression, that led us to the idea of creating Charter 77, whose inception we today publicly announce.

Charter 77 is a loose, informal and open association of people of various shades of opinions, faiths and professions united by the will to strive individually and collectively for the respecting of civil and human rights in our own country and throughout the world—rights accorded to all people by the [International Covenant on Civil and Political Rights and the International Covenant on Economic, Social and Cultural Rights], by the Final Act of the Helsinki conference and by numerous other international documents opposing war, violence and social or spiritual oppression, and which are comprehensively laid down in the United Nations Universal Declaration of Human Rights.

Charter 77 springs from a background of friendship and solidarity among people who share our concern for those ideals that have inspired, and continue to inspire, their lives and their work.

Charter 77 is not an organization; it has no rules, permanent bodies or formal membership. It embraces everyone who agrees with its ideas and participates in its work. It does not form the basis for any oppositional political activity. Like many similar citizen initiatives in various countries, West and East, it seeks to promote the general public interest.

It does not aim, then, to set out its own platform of political or social reform or change, but within its own field of impact to conduct a constructive dialogue with the political and state authorities, particularly by drawing attention to individual cases where human and civil rights are violated, to document such grievances and suggest remedies, to make proposals of a more general character calculated to reinforce such rights and machinery for protecting them, to act as intermediary in situations of conflict which may lead to violation of rights, and so forth.

By its symbolic name, Charter 77 denotes that it has come into being at the start of a year proclaimed as Political Prisoners' Year—a year in which a conference in Belgrade is due to review the implementation of the obligations assumed at Helsinki.

As signatories, we hereby authorize Professor Dr. Jan Patočka, Václav Havel and Professor Jiří Hájek to act as the spokespersons for the Charter. These spokespersons are endowed with full authority to represent it *vis-à-vis* state and other bodies, and the public at home and abroad, and their signatures attest to the authenticity of documents issued by the Charter. They will have us, and others who join us as their colleagues, taking part in any necessary negotiations, shouldering particular tasks and sharing every responsibility.

We believe that Charter 77 will help to enable all the citizens of Czechoslovakia to work and live as free human beings.

Prague, January 1, 1977

Preamble to the Constitution of Mongolia 1992

We, the people of Mongolia:

- Consolidating the independence and sovereignty of the nation,
- Cherishing human rights and freedoms, justice and national unity,
- Inheriting the traditions of national statehood, history and culture,
- Respecting the accomplishments of human civilization,
- Aspiring to the supreme objective of building a humane and democratic civil society in the country,

Hereby proclaim the Constitution of Mongolia.

The Ten Commitments

COPENHAGEN DECLARATION AND PROGRAMME OF ACTION,
WORLD SUMMIT FOR SOCIAL DEVELOPMENT, 1995

COMMITMENT 1

We commit ourselves to creating an economic, political, social, cultural and legal environment that will enable people to achieve social development.

COMMITMENT 2

We commit ourselves to the goal of eradicating poverty in the world, through decisive national actions and international cooperation, as an ethical, social, political and economic imperative of human kind.

COMMITMENT 3

We commit ourselves to promoting the goal of full employment as a basic priority of our economic and social policies, and to enabling all men and women to attain secure and sustainable livelihoods through freely chosen productive employment and work.

COMMITMENT 4

We commit ourselves to promoting social integration by fostering societies that are stable, safe and just and that are based on the promotion and protection of all human rights, as well as on non-discrimination, tolerance, respect for diversity, equality of opportunity, solidarity, security, and participation of all people, including disadvantaged and vulnerable groups and persons.

COMMITMENT 5

We commit ourselves to promoting full respect for human dignity and to achieving equality and equity between women and men, and to recognizing and enhancing the participation and leadership roles of women in political, civil, economic, social and cultural life and in development.

COMMITMENT 6

We commit ourselves to promoting and attaining the goals of universal and equitable access to quality education, the highest attainable standard of physical and mental health, and the access of all to primary health care, making particular efforts to rectify inequalities relating to social conditions and without distinction as to race, national origin, gender, age or disability; respecting and promoting our common and particular cultures; striving to strengthen the role of culture in development; preserving the essential bases of people-centred sustainable development; and to social development. The purpose of these activities is to eradicate poverty, promote full and productive employment and foster social integration.

COMMITMENT 7

We commit ourselves to accelerating the economic, social and human resource development of Africa and the least developed countries.

COMMITMENT 8

We commit ourselves to ensuring that when structural adjustment programmes are agreed to they include social development goals, in particular eradicating poverty, promoting full and productive employment, and enhancing social integration.

COMMITMENT 9

We commit ourselves to increasing significantly and/or utilizing more efficiently the resources allocated to social development in order to achieve the goals of the Summit through national action and regional and international cooperation.

COMMITMENT 10

We commit ourselves to an improved and strengthened framework for international, regional and subregional cooperation for social development, in a spirit of partnership, through the United Nations and other multilateral institutions.

Constitution of the Republic of South Africa
FOUNDING PROVISIONS

REPUBLIC OF SOUTH AFRICA

The Republic of South Africa is one sovereign democratic state founded on the following values:

(a) Human dignity, the achievement of equality and advancement of human rights and freedoms.

(b) Non-racialism and non-sexism.

(c) Supremacy of the Constitution and the rule of law.

(d) Universal adult suffrage, a national common voters roll, regular elections, and a multi-party system of democratic government, to ensure accountability, responsiveness and openness.

SUPREMACY OF CONSTITUTION

This Constitution is the supreme law of the Republic; law or conduct inconsistent with it is invalid, and the duties imposed by it must be performed.

CITIZENSHIP

(1) There is a common South African citizenship.

(2) All citizens are:

(a) equally entitled to the rights, privileges and benefits of citizenship; and

(b) equally subject to the duties and responsibilities of citizenship.

(3) National legislation must provide for the acquisition, loss and restoration of citizenship.

NATIONAL ANTHEM

The national anthem of the Republic is determined by the President by proclamation.

NATIONAL FLAG

The national flag of the Republic is black, gold, green, white, red and blue, as described and sketched in Schedule 1.

LANGUAGES

(1) The official languages of the Republic are Sepedi, Sesotho, Setswana, siSiswati, Tshivenda, Xitsonga, Afrikaans, English, isiNdebele, isiXhosa and isiZulu.

(2) Recognising the historically diminished use and status of the indigenous languages of our people, the state must take practical and positive measures to elevate the status and advance the use of these languages.

(3) National and provincial governments may use particular official languages for the purposes of government, taking into account usage, practicality, expense, regional circumstances, and the balance of the needs and preferences of the population as a whole or in respective provinces; provided that no national or provincial government may use only one official language. Municipalities must take into consideration the language usage and preferences of their residents.

(4) National and provincial governments, by legislative and other measures, must regulate and monitor the use by those governments of official languages. Without detracting from the provisions of subsection (2), all official languages must enjoy parity of esteem and must be treated equitably.

(5) The Pan South African Language Board must

    (a) promote and create conditions for the development and use of

        (i) all official languages;

        (ii) the Khoi, Nama and San languages; and

        (iii) sign language.

    (b) promote and ensure respect for languages, including German, Greek, Gujarati, Hindi, Portuguese, Tamil, Telugu, Urdu, and others commonly used by communities in South Africa, and Arabic, Hebrew, Sanskrit and others used for religious purposes.

1996

The La Pietra Recommendations

1. The OECD should ensure that bribe payments to foreign political parties and their officials are effectively prohibited by its instruments. Such a prohibition should cover bribe payments made "to obtain or retain business or other improper advantage" in order to have the same scope as the prohibition against the bribing of foreign public officials.

2. Governments should take effective action to implement such a prohibition in a manner consistent with their legal systems. In some countries such action could include a prohibition against "trading in influence," as provided for in the Council of Europe's Criminal Law Convention Against Corruption.

3. In order to achieve greater transparency, political parties in the signatory states of the OECD Convention should be required to make prompt and appropriate disclosure of contributions and expenditures. Corporations should also be required publicly to report political contributions and to comply with reporting and other requirements imposed by the countries where such contributions are made.

4. The signatory states of the OECD Convention should prohibit corporations based in their own countries from making political party contributions in violation of the laws of the foreign countries where the contributions are made.

5. The development of effective mechanisms to deal with bribery within the private sector is a matter of growing urgency. Action in this area may also be a means by which to address aspects of political party corruption.

The participants agreed that their proposals should be submitted formally to the OECD Working Group on Bribery. They also agreed to function as a continuing advisory group to assist Transparency International in promoting reform of political financing, at the OECD and in other national and international fora.

La Pietra, Italy
14 October 2000

These recommendations were made by participants in a meeting sponsored by Transparency International at the Villa La Pietra, Florence, Italy, October 12-14, 2000. The purpose of the meeting was to review issues relating to corruption and political party financing, particularly in the context of the *OECD[1] Convention on Combating Bribery of Foreign Public Officials in International Business Transactions.*

A Joint Civil Society Statement on the Tragedy in the United States

Following the attacks in the United States on September 11, [2001], CIVICUS convened a global meeting of civil society organisations (CSOs) in London. With the support of Actionaid and other transnational CSOs, CIVICUS facilitated the drafting of a 'Joint Civil Society Statement on the Tragedy in the United States'. This statement has been endorsed by hundreds of organizations and individuals around the world,

---

[1] Organization for Economic Co-Operation and Development

and has been presented to national and international policy- and decision-makers as a united appeal by civil society activists. Below is the statement....

In the wake of the tragic events that took place in the United States of America on 11th September 2001, we wish to extend our deepest condolences to all who have lost loved ones and to the millions more whose lives have been affected. The horrific scenes we have witnessed remind us that all too often, in many places around the world, innocent people are the victims of conflict and aggression beyond their control.

During this time of shared grief, we pay tribute to citizens, non-profit organizations and rescue workers whose acts of bravery and volunteerism sum up the best of our common humanity. We urge continued support for the important work being done by a range of civil society organizations to help people affected by this current crisis as well as by the increasing political violence around the world.

At the global level, we want to raise our voices for peace, justice, human rights and the rule of law. Those who have planned, carried out or abetted these appalling crimes must be brought to justice. This tragedy makes plain the need for a system of international justice, relying on rules of evidence, proof of guilt, respect for rights and due judicial process.

We should resist efforts to target people because of their race, religion, ethnic background or appearance, including immigrants in general and people of the Islamic faith and Arab community in particular. We note with great concern the attacks against people believed to be Muslims or from the Arab community and the desecration of mosques and Sikh Temples.

Great care must be taken in the use of language and images. Neither justice nor peace will be served by the demonisation of particular communities. As leaders in civil society, we have an obligation to ensure that every part of the community is respected, that its voice can be heard, and that human rights and public safety for all are upheld. We appeal to the media to act responsibly in their use of imagery or inflammatory language. We also wish to stress the vital role of information and communications to promote informed debate and decision-making.

While emotions are running high, we urge restraint on the part of political leaders. To react with wisdom and long-term effect, leaders must not act in haste, unilaterally, or indiscriminately. We call for a strong commitment to human rights, international law and humanitarian concern in any actions that are taken. We should be motivated by the demand for justice, not revenge, and by the pursuit of peace, exhausting all peaceful measures so that many more innocent victims do not suffer.

We feel strongly that there is no purely military solution to the kinds of acts that we saw last week. Indeed, the blunt instrument of war may further intensify a cycle of violence and attract new recruits to terror.

We do not underestimate the difficulty or the urgency of the task facing political leaders. But we are convinced that a safer world for all can only be achieved by the extension of human rights and the rule of law. As they act to prevent such attacks in the future, we urge governments to uphold the fundamental civil liberties that underpin democratic participation. We believe that in a world afflicted by vast inequality, governments and citizens alike have a responsibility to work for sustainable development and social inclusion. Across the whole range of non-profit activities for the public good, we encourage civil society organizations to redouble their efforts to weave anew the torn fabric of our lives.

We appeal to world leaders to protect and strengthen the institutions of civil society. We believe firmly that robust local and national communities linked internationally and inspired by an ethos of compassion and tolerance are our best defence against those who would sow hate and destruction.

A key strength of civil society is its diversity. We, as a group of concerned organisations, encourage our colleagues in civil society across the world to give practical expression to the objectives of this statement in ways they deem most appropriate. In addition, we invite other organisations to add their endorsement to this statement.

Finally, we hope that from the pain and sorrow of recent events hope may yet rise again for the establishment of a more peaceful, just and sustainable world order.

Bibliography

Almond, Gabriel A. and Sidney Verba. *The Civic Culture: Political Attitudes and Democracy in Five Nations.* Rev. ed. Newbury Park, California: Sage Publications, 1989.

Achebe, Chinua. *A Man of the People.* Garden City, New York: Anchor Books, 1967.

Achebe, Chinua. *Ant Hills of the Savannah.* New York: Doubleday & Co., 1989.

Arblaster, Anthony. *Democracy.* Minneapolis: University of Minnesota Press, 1989.

Arendt, Hannah. *Eichmann in Jersualem: A Report on the Banality of Evil.* New York: Penguin, 1977.

Arendt, Hannah. *Origins of Totalitarianism.* Orlando, Florida: Harcourt Brace & Co., 1973.

Arendt, Hannah. "The Public Realm." *The Human Condition.* Chicago: University of Chicago Press, 1958.

Aristotle. *Politics.* Translated by Ernest Baker. New York: Oxford University Press, 1995.

Arrow, Kenneth Joseph. *Social Choice and Individual Values.* New York: Wiley, 1963.

Attali, Jacques. *Millennium: Winners and Losers in the Coming World Order.* Translated by Leila Conners and Nathan Gardels. New York: Times Books, 1991.

Ayittey, George B.N. *Africa in Chaos.* New York: St. Martin's Books, 1998.

Ayittey, George B.N. *Indigenous African Institutions.* Irvington-on-Hudson, New York: Transnational Publishers, Inc., 1991.

Axtmann, Roland. *Balancing Democracy.* London: Continuum, 2001.

Barber, Benjamin R. *Aristocracy of Everyone: The Politics of Education and the Future of America.* New York: Ballantine Books, 1992.

Barber, Benjamin R. *Jihad vs. McWorld.* New York: Ballantine Books, 2001.

Barber, Benjamin R. *Strong Democracy.* Berkeley: University of California Press, 1984.

Bellah, Robert N., Richard Madsen, William M. Sullivan, Ann Swidler, Steven M. Tipton. *Habits of the Heart*. Berkeley, California: University of California Press, 1996.

Bellah, Robert N., Richard Madsen, William M. Sullivan, Ann Swidler, Steven M. Tipton. *The Good Society*. New York: Alfred Knopf, 1991.

Berlin, Isaiah. *Four Essays on Liberty*. Oxford: Oxford University Press, 1979.

Boulding, Elise. *Building a Global Civic Culture*. New York: Columbia University Press, 1980.

Bryan, Frank and John McClaughry. *The Vermont Papers: Recreating Democracy on a Human Scale*. Post Mills, Vermont: Chelsea Green Publishing Co., 1989.

Bryson, John. *Leadership for the Common Good: Tackling Public Power in a Shared Power World*. San Francisco: Jossey-Bass, 1990.

Building Civil Society Worldwide: Strategies for Successful Communications. Washington, D.C.: CIVICUS, 1997.

Carley, Michael, Paul Jenkins, and Harry Smith. *Urban Development and Civil Society: The Role of Communities in Sustainable Cities*. Sterling, Virginia: Earthscan Publications, 2001.

Chrislip, David and Carl Larson. *Collaborative Leadership: How Citizens and Civic Leaders Can Make a Difference*. San Franciso: Jossey-Bass, 1994.

Dahl, Robert. *On Democracy*. New Haven, Connecticut: Yale University Press, 1998.

Dahl, Robert. *Polyarchy: Participation and Opposition*. New Haven, Connecticut: Yale University Press, 1971.

Dennis, Everette E. and Robert W. Snyder, eds. *Media & Democracy*. New Brunswick, New Jersey: Transaction Publishers, 1998.

De Ruggiero, Guido. *The History of European Liberalism*. Translated by R.G. Collingwood. London: Oxford University Press, 1927.

Dewey, John. *The Public and Its Problems*. Athens, Ohio: Swallow Press, 1954.

Diamond, Larry and Mark F. Plattner. *Nationalism, Ethnic Conflict and Democracy*. Baltimore: The Johns Hopkins University Press, 1994.

Dyson, Freeman. *Imagined Worlds*. Cambridge: Harvard University Press, 1997.

Eade, Deborah. *Development, NGOs, and Civil Society*. Oxford: Oxfam, 2000.

Eberly, Don E. *The Essential Civil Society Reader*. New York: Rowman and Littlefield Publications, Inc., 2000.

Eberly, Don E., ed. *Restoring the Good Society*. Grand Rapids, Michigan: Baker Books, 1994.

Edwards, Michael. *Future Positive*. London: Earthscan Publications Ltd., 1999.

Edwards, Michael and John Gaventa. *Global Citizen Action*. Boulder, Colorado: Lynne Rienner Publishers, 2001.

Esposito, John L. and John O. Voll. *Islam and Democracy*. New York: Oxford University Press, 1996.

Etzioni, Amitai. *The Spirit of Community: The Reinvention of American Society*. New York: Simon & Schuster, 1993.

Fang, Lizhi. *Bringing Down the Great Wall*. Translated and edited by James H. Williams. New York: Knopf, 1996.

Farrar, Cynthia. *The Origins of Democratic Thinking: The Invention of Politics in Classical Athens*. Cambridge: Cambridge University Press, 1988.

Fox, Leslie and Bruce Shearer, eds. *Sustaining Civil Society: Strategies for Resource Mobilization*. Washington, D.C.: CIVICUS, 1997.

Frantzich, Stephen E. *Citizen Democracy*. New York: Rowman and Littlefield Publishers, Inc., 1999.

Freedom Forum Media Studies Center. "Media and Democracy." *Media Studies Journal*. New York: Columbia University, 1995.

Gardner, Howard, Mihaly Csikszentimihalyi, and William Damon. *Good Work: When Excellence and Ethics Meet*. New York: Basic Books, 2001.

Gardner, John W. *On Leadership*. New York: The Free Press, 1990.

Garton Ash, Timothy. *The Magic Lantern: The Revolution of '89 Witnessed in Warsaw, Budapest, Berlin and Prague*. New York: Random House, 1990.

Gellner, Ernest. *Conditions of Liberty, Civil Society and Its Rivals*. London: Penguin Books, 1996.

Glendon, Mary Ann. *Rights Talk: The Impoverishment of Political Discourse*. New York: The Free Press, 1991.

Goldfarb, Jeffrey. *After the Fall: The Pursuit of Democracy in Central Europe*. New York: Basic, 1992.

Gratz, Roberta Brandes. *A Frog, a Wooden House, a Stream and a Trail: Ten Years of Community Revitalization in Central Europe*. New York: Rockefeller Brothers Fund, Inc., 2001.

Gutmann, Amy. "The Challenge of Multiculturalism in Political Ethics." *Philosophy and Public Affairs*. Vol. 22, No. 3. (Summer, 1993).

Habermas, Jürgen. *The Structural Transformation of the Public Sphere*. Cambridge, Massachusetts: MIT Press, 1989.

Hamilton, Alexander, James Madison, and John Jay. *The Federalist Papers*. Edited by Clinton Rossiter. New York: New American Library, 1961.

Harris, Sam. *Reclaiming Our Democracy: Healing the Break Between People and Government*. Philadelphia: Camino Books, 1994.

Hardt, Michael, and Negri, Antonio. *Empire* Cambridge, Massachusetts: Harvard University Press, 2000.

Heifetz, Ronald. *Leadership Without Easy Answers*. Cambridge, Massachusetts: Belknap Press, 1994.

Herz, John, ed. *From Dictatorship to Democracy: Coping with the Legacies of Authoritarianism and Totalitarianism*. Westport, Connecticut: Greenwood, 1982.

Hoffman, Eva. *Exit into History: A Journey Through the New Eastern Europe*. New York: Viking, 1993.

Holbrooke, Richard. *To End a War*. New York: Random House, 1998.

Horwitz, Robert H., ed. *The Moral Foundations of the American Republic*. 3rd ed. Charlottesville: University of Virginia Press, 1986.

Howell, Jude. *Civil Society and Development: A Critical Exploration*. Boulder, CO: Lynne Rienner Publishers, 2001.

Huntington, Samuel P. *The Third Wave: Democratization in the Late Twentieth Century*. Norman, Oklahoma: University of Oklahoma Press, 1991.

Isaac, Katherine. *The Death of Common Sense*. New York: Random House, 1992.

Kaplan, Robert. *The Ends of the Earth*. New York: Random House, 1996.

Kaufman, Michael T. *Mad Dreams, Saving Graces: Poland: A Nation in Conspiracy*. New York: Random House, 1989.

Kaye, Harvey J. *Are We Good Citizens?* New York: Teachers College Press, 2001.

Korten, David C. *When Corporations Rule the World*. San Francisco: Berrett-Koehler. 1995.

Kriseová, Eda. *Václev Havel: The Authorized Biography*. New York: St. Martin's. 1991.

Landes, David S. *The Wealth and Poverty of Nations: Why Some Are So Rich and Some So Poor*. New York: W.W. Norton, 1998.

Legal Principles for Citizen Participation: Toward a Legal Framework for Civil Society Organizations. Washington, D.C.: CIVICUS, 1997.

Locke, John. *The Second Treatise of Government.* New York: Liberal Arts Press, 1956.

Marcus, George E. and Russell L. Hanson, eds. *Reconsidering the Democratic Public.* University Park, Pennsylvania: The Pennsylvania State University Press, 1993.

Masaryk, Tomás G. *The Ideals of Humanity and How to Work.* New York: Arno Press, 1971

Matynia, Elzbieta, ed. *Grappling with Democracy: Deliberations on Post-Communist Societies.* Prague: SLON Publishing, 1996.

McDonald, Forrest. *Novus Ordo Seclorum: The Intellectual Origins of the Constitution.* Lawrence, Kansas: University of Kansas Press, 1985.

Michnik, Adam. *Letters from Prison and Other Essays.* Berkeley: University of California Press, 1986.

Michnik, Adam. *Letters from Freedom: Post-Cold War Realities and Perspectives (Societies and Culture in East-Central Europe, No. 10).* Berkeley, California: University of California Press, 1998.

Milosz, Czeslaw. *The Captive Mind.* New York: Vintage, 1953.

Monroe, James A. *The Democratic Wish: Popular Participation and the Limits of American Government.* New York: Basic Books, 1990.

Morison, Samuel E., ed. *Sources and Documents Illustrating the American Revolution, 1764-1788, and the Formation of the Federal Constitution.* New York: Oxford University Press, 1965.

Mouffe, Chauntal, ed. *Dimensions of Radical Democracy: Pluralism, Citizenship, Community.* London: Verso, 1995.

The New Civic Atlas: Profile of Civil Society in 60 Countries. Washington, D.C.: CIVICUS, 1997.

O'Connell, Brian. *Civil Society: The Underpinnings of American Democracy.* London: University Press of New England and Tufts University, 1999.

Oliveira, Miguel Darcy de, and Rajesh Tandon, coordinators. *Citizens of the Postmodern Age.* Baltimore: The Johns Hopkins University Press, 1992.

Oliveira, Miguel Darcy de, and Rajesh Tandon, coordinators. *Citizens Strengthening Global Civil Society.* Washington World Alliance for Citizen Participation, 919 18th Street, N.W., Washington, D.C., 1994.

Perez-Diaz, Victor M. *The Return of Civil Society: The Emergence of Democratic Spain.* Cambridge, Massachusetts: Harvard University Press, 1993.

Plato. *The Republic of Plato.* Edited by Francis MacDonald Cornford. London: Oxford University Press, 1966.

Popper, Karl. *The Open Society and Its Enemies*. 5th ed., rev. Princeton: Princeton University Press, 1966.

Putnam, Robert D. *Making Democracy Work*. Princeton: Princeton University Press, 1993.

Putnam, Robert D. *Bowling Alone: The Collapse and Revival of America*. New York: Simon and Schuster, 2000.

Quigley, Charles N. and Charles F. Bahmueller, Ph.D., eds. *CIVITAS: A Framework for Civic Education*. Calabasas, California: Center for Civic Education, 1991.

Ravitch, Diane, ed. *The American Reader: Words that Moved a Nation*. New York: HarperCollins, 1990.

Revel, Jean-Francoise, with the assistance of Branko Lazitch. *How Democracies Perish*. Translated by William Byron. Garden City, New York: Doubleday, 1984.

Salamon, Lester and Helmut Anheier. *Defining the Non-Profit Sector: A Cross-National Analysis*. New York: Manchester University Press, 1997.

Sandel, Michael J. *Democracy's Discontent: American in Search of a Public Philosophy*. Cambridge, Massachusetts: Belknap Press of Harvard University, 1996.

Sandel, Michael J. *Liberalism and the Limits of Justice*. Cambridge: Harvard University Press, 1991.

Seligman, Adam B. *The Idea of Civil Society*. New York: The Free Press, 1992.

Shklar, Judith N. *American Citizenship: The Quest for Inclusion*. Cambridge: Harvard University Press, 1991.

Shorris, Earl. *New American Blues: A Journey Through Poverty to Democracy*. New York: W.W. Norton, 1997.

Smyre, Rick. *Consensus Democracy*. Gastonia, North Carolina: Communities of the Future, 1995.

Sokolowski, S. Wojciech. *Civil Society and the Professions in Eastern Europe: Social Change and Organizational Innovation in Poland*. New York: Kluwer Academic/Plenum Publishers, 2001.

Soros, George. The Crisis of Global Capitalism: Open Society Endangered. New York: Perseus Books Group, 1998.

Taylor, Charles. *Multiculturalism: Examining the Politics of Recognition*. Princeton: Princeton University Press, 1994.

Thomson, Ken. *From Neighborhood to Nation: The Democratic Foundations of Civil Society*. Hanover, NH: University Press of New England, 2001.

Thurow, Lester. *The Future of Capitalism*. New York: William Morrow and Co., 1996.

Tocqueville, Alexis de. *Democracy in America*. New York: Vintage Books Edition, 1990.

Truth and Justice, The Delicate Balance: The Documentation of Prior Regimes and Individual Rights. Budapest: Institute for Constitutional and Legislative Policy, Central European University, 1993.

Tully, Jane. *Community Foundations Around the World: Building Effective Support Systems*. Washington, D.C.: Council on Foundations, 1997.

UN Commission on Global Governance. *Our Global Neighborhood*. Oxford: Oxford University Press, 1995.

Voegelin, Eric. *New Science of Politics, An Introduction*. Chicago: University of Chicago Press, 1952.

Walzer, Michael. *On Toleration*. New Haven: Yale University Press, 1997.

Walzer, Michael. *Thick and Thin: Moral Argument at Home and Abroad*. Notre Dame: University of Notre Dame Press, 1994.

Warren, Mark. *Democracy and Association*. Princeton: Princeton University Press, 2001.

Webber, Stephen and Ilkka Liikanen, eds. *Education and Civic Culture in Post-Communist in Societies*. Basingstoke: Palgrave, 2001.

Whitman, Walt. *Democratic Vistas*. New York: Liberal Arts Press, 1949.

Wolfe, Alan. *Whose Keeper? Social Science and Moral Obligation*. Berkeley: University of California Press, 1989.

Yankelovich, Daniel. *Coming to Public Judgment: Making Democracy Work in a Complex World*. Syracuse: Syracuse University Press, 1991.

Zakaria, Fareed. "The Culture of Islamic Hate." *Newsweek*. Vol. 133, No. 16. (October 15, 2001)

Web Sites

Academics Consortium Project in Civics Education.
http://civics.edfac.usyd.edu.au

ActionAid. http://www.actionaid.org

The Adam Institute. http://www.adaminstitute.org.il (Israel)

Carnegie Endowment for Peace. http://www.ceip.org

Center for Citizenship Education. http://www.ceo.org.pl (Poland)

Center for Civic Networking. http://www.civic.net:2401/ccn.html

Center for Civil Society International. http://www.friends-partners.org

Center for Democracy & Citizenship. http://www.publicwork.org

Center for Living Democracy. http://www.livingdemocracy.org

The Centre for Citizenship Development.
http://www.cam.anglia.ac.uk/hums/citizen/home.htm

Centre for Youth & Social Development.
http://www.pria.org/Partners/CYSD/cysdhome.htm

Charities Aid Foundation. http://www.charitynet.org/aboutcaf.asp

Civic Practices Network. http://www.cpn.org/cpn/index.html

Civics Online. http://civics-online.org

CIVICUS. http://www.civicus.org

CIVITAS. http://www.civitas.org

CIVNET. http://www.civnet.org

Close Up Foundation. http://www.closeup.org

The Commonwealth. http://www.thecommonwealth.org

Conciencia. http://www.concienciadigital.com.ar (South America)

Council for Education in World Citizenship. http://www.cewc.org.uk

Democracy. http://www.abc.net.au/civics/demos/default.htm (Australia)

The Democracy Center. http://www.democracytr.org (Latin America, Brazil)

Dissent. http://www.dissentmagazine.org

European Foundation Centre. http://www.efc.be

Foreign Affairs. http://www.foreignaffairs.org

Foreign Policy. http://www.foreignpolicy.com

Freedom House. http://www.freedomhouse.org

Institute for Democracy in South Africa. http://www.idasa.org.za

Institute for the Study of Civic Values. http://www.iscv.org

International IDEA. http://www.idea.int

International Institute for Democracy. http://iidemocracy.coe.int

National Endowment for Democracy. http://www.ned.org

Pact, Inc. http://www.pactworld.org

Salzburg Seminar. http://www.salsem.ac.at

Society for Participatory Research in Asia (PRIA). http://www.pria.org

Trust in Government Project.
http://www.gspa.washington.edu/trust/links/capital.html

United Nations. http://www.un.org

Voice International. http://www.voiceinternational.org

World Movement for Democracy. http://www.wmd.org